Knowledge Development in Marketing

The MSI Experience

Paul N. Bloom
University of North Carolina

Lexington Books
D.C. Heath and Company/Lexington, Massachusetts/Toronto

Library of Congress Cataloging-in-Publication Data

Bloom, Paul N.
    Knowledge development in marketing.

    Bibliography: p.
    Includes index.
    1. Marketing research.   2. Marketing Science
Institute.   I. Marketing Science Institute.   II. Title.
HF5415.2.B57   1987   658.83   85-45938
ISBN 0-669-12581-4 (alk. paper)

Published simultaneously in Canada
Printed in the United States of America
Casebound International Standard Book Number: 0-669-12581-4
Library of Congress Catalog Card Number: 85-45938

The paper used in this publication meets the minimum requirements of American
National Standard for Information Sciences—Permanence of Paper for Printed
Library Materials, ANSI Z39.48-1984. ∞ ™

87 88 89 90 91 8 7 6 5 4 3 2 1

To Diane and Jonathan

Contents

Figures

Tables

Preface

What we know about marketing is continuously growing and evolving. A substantial number of individuals and institutions are now working to develop knowledge about marketing, and they have had considerable success in helping us understand some inherently complex and puzzling phenomena. But in spite of much progress, there are those who are dissatisfied with how knowledge development has proceeded in the marketing discipline. Academics frequently question one another about the topics, methods, and procedures used in researching new marketing knowledge. At the same time, practitioners frequently question the practical relevance of what academics do, while academics chastise practitioners for not sharing what they have learned in the "real world." The conclusion of a recent blue-ribbon commission, formed to evaluate the overall relationship among business, government, and academia, seems to apply to the situation in marketing:

> The challenge is to create the mechanisms through which the expertise
> and knowledge of each sector can be combined and applied by all sectors
> to the challenges of innovation, economic revitalization, and competitive-
> ness. (Business-Higher Education Forum, 1983, p. 28)

This book examines the knowledge development system in marketing, paying particular attention to one mechanism that has been established to encourage joint efforts between practitioners and academics. That mechanism is the Marketing Science Institute. The manner in which knowledge has been created through a host of MSI-supported research projects is described in some detail. The hope is that this material will stimulate readers to form insights about how knowledge development in the discipline might be improved.

This book is an outgrowth of a project that was commissioned by the Marketing Science Institute. MSI celebrated its twenty-fifth anniversary in 1986 and, in honor of this event, decided to publish a volume summarizing the research it has supported through the years. I was asked to write such a summary, but decided—with MSI's encouragement—to do a more extensive project. Rather than simply write short descriptions of study after study, I decided it would make more interesting and useful reading to provide some background on how various research projects got started and what became of those projects. Thus, the book could make a contribution to the growing discussion about how to improve scholarly research in marketing.

Writing a book like this has required the support of an extensive number of people. Alden Clayton, MSI's recently retired President, deserves the first acknowledgement, since it was he who originally asked me to pursue the project. Alden has provided perceptive advice and encouragement throughout the effort. His faith in me is deeply appreciated.

Other members of the MSI "family" whose thinking and reinforcement have helped tremendously include past Executive Directors Stephen A. Greyser (Harvard) and Louis W. Stern (Northwestern), and present Executive Director John Farley (Columbia). Also, Diane Schmalensee (Vice President, Research Operations), Muriel Saver (Director of Communications), and Sherry Oliver (Office Manager) have offered valuable ideas and support. Katherine Jocz (Manager of Research Operations) has helped with editing, fact finding, and a variety of other tasks. Robert Seith (Editorial Director) saw the book through production.

I obviously owe a debt of gratitude to the many people who agreed to be interviewed. Their names appear in the text. I thank them for their time and candid remarks.

The bulk of the telephone interviews were conducted by Meme Drumwright (Harvard) while she served as my graduate assistant. She did a superior job of drawing people out and making them feel comfortable with the subject matter. Carolyn Costley, another graduate assistant, also performed very capably in conducting a smaller share of the interviews. A third graduate assistant was Drue Schuler, who did an excellent job of helping me prepare the extensive bibliography of this book.

I would be remiss not to mention several of my supportive colleagues at the University of North Carolina. I would particularly like to thank Fritz Russ, Nick Didow, Merrie Brucks, William Perreault, and David Hughes. In addition, the School of Business Administration at UNC has provided release time and financial support to help me complete this effort.

Finally, I would like to dedicate this book to my wife, Diane, and my son, Jonathan. They have patiently accepted the loss of time with me and the distracted thoughts this project has created. I plan to make it up to them.

1
Introduction

T he academic discipline of marketing has become relatively mature.
Serious scholarly research has been pursued by marketing
academics for several decades now, and this work has been ac-
companied by a proliferation of journals, proceedings, monographs, and
other academic publications. Recently, the discipline seems to have
undergone a "mid-life crisis," since considerable effort has been devoted
to examining what all this research activity has accomplished. Conference
sessions and journal articles have been regularly exploring the nature of
scholarly inquiry in marketing. They have discussed what the theories,
methods, findings, and dissemination vehicles of the discipline are
contributing to the development of verifiable and useful knowledge about
marketing phenomena (e.g., Arndt, 1985; Hirschman, 1986; Anderson, 1986;
Brinberg and Hirschman, 1986). In addition, a major commission—formed
in the late 1970s by the American Marketing Association (AMA) and the
Marketing Science Institute (MSI)—has conducted a rather global
assessment of the effectiveness of research and development for
marketing management (see Myers, Massy, and Greyser, 1980). Most
recently, the AMA organized a Development of Marketing Thought Task
Force that has investigated topics such as research funding sources,
doctoral training, academic-practitioner interaction, the publication
system, and professorial "burnout" (see Monroe, 1986).

Much of the recent discussion has, frankly, been quite critical of
marketing's knowledge development system. For instance, the AMA Task
Force reached the following assessments about certain "structural
impediments to the development of marketing knowledge:"

1. Overall, the field of marketing is not investing sufficient resources in
   the systematic development of knowledge.
2. Problems exist with the communication of ideas and findings.
3. The allocation of time and effort by contributors is often a problem.

4. The efficiency or productivity of development efforts appears low.
5. Incentive and reward systems have institutionalized a restrictive approach to knowledge development. (Wilkie, 1986, p. 1)

These statements reflect feelings about how the entire discipline has performed, and are not meant to suggest anything about the contributions of individual research projects. Certainly, there have been many studies that have illustrated productive approaches for others to follow in the future.

This book describes how a particular set of academic research studies in marketing *actually were* initiated, pursued, disseminated, and utilized. The set of studies examined—those supported by MSI—can safely be said to include many significant contributions to the discipline. MSI has spent the last twenty-five years deploying a variety of funding and communication approaches to improve knowledge development in marketing. Thus, descriptions of how some of this work evolved should prove helpful for generating ideas on how to improve knowledge development in marketing. In particular, reviewing this body of work should provide insights into what can be accomplished by addressing the AMA Task Force's first two assessments and providing academic researchers with more resources and improved communication vehicles.

The specific objectives of this book are presented in the next section. This is followed by a section providing background on some of the major structural features of the knowledge development system in marketing and on MSI. An overview of the project's guiding theoretical perspectives, methods, and results is presented in chapter 2.

Objectives

The objectives of this book are:

1. to describe how academic research in marketing has been initiated, pursued, disseminated, and utilized;
2. to summarize the topics, methods, and findings of the set of research studies supported by the Marketing Science Institute over the last twenty-five years;
3. to assess what the Marketing Science Institute has contributed to knowledge development in marketing.

The research approach used in seeking these objectives is described in detail in chapter 2. In brief, the emphasis was on obtaining new ideas and insights rather than on gathering definitive results. An exploratory investigation, relying on methods such as in-depth interviews, seemed called for given (1) the limited amount of previous research on the knowledge development process in marketing and (2) the difficulty of conducting a rigorous evaluation of MSI's contributions, since there is no way of estimating what knowledge development would have occurred over the last twenty-five years in MSI's absence.

This book should be of interest to several audiences. First, doctoral students and faculty members in marketing may find the descriptions of the knowledge creation process helpful for guiding them on how to initiate more fruitful research projects of their own. These people might also find the summaries of the MSI work useful for gaining background on what research has been done in particular areas.

A second audience includes practitioners of marketing. Many of the people who do marketing in the real world know little about how academics conduct research. Indeed, there are numerous misconceptions about what actually goes on in the "ivory tower" of academia. This book should help to clarify what academics do, and it should also provide a way of learning about a significant body of academic research.

Finally, this book may be of interest to scholars from a variety of disciplines who are interested in the sociology of knowledge. There is a growing body of research on this subject which has appeared in journals like *Knowledge*, and this book may serve as a type of "case study" of the sociology of knowledge in a particular discipline.

Some Background on Marketing's Knowledge Development System

Knowledge has been defined by sociologist Daniel Bell as:

> A set of statements of facts or ideas, presenting a reasoned judgment or an experimental result, which is transmitted to others through some communication medium. . . . [It] consists of new judgments (research and scholarship) or new presentations of old judgments (textbooks and teaching). (Bell, 1973, p. 175)

The field of marketing has a highly complex system of allowing "organized statements of facts or ideas" to develop, either as (1) "new judgments" within the minds of researchers, or (2) "new presentations" within the minds of students and practitioners. Some of the key structural features of this knowledge development system are reviewed in the remainder of this chapter, with the dynamics of this system—or the manner in which research gets initiated, pursued, disseminated, and utilized—being the

concern of subsequent chapters. The major features of the following individuals and institutions are described:

1. Marketing academics
2. Professional associations
3. Publishers
4. Marketing practitioners
5. Funding sources of academic research in marketing

A short history and description of MSI conclude the chapter.

Marketing Academics

Professors, instructors, and doctoral students within colleges and universities conduct research projects, write articles and books, edit and review
articles and papers, organize conferences and workshops, make scholarly
presentations, and teach seminars and classes. They are an extremely
diverse group who work for extremely diverse institutions. There are
academics who spend most of their time pouring over computer outputs
or writing highly technical papers, and there are those who spend most
of their time working with students and teaching classes. Still others spend
substantial amounts of time doing consulting or training for marketing
practitioners. Some try to do all of these things, or emphasize different
activities during different stages of their careers. The choices they make
on how to spend their time are influenced greatly by the types of
institutions with which they are associated, since some schools are more
research-oriented, teaching-oriented, or consulting-oriented than others,
and hand out rewards and promotions accordingly.

The academic who participates in marketing's knowledge development system typically works in a school or college of business administration or management—although there are a few contributors to the
system who work in departments of journalism, communications, consumer economics, psychology, management science, or something else.
Most of these people have obtained or are working on doctoral degrees
in marketing, but there are many important contributors who have
received degrees in other disciplines. Marketing academics vary greatly
in the amount of real-world work experience they possess. Many have
put in several years or more in industrial positions. But many others have
gained most of their practical experience through consulting assignments.

Professional Associations

There are several professional associations that are concerned with advancing knowledge development in marketing. They all conduct

conferences at which academics (and practitioners) can interact with one another, and most publish conference proceedings and journals to facilitate the dissemination of knowledge. The major associations are:

1. *American Marketing Association:* This large association holds two major conferences every year for marketing academics and several other conferences attended by both academics and practitioners. It typically publishes proceedings of its conferences. Its other major publications are two scholarly journals, the *Journal of Marketing* and the *Journal of Marketing Research,* and two newsletters, the *Marketing News* and the *Marketing Educator.* The association runs a dissertation competition every year to recognize the best doctoral thesis on a marketing topic, and it also sponsors an annual doctoral consortium, where accomplished doctoral students and faculty from a variety of schools come together for an intensive exchange of ideas.

2. *Association for Consumer Research:* This more interdisciplinary association—with members from the fields of marketing, psychology, consumer economics, sociology, and other disciplines—focuses on advancing research on consumer behavior. It is a much smaller and more academically oriented organization than the American Marketing Association, with a much lower percentage of practitioners among its members. It holds an annual conference that has published proceedings, and it publishes the *Journal of Consumer Research* and a newsletter. It also runs an annual dissertation competition.

3. *Academy of Marketing Science:* This is primarily an academic association that holds an annual conference every year with published proceedings. It publishes the *Journal of the Academy of Marketing Science* and a newsletter. It also runs an annual dissertation competition.

4. *The Marketing Science Group of ORSA/TIMS:* The Operations Research Society of America and The Institute of Management Sciences collaborate to run an annual conference and publish the journal *Marketing Science.* The research discussed in these outlets tends to be quantitative.

Other associations that are part of marketing's knowledge development system include the Southern Marketing Association (which runs an annual conference for academics and helps in publishing the *Journal of Business Research*), the Advertising Research Foundation (which runs conferences primarily for practitioners and publishes the *Journal of Advertising Research*), and the American Council on Consumer Interests (which runs both academic and practitioner conferences and publishes the *Journal of Consumer Affairs*).

These associations rely very heavily on their member academics, and also on member practitioners, to do much of their work. These members serve as editors of journals, chairpersons of conferences, reviewers of prospective journal articles and conference papers, judges of dissertation competitions, and officers of the associations. Several associations even have members editing and publishing their newsletters and organizing membership drives.

A feature of the publications of most of these associations that deserves mention is that reviews are done in a "double-blind" manner. That is, reviewers of prospective conference papers and journal articles do not know whose paper they are reviewing, nor are authors told who reviewed their manuscripts. Another somewhat distinctive feature is that most of these associations (e.g., AMA and the Association for Consumer Research) will not permit a paper that has been published in a conference proceedings to be republished in a journal.

Publishers

In addition to the professional associations, which publish conference proceedings, journals, newsletters, and some books, there are several other organizations which regularly publish material that contributes to knowledge development in marketing. These include:

1. *Divisions of research of universities and business schools.* Scholarly journals like the University of Chicago's *Journal of Business* and the University of Michigan's *Journal of Public Policy and Marketing* are published by these operations. They tend to use academic editors and academic reviewers. Other magazines like the *Harvard Business Review* rely heavily on a staff of full-time editors to make editorial judgments. Universities also frequently publish and distribute working papers of faculty, and they will occasionally publish a research monograph or book.

2. *Business periodical publishers.* There are a number of for-profit organizations that publish journals aimed at both the academic and practitioner markets. These include the operations that publish *Industrial Marketing Management* and the *Journal of Consumer Marketing.*

3. *Research Monograph Publishers.* Publishers such as Lexington Books, Ballinger, JAI Press, and Praeger have published an assortment of scholarly monographs or books that report the results of more extensive research studies.

4. *Textbook Publishers.* Several large publishers regularly publish mark-eting texts. There are now numerous different texts available for teaching just about any marketing course offered.

5. *Marketing Science Institute.* MSI produces a working paper series of reports on MSI-funded projects and, on occasion, other research efforts. Copies are sent to practitioners affiliated with companies that support MSI, and additional copies are sent to more than 300 aca-demics. The papers are also sold to the public for a nominal fee.

Practitioners

There has always been a small cadre of practitioners who have tried to contribute to knowledge development in marketing by publicly speaking and writing on various topics. Moreover, there are some consulting or marketing research firms that have contributed valuable studies to the marketing literature. However, the bulk of the practitioner community has contributed to marketing's knowledge development system in a less visible way, such as by sharing ideas and experiences with academics during conferences, workshops, consulting assignments, or research projects. MSI, AMA, and other organizations have often sponsored events or programs designed to encourage practitioners to share their new ideas, data, or results.

Research Funding Sources

The marketing discipline is not blessed with abundant sources of fund-ing for scholarly research. Unlike the case in many other fields, no government agencies or foundations regularly provide funding for marketing investigations. At one time, the National Science Foundation and a few other federal agencies frequently offered support for research related to marketing, but in recent times federal funding for marketing studies has been very limited. Other potential sources of funding—such as the American Association of Advertising Agencies, the Association of National Advertisers, and the Advertising Research Foundation—have supported only an occasional academic project over the years. And professional societies like the American Marketing Association have never made a practice of funding academic research.

The lack of funding has led most marketing academics to rely on (1) their universities for small grants to support their research activities, (2) their consulting contacts, who have occasionally allowed them to incorporate scholarly research aspects into practical consulting projects,

(3) MSI. There is a new corporate-funded Institute for the Study of Business Markets at Pennsylvania State University, which intends to fund research on industrial marketing topics, but it is still too early to tell what kind of funding it will make available.

The Marketing Science Institute

MSI has completed twenty-five years as one of the only funding sources available for doing scholarly research in marketing. The Institute was the brainchild of the late Thomas McCabe, Sr., former President of Scott Paper Company, who through discussions with leading marketing thinkers of his era like Wroe Alderson (Wharton), Albert Wesley Frey (Pittsburgh), and John Howard (then at Pittsburgh), came to believe in the need for an organization that would sponsor and conduct more basic research in marketing. McCabe wanted to establish something that went beyond being merely a bridge between academics and practitioners. He hoped to help these two constituencies become of one mind. In 1960, Frey and Howard completed a survey of leading marketing practitioners and academics to help McCabe formalize his ideas, and in 1961 he began to enlist the support of other corporate leaders.

The proposal McCabe showed to potential sponsors of "The Institute for Science in Marketing" contained the following statement of objectives:

> The proposed Institute would work toward the advancement of productivity and efficiency in marketing by conducting *research* and *educational activity* designed (1) to contribute to the emergence of a definitive science of marketing and (2) to stimulate increased application of scientific techniques to the understanding and solving of current marketing problems. Emphasis would be upon creative, original thinking—not on organizing and reporting otherwise available material. (McCabe, 1961, p. 1)

The benefits offered by this new nonprofit institute were to be many. Sponsoring member companies would benefit from research that they could not accomplish single-handedly. Trustees representing the companies would gain increased sophistication and personal growth. Academics would benefit by tapping into the business community for financial support and a link to the real world. And on a broader scale, MSI's research results would be used to improve the working of the free-enterprise system and guide public policy decisions.

Twenty-nine companies responded to McCabe's appeal and agreed to become five-year charter members. The "Marketing Science Institute" was then set up in Philadelphia to be near Scott Paper and The Wharton

School of the University of Pennsylvania. Wendell R. Smith was hired as the first President, overseeing a small group of full-time researchers and support staff. Patrick Robinson was the first Research Director for MSI and took a leadership role in the development of a broad program of research.

The initial activity of MSI focused on rather large research projects that produced several long books. These were done primarily by full-time MSI staff, with Wharton marketing faculty members making substantial contributions in a few cases. In 1967, after five years had been completed and member companies were being asked to continue their support, a need to explore new directions was identified. Among other things, Wendell Smith had decided to leave MSI to become dean of the business school at the University of Massachusetts. A consensus emerged for moving MSI up to Cambridge, Massachusetts to have a connection with the Harvard Business School—it was felt that a closer affiliation with a major university would lend additional legitimacy to MSI's mission. Harvard was eager to have MSI, seeing it as a vehicle for improving the research productivity of its marketing faculty. In 1968, MSI moved its offices to Cambridge and Harvard professor Robert Buzzell became its Executive Director.

Buzzell steered MSI away from publishing books written by MSI staffers, and instead encouraged the publication of less ambitious, but significant, working papers (that might later be published in journals) written primarily by full-time academics. He got Harvard faculty and doctoral students heavily involved with developing these papers, while at the same time making greater use of the advice of the trustees from member companies about what these papers should address.

Buzzell's successor, Harvard professor Stephen A. Greyser, took over in 1972 and began to formalize the advisory role of the trustees by setting up a "research priorities" program that identified topics about which proposals would be welcomed. Greyser worked closely with Thomas McCabe, Jr., who had become MSI's President, in seeking guidance from the member companies and maintaining their enthusiasm. In 1974, they brought in Alden Clayton from Lever Brothers as MSI's Director of Research Operations to help in working with the member companies and, also, in expanding the number of non-Harvard academics receiving MSI support. Functions such as mini-conferences and workshops, which encouraged interaction between academics and practitioners from the member companies, were conducted with increasing frequency.

The trends toward seeking more guidance on topic selection from member companies and supporting a broader range of academics have continued through the executive directorships of Harvard's Raymond Corey (1981–83), Northwestern University's Louis W. Stern (1983–85), and

Columbia University's John Farley (1985–87). Alden Clayton remained with MSI through all these years, retiring as its President at the end of 1986. At that time, MSI had ten staff members. It was guided by the advice of six steering groups, each made up of distinguished academics and representatives from member companies. More than twenty universities and forty member companies (see table 1–1) were represented on these steering groups, which were established to:

1. identify key issues and stimulate research interest;
2. identify promising academic researchers;
3. review proposals and publication submissions;
4. help develop, guide, and sometimes fund research projects.

The six groups focus on issues of concern to consumer durables, business-to-business, consumer services, and packaged goods marketers, and on more general issues related to advertising and marketing strategy.

Although MSI typically supports projects that result in short working papers, from time to time projects have produced longer research monograph-type books. These projects have typically been supported by special grants from MSI member companies for amounts up to $50,000 (or occasionally more). However, the vast majority of MSI-supported projects have been completed with small grants in the $4,000 to $5,000 range. And recently, MSI has made available even smaller grants as part of new programs to (1) award small grants to winners of a doctoral dissertation proposal competition and (2) award small grants for paying subject fees for experimental research.

The typical MSI project evolves from a dialogue among academic researcher(s), MSI staff, and member-company personnel. Academics write proposals in response to MSI's Research Priorities statement, and approximately one in five receives funding after a first submission. MSI staff often request resubmissions of proposals, and by working together approximately one in three applicants is able to design projects deemed worthy of some financial support. Once the projects are well under way, progress reports in the form of mini-conferences or workshops for member-company personnel are usually held, providing an opportunity for feedback to the researcher(s) and, where appropriate, a chance to request additional funding. Upon completion of a project, MSI typically issues a working paper, which is distributed to academics and practitioners. Presentations on completed projects are also often made at MSI conferences and meetings. Since MSI has not restricted the researchers it supports from republishing their MSI working papers in scholarly

Table 1–1
MSI Member Companies, January 1987

AT&T	IBM Corporation
Avon Products, Inc.	John Hancock Mutual Life Insurance
Bank of America	Company
Bank of Boston	S.C. Johnson & Son, Inc.
Beatrice-Hunt Foods, Inc.	Leo Burnett USA
Bell & Howell Company	Lever Brothers Company
Borg-Warner Chemicals, Inc.	Mars Information Services Group
Campbell Soup Company	McDonnell Douglas - Information Systems
Capital Cities/ABC, Inc.	Group
CBS Inc.	Metropolitan Life and Affiliated Companies
CIGNA Corporation	New York Stock Exchange
Dun & Bradstreet	The NutraSweet Company
E.I. DuPont De Nemours & Co. (Inc.)	Pepsico, Inc.
Eastman Kodak Company	Polaroid Corporation
Ford Motor Company	The Procter &.Gamble Company
General Electric Company	The Quaker Oats Company
General Foods Corporation	R.J. Reynolds Industries, Inc.
General Motors Corporation	Ryder System, Inc.
The Gillette Company	SAMI/Burke, Inc.
GTE	Sears, Roebuck and Co.
Harris Corporation	The Travelers Insurance Company
Hewlett-Packard Company	Whirlpool Corporation

journals, proceedings, or books, the projects often end up producing journal articles or other non-MSI publications.

It is difficult to put a label on the type of research MSI tends to fund. A recent statement by MSI's Executive and Research Policy Committee describes the research domain it seeks to cover in the following way:

> We very clearly intend to exclude from the MSI research domain many kinds of business research projects that may well have great value to individual companies as well as great intellectual or technical merit—on the grounds that they do not contribute to the development of theory, basic knowledge, or techniques that have a reasonable prospect of being applied (over some reasonable time horizon) to understanding and/or solving marketing problems affecting more than one company or improving marketing education.
>
> We equally clearly intend to exclude from the MSI research domain many kinds of academic projects that may well have great intellectual or technical merit—on the grounds that there is not a clear connection between the subject of the research and its eventual marketing application.
>
> Since there is no precise definition of the boundary of the MSI research domain on either side, periodic questioning is necessary to test our sense of where the boundaries ought to be. Hence the need and value of MSI's institutional arrangements—priority setting, steering committees, mini-conferences, advisory councils, etc., to provide vehicles for

collaborative decision making about where the boundaries ought to be for a particular zone of research. (Marketing Science Institute, 1985, p. 16)

Among other things, the remainder of this book contains an attempt to categorize and summarize the domain of research MSI has supported in the past.

2

Overview of the Study: Perspectives, Methods, and Results

The preceding chapter introduced some of the key structural features of the knowledge development system in marketing. To gain a better understanding of the *dynamics* of this system—or of how the knowledge development *process* works—a multi-phase study was conducted. This study addressed the following basic questions:

1. Where and how do the ideas for research efforts originate?
2. Why are certain topics and projects pursued?
3. Who and what influence researchers in their decisions about what topics, theories, and methods to employ in their investigations?
4. How do the results of research projects tend to be disseminated?
5. What research has stimulated further research by other individuals?
6. How do practitioners use the findings of scholarly research efforts?
7. Who and what influence research utilization by practitioner?

An attempt was made to answer these questions only for the knowledge development activities that have been touched in some way by the Marketing Science Institute. This focus led the study to possess a large component of "evaluation research," since addressing questions 3, 5, and 7 for MSI-supported studies would, naturally, tend to lead to judgments about MSI's contributions. But the study was intended to be much more than an evaluation of MSI. And to the extent that MSI-supported research is representative of research in the marketing discipline as-a-whole—an issue which is addressed later in this chapter—the study can legitimately be seen as an attempt to improve our understanding of how knowledge gets developed in the entire marketing discipline.

The study consisted of the following overlapping phases:

1. a literature review of relevant works on knowledge development, knowledge use, the sociology of knowledge, philosophy of science,

organizational behavior, creativity, marketing history, marketing theory, and several other areas;

2. in-depth telephone interviews with fifty-six former and current MSI researchers;

3. an examination of annotated resumes from forty-seven of these fifty-six former and current MSI researchers;

4. in-depth telephone interviews with ten former or current editors of the *Journal of Marketing, Journal of Marketing Research,* and *Journal of Consumer Research;*

5. an examination of the sales records for MSI working papers;

6. in-depth telephone interviews with thirty-six practitioners from MSI member companies;

7. a review of all the works published by MSI.

This chapter provides an overview of how the study was conducted and what was discovered. The discussion is broken into two major parts: (1) *knowledge creation,* or how research gets initiated and pursued, and (2) *knowledge use,* or how research gets disseminated and utilized. In each part, theoretical perspectives that guided the investigation are addressed first, followed by a description of the methods employed and a brief summary of the major findings. A more comprehensive summary of the findings is presented in the final chapter (chapter 11).

Perspectives on Knowledge Creation

Little has been written about many of the details of how marketing academics go about creating knowledge. Of course, authors frequently describe why specific methods (e.g., samples, experimental designs, measurement scales, analysis techniques) have been selected for their studies. Moreover, the *philosophies of science* explicitly or implicitly underlying choices of research methods have received considerable commentary in recent marketing publications (e.g., Arndt, 1985; Hirschman, 1986; Anderson, 1986). But only limited attention has been paid to some of the more mundane and practical aspects of doing research in marketing such as:

1. Where and how do the ideas for research efforts originate?

2. Why are certain topics and projects pursued?

3. Who and what influences researchers in their decisions about what topics, theories, and methods to employ in conducting their investigations?

Unfortunately, these questions have also received only limited attention in other academic disciplines. Nevertheless, it is possible to draw from a variety of sources to formulate *potential* answers. Three models that present these potential answers are introduced below. They are labeled:

1. The Garbage Can Model
2. The Creativity Model
3. The Entrepreneur Model

Each model draws on a different body of literature for its key notions. A fourth model, to be introduced later, attempts to integrate features of all the models.

The Garbage Can Model

The field of organizational behavior has generated a few recent papers concerned with describing the knowledge creation process. One such paper by Martin (1982) proposes a "garbage can" model of the research process. This label and many of the features of the model are borrowed from the work on organizations done by March and his colleagues (Cohen et al., 1972; March and Olsen, 1976). The main idea of this model is that decisions by researchers about what to study, how to study it, where to study it, and so forth are not made in an especially rational manner—just as decision making in organizations often lacks rationality. According to Martin (1982), textbook advice about how to conduct research in a rational, systematic fashion is rarely followed.

Instead of rationality in the research process, Martin sees considerable amounts of "organized anarchy." She adopts the metaphor of the "garbage can" to convey the notion that what happens in the research process tends to be the result of an almost random throwing together of several factors. As she puts it:

> The garbage can model conceptualizes research decisions as the product of Brownian motion, whereby the four variables (theoretical problems, resources, methodological choices, and solutions) attach and unattach themselves. (Martin, 1982, p. 33)

Figure 2–1 contains a representation of this model.

Martin stresses how the four variables can connect with and influence one another in a myriad of ways. In some cases, resources—which she defines to include intellectual, financial, and data resources—serve only a facilitating role in connecting problems with methods and solutions.

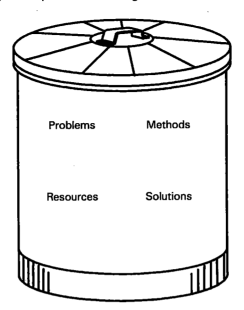

Figure 2-1. The Garbage Can Model

In other cases, resources can be a driving force behind choices of problems and methods, as researchers take actions such as:

1. choose problems they have worked on in the past in order to enhance their efficiency and productivity;
2. choose problems that colleagues can help them address;
3. choose problems for which ample funding has been made available;
4. choose problems about which data exist;
5. choose methods that they have used many times before, regardless of how appropriate they may be for a problem;
6. choose methods that funding agencies prefer; or
7. choose methods that utilize existing facilities (e.g., a survey research center).

Similarly, methods can influence the choice of problems, as researchers may search around for problems to "hit" with their methodological "hammers." Moreover, solutions—as well as failures and surprise findings—can have a major impact on what problems and methods are turned to next.

What is unclear from Martin's description of the garbage can model is (1) how often certain kinds of connections between the variables can be expected to occur and (2) what factors, if any, are most influential in determining the sequence of connections. Is the process essentially a random one, where personal idiosyncrasies and unplanned circumstances (Kulka, 1982) lead to constantly changing knowledge creation approaches? Or is the Brownian movement pushed into certain recurrent patterns by either societal forces or individual actions?

The Creativity Model

Some insights into what factors might influence the Brownian movement of the knowledge creation process to form recurrent patterns can be obtained from examining the literature on creativity. Researchers in a number of different disciplines have studied the creative process, attempting to learn what leads to more creative output from both individuals (Stein, 1974; Amabile, 1983, 1985) and organizations (Campbell, Daft, and Hulin, 1982). One interesting model of the creative process proposed by Amabile (1983), a social psychologist, is presented in figure 2-2. The model describes a way in which cognitive abilities, personality characteristics, and social factors might contribute to different stages of the creative process.

Amabile's "componential framework" identifies three key factors which influence creativity:

1. *Domain-relevant skills*: "The set of cognitive pathways for solving a given problem or doing a given task. . . . The larger the set, the more numerous the alternatives available for producing something new, for developing a new combination of steps." (Amabile, 1983, p. 363) The set may include knowledge about the domain, technical skills required to work in the domain, or special domain-relevant "talent." The level of these skills depends on innate cognitive abilities, innate perceptual and motor skills, and formal and informal education.

2. *Creativity-relevant skills*: These include (*a*) having an appropriate cognitive style which accommodates doing things like "breaking set" during problem-solving, keeping response options open for a long time, and suspending judgment, (*b*) having implicit or explicit knowledge of heuristics for generating novel ideas, and (*c*) having a conducive work style. The level of these skills depends on training, experience in idea generation, and personality characteristics.

3. *Task motivation*: This consists of a person's attitude toward the task and the perceptions held of his or her own motivations for undertaking the task. The level of motivation depends on (*a*) the person's initial level of intrinsic motivation toward the task, (*b*) the presence or absence of salient extrinsic constraints in the social environment, and (*c*) the person's ability to cognitively minimize extrinsic constraints.

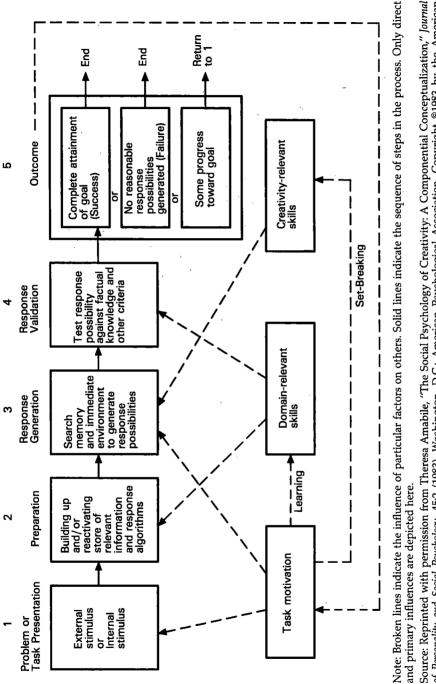

Figure 2-2. Componential Framework of Creativity

Note: Broken lines indicate the influence of particular factors on others. Solid lines indicate the sequence of steps in the process. Only direct and primary influences are depicted here.

Source: Reprinted with permission from Theresa Amabile, "The Social Psychology of Creativity: A Componential Conceptualization," *Journal of Personality and Social Psychology,* 45:2 (1983), Washington, D.C.: American Psychological Association. Copyright ©1983 by the American Psychological Association. Reprinted with permission of the publisher and author.

These factors are supposed to vary in influence depending on the stage of the creative process. For example, task motivation is seen as an especially important factor in the first stage (task presentation), when high levels of intrinsic motivation can get the creative process moving rapidly. On the other hand, domain-relevant skills are seen as especially important in the second stage (preparation), which can be completed very rapidly if these skills are abundant.

Many of Amabile's ideas—which require a much lengthier explanation to be appreciated fully—are relevant to the knowledge creation process in marketing. Her model suggests notions such as:

1. Researchers will produce more creative results in a more efficient manner when they pursue topics and methods that they have pursued before (i.e., when they have domain-relevant skills).
2. Researchers will produce more creative results when they pursue projects because of personal curiosity or interests (i.e., intrinsic motivation).
3. "Publish or perish," salary increases, grant support, consulting opportunities, and other forms of extrinsic motivation frequently inhibit the production of creative results.
4. Wide-ranging, unstructured exploration for ideas will tend to produce more creative results than narrow, structured efforts.

Her model also suggests that there is a definite, underlying, purposive character to any creative process, even though at times the process may (and perhaps should) have a floundering quality to it. A researcher proceeds step-by-step toward reasonably well-defined goals. Thus, the process may not be as non-rational and random as the garbage can model proposes.

The Entrepreneur Model

The entrepreneur model tends to place even greater emphasis on the purposive character of the knowledge creation process. It views knowledge creation as, quite simply, an entrepreneurial process. Researchers are seen as essentially "marketers of ideas" who regularly search for ways to obtain substantial "returns" on their investment of time in doing research. This model is drawn from the article "Is Science Marketing?" by Peter and Olson (1983), where they argue that successful scientists "must (at least implicitly) develop and carry out a marketing strategy to promote their theories" (Peter and Olson, 1983, p. 112). The model is also consistent with the viewpoint adopted by Garvey (1979) based on his research on the knowledge creation process in several disciplines. Garvey points out that the scientist is like "members of other professions, much involved in a competitive social world in which he is motivated by the desire to be successful" (Garvey, 1979, p. 1).

This model suggests that marketing academics are goal-driven, opportunistic people. Many are seeking self-serving goals such as job security (tenure), promotions, salary increases, big consulting fees, prestige, and power. But many others are primarily striving toward satisfying their own curiosity or attaining more noble goals, such as making a contribution to the marketing discipline or to society (Olson and Peter, 1983). Depending upon their goals, academics will pursue different approaches toward generating new research ideas (i.e., market opportunity analysis), conducting their research (i.e., new product development), circulating their unrefined ideas or preliminary results (i.e., test marketing), choosing publication outlets (i.e., selecting channels of distribution), and communicating with others about their research (i.e., promotion and personal selling).

For example, the academic who is driven primarily by a desire for big consulting fees will tend to look for ideas by observing what practitioners are most concerned about. This person will often pay less attention to theory and rigorous methodology in conducting research, and will tend to be reluctant to discuss or reveal preliminary ideas or results (out of fear that someone may steal them and make money off them). Practitioner-oriented journals and trade magazines will be sought as publication outlets by this person, who will also attempt to make many speeches and appearances before practitioners.

At another extreme would be the academic who has an overriding goal of providing service to the marketing discipline. This person will tend to circulate widely, seeking opportunities to discover new research ideas by talking to colleagues, attending conferences, interacting with practitioners, and so forth. In other words, the person will tend to engage in what Campbell, Daft, and Hulin (1982) have labeled "activity," which they found to be the most important antecedent to "significant" research in a study of highly regarded academics in the field of organizational behavior. This person will also place great emphasis on theory and rigorous methods, and he or she will speak freely with others about ideas and findings. The most prestigious scholarly journals will be sought as publication outlets, and numerous appearances will be made at academic conferences to communicate what has been discovered and encourage others to pursue similar lines of research.

Academics with other goals might operate still differently. Thus, young academics seeking tenure may tend to work primarily on low-risk projects that involve collaboration with successful senior colleagues and do not require very much generation of original research ideas. And those who seek prestige and power may choose to do research in areas where large financial grants are available. In short, this model suggests that academics will tailor their idea marketing program to facilitate the efficient attainment of their personal goals.

An Integrated Model

Figure 2–3 displays a fourth, integrated model of the knowledge creation process in marketing. The model attempts to bring together several key features of the other three models, especially (1) the occurrence of frequent random or unplanned events, which is emphasized in the garbage can model, (2) the importance of prior research activity and task motivation, which are emphasized in the creativity model, and (3) the importance of goal-directed, opportunistic behavior, which is emphasized in the entrepreneur model.

The integrated model suggests that the knowledge creation process has six major "actors" and four major sub-processes. The major actors are:

1. *The Individual Researcher*: Several characteristics of this person have a significant impact on the process. Of particular importance are (*a*) career goals, (*b*) task motivation, (*c*) previous research experiences, (*d*) previous work experiences, and (*e*) creative skills.

2. *Other Researchers*: These include colleagues at the same school, researchers at other schools, reviewers and editors of journals, and reviewers for promotion decisions.

3. *University Administrators*: The important characteristics of this group are (*a*) their standards for determining promotions and salary increases and (*b*) the support they provide for doing research.

4. *Funding Sources*: These can be organizations such as MSI, other research organizations within the government and nonprofit sector, and any other organization willing to pay for a research study by an academic.

5. *Practitioners of Marketing*: These include people from both the profit-making and nonprofit sector.

6. *Society*: Economic, political, cultural, and social institutions.

The major sub-processes are:

1. *Environmental Scanning*: The activities performed by the researcher in the hope of connecting with a research idea. These activities may include reading both scholarly work and trade publications, attending conferences and seminars, talking with practitioners, and interacting with colleagues and students.

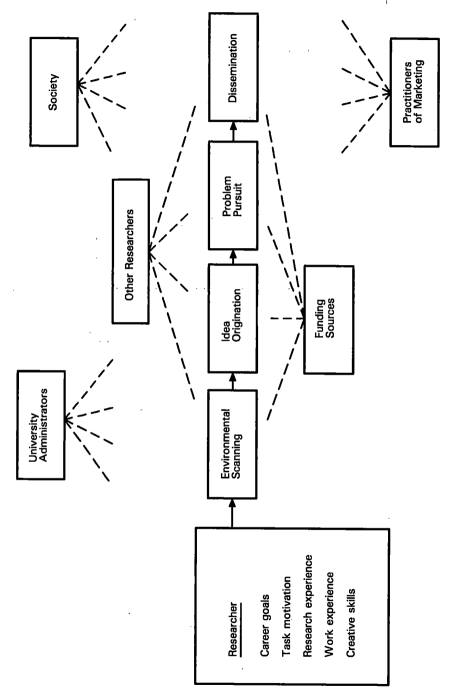

Figure 2–3. An Integrated Model of the Knowledge Creation Process

2. *Idea Origination*: The event or sequence of events that first sparks the interest in a research idea.

3. *Problem Pursuit*: The activities involved in implementing a research idea, including tasks such as conceptualizing theories or models, formulating research designs, collecting data, and analyzing results.

4. *Dissemination*: The activities involved in writing, publishing, and speaking about research results.

The solid line in figure 2–3 going from the individual researcher though the four sub-processes is included to suggest that characteristics of the individual researcher have the most influence on the overall process. The broken lines emanating from all the actors are included to suggest that the actors influence both the process and one another, but not in persistent or direct ways. The idea here is that influence can take complicated forms and can often occur because of unpredictable encounters or circumstances.

Many of the key notions in the model have been introduced in the discussion about the first three models. Thus, only a brief review of the major influences on each of the four sub-processes is presented below.

Environmental Scanning. The personal characteristics of researchers will have the greatest influence on where and how scanning for research ideas is conducted. In general, one could expect more widespread, interactive scanning from researchers who have noble career goals, intrinsic motivation, and strong creative skills (e.g., the ability to suspend judgment). Of course, the other actors will have an influence on the formation of these personal characteristics. For example, university administrators who enforce strong "publish or perish" standards may encourage nontenured researchers to adopt self-serving goals and an extrinsic motivation. Or experienced colleagues may teach young researchers creative skills and may encourage them to be driven by curiosity and intrinsic motivation.

The other actors in the model can also influence environmental scanning in a more direct fashion. For example, university administrators can provide funds for travel to conferences, bibliographic search services, or guest speakers. Similarly, funding sources can run conferences and publish proceedings to facilitate interaction among researchers.

Idea Origination. Personal characteristics can frequently influence this sub-process, as researchers may have their interests sparked by previous research or work experiences. For instance, an unanticipated finding in a research study could stimulate a whole new line of research in another direction. Ideas can also be sparked by events in society, requests for proposals from funding sources (e.g., MSI's "Research Priorities" document), and unplanned, serendipitous encounters with other researchers or practitioners.

Problem Pursuit. The manner in which a research idea is implemented can be influenced by a host of factors. Among the factors that are likely to be most influential are (1) the researcher's previous research experiences, which may lead the researcher to probe areas and employ methods that he or she has used before successfully; (2) the career goals of the researcher, which can influence the degree of rigor and the speed with which an idea is pursued; and (3) the theoretical and methodological preferences of respected other researchers and/or funding sources.

Dissemination. The career goals of a researcher are likely to have a major influence over where he or she attempts to publish or speak about completed research. But an even greater influence on this sub-process is probably exerted by those other researchers who serve as reviewers and editors of journals and conference proceedings. In addition, a funding source such as MSI, which publishes a working paper series, can be influential on dissemination.

Method of Studying Knowledge Creation

A qualitative telephone survey was conducted to help further refine some of the notions about the knowledge creation process that were distilled from the literature review and included in the integrated model. Such a survey was viewed as a necessary step before specific hypotheses about knowledge creation could be proposed and tested in a rigorous fashion in a subsequent study. Fifty-nine in-depth telephone interviews were conducted with marketing academics who had at some time received funding from MSI. A total of fifty-six people participated in these interviews, since three individuals were interviewed about two different research projects on which they had worked.

Sample

A judgment sampling approach was used to determine who would be interviewed. The names of all academics who had received support from MSI were reviewed by MSI's management, and a subset was identified consisting of those who had done more extensive projects and were still active in academia. An effort was also made to include several people who had worked in each of the eight topic areas treated in this volume. Although a few important researchers or projects may have been overlooked in selecting the sample, no bias was introduced into the study because of nonresponse. One-hundred percent of the people contacted agreed to be interviewed. The names of the interviewees—as well as their current affiliations—are presented in table 2-1.

Table 2–1
Academic Researchers Who Were Interviewed

Name	Affiliation in 1986
Mark S. Albion	Harvard
Alan R. Andreasen	UCLA
John E. G. Bateson	London Business School
George E. Belch	San Diego State
Thomas V. Bonoma	Harvard
Robert D. Buzzell	Harvard
Darral G. Clarke	Brigham Young
Ronald C. Curhan	Boston University
E. Raymond Corey	Harvard
Victor J. Cook	Tulane
John A. Czepiel	N.Y.U.
George S. Day	Toronto
Rohit Deshpande	Dartmouth
Peter Dickson	Ohio State
Paul W. Farris	Virginia
Neil M. Ford	Wisconsin
Paul E. Green	Wharton
Stephen A. Greyser	Harvard
David Hughes	North Carolina
H. Keith Hunt	Brigham Young
Thomas P. Hustad	Indiana
Thomas C. Kinnear	Michigan
Robert Kopp	Babson
Christopher H. Lovelock	———
Eleanor G. May	Virginia
Leigh McAlister	Texas (Austin)
David B. Montgomery	Stanford
Rowland T. Moriarty	Harvard
Scott Neslin	Dartmouth
Jerry Olson	Penn State
C. Whan Park	Pittsburgh
Edgar Pessemier	Virginia
Lynn W. Phillips	Stanford
John A. Quelch	Harvard
Vithala R. Rao	Cornell
Michael L. Ray	Stanford
David J. Reibstein	Wharton
Thomas S. Robertson	Wharton
Adrian B. Ryans	Toronto
Alan G. Sawyer	Florida
Subrata Sen	Yale
Benson P. Shapiro	Harvard
Allan D. Shocker	Washington
Robert E. Spekman	U.S.C.
Louis W. Stern	Northwestern
Daniel B. Wackman	Minnesota
Orville C. Walker, Jr.	Minnesota
Scott Ward	Wharton
Frederick E. Webster, Jr.	Dartmouth
Charles B. Weinberg	British Columbia
Barton A. Weitz	Florida
William L. Wilkie	Florida
Frederick Wiseman	Northeastern
George S. Yip	———
Gerald Zaltman	Pittsburgh
Valarie A. Zeithaml	Duke

The interviewees include some of the more highly regarded researchers in the discipline. For instance, twelve of them—Green, Robertson, Pessemier, Montgomery, Webster, Wilkie, Ward, Ray, Day, Zaltman, Buzzell, and Stern—were among the thirty most frequently cited authors in marketing between 1972 and 1975, according to a 1979 study by Robinson and Adler (1979). The sample clearly does *not* contain a representative group of marketing faculty, making it difficult to say that the results of the survey apply to the entire marketing academic community. However, it does seem reasonable to say the sample is a fairly representative group of *leaders* of knowledge development in marketing, whose approaches to knowledge creation are probably emulated by many of their students and colleagues. Thus, the survey results should provide insights about how a substantial portion of the marketing academic community creates knowledge.

It should also be noted that the examined projects are not representative of all research projects conducted by marketing academics. On average, these projects probably contain better-quality research, both because more highly regarded researchers were involved and because MSI is reasonably selective in making funding decisions. In fact, as discussed later in this volume, these projects seem to have produced numerous articles in the major marketing journals, including several that won awards.

Another feature that makes the examined projects less representative is that all have aspects that are intended to be of great interest to the practitioners who provide MSI's funding. By and large, the studies were designed to be what Myers, Massy, and Greyser (1980) have described as "problem-oriented." That is, the studies were designed to provide insights that would be valuable for solving problems within several organizations, not just within a single organization (i.e., applied research) or within no organization at all (i.e., basic research).

Interview Procedure

All of the interviews were conducted during 1985 by two doctoral students in marketing from the University of North Carolina. These experienced interviewers telephoned each of the researchers, introduced themselves, and described the survey as an MSI-supported project designed to learn more about the origins and impact of MSI projects. After obtaining permission to tape-record the responses, they went through a structured interview consisting completely of open-ended questions designed to obtain descriptions of the knowledge-creation process. Follow-up questions or probes were also employed to make sure certain ideas generated from the literature review were explored. A listing of the questions asked on knowledge creation is found in table 2–2. Other questions that were asked about the impact of MSI-supported research are described later in this chapter.

Table 2–2
Questions on Knowledge Creation Asked of Academic Researchers

1. What were some of the things that first sparked your interest in _____ ? (Open-ended)

   Probe: Let me read off some other things that may have sparked your interest in this topic. Was your interest sparked by . . .
   a. Research you conducted on a different, but related topic?
   b. Discussions with colleagues, students, or former professors?
   c. Personal experiences as a consultant or practicing marketer?
   d. Personal experiences as a consumer or citizen?
   e. Learning about the availability of funding to do research on this topic?

2. At some point, you decided to make a significant "investment" of your time on this topic. What were some of the factors that influenced you to focus on this topic over others with which you had some interest? (Open-ended)

   Probe: Let me read off some other factors that may have influenced your decision to invest time on this topic. Were you influenced by . . .
   a. A belief that the topic had potential for generating scholarly publications?
   b. A belief that the topic had potential for receiving grant or funding support?
   c. The actual winning of financial support?
   d. Personal encouragement from other academicians?
   e. Personal encouragement from practitioners?
   f. A belief that the topic had potential for generating consulting opportunities?
   g. Just plain curiosity?

3. Were you influenced very much by work from disciplines other than marketing?

4. Were you influenced very much by previous work that had been done in the marketing discipline?

5. Were you influenced very much in the design of your research by MSI staff members, personnel from MSI member companies, or academicians you met at MSI-sponsored events?

The interviews went smoothly; the researchers seemed to enjoy telling the doctoral students about the origins of their projects. Most of the interviews lasted between twenty and thirty minutes. Interviews were always transcribed within a few days of their completion.

Analysis

Since the survey was viewed essentially as a qualitative research effort, statistical analysis of the responses was not a major goal. What was primarily sought were "oral histories" of what had transpired in a variety of research projects. These histories are reported in the eight chapters of this book that cover how knowledge developed in eight different research areas (chapters 3–10). The chapters attempt to tell the story of (1) how research has evolved in each area, (2) how certain researchers began working in that area, (3) what role MSI played in the research efforts, and (4) what the research effort seemed to discover (based on the review of MSI working papers).

Although of secondary interest, aggregation of the responses was performed in the hope of detecting certain trends and patterns. One of the interviewers and the author collaborated on content analyzing the open-ended responses. Categories were established for each question, and frequencies with which responses fell within each category were tallied. No attempt was made to examine whether the judgments of these coders corresponded with those of coders who had not had a heavy involvement with the data collection. Training independent coders was viewed as an expensive task that would add only a limited amount of valuable information to an exploratory effort.

Summary of Results on Knowledge Creation

The interviews produced few surprises in terms of how people described their knowledge-creation experiences. The factors that were expected to influence the process (i.e., those in the integrated model) seemed to do so, while no new factors were identified. Tables 2–3 to 2–8 summarize the findings from the portions of the interviews dealing with knowledge creation.

The most frequently heard responses to the unprompted question about what first sparked researchers' interest in a topic had to do with previous research experiences and interaction with colleagues. In addition, work experience, funding opportunities, desire to make a contribution, mentor advice, and serendipity seemed to play a role for many of the respondents (see table 2–3). When prompted, over 75 percent said discussions with colleagues played an important role in sparking their interest. Prompting also revealed that previous research experiences, work experiences, and funding provided sparks for a high proportion of the respondents (see table 2–4).

When asked why they invested their time in a particular idea or topic, the most frequently mentioned, unprompted reason had to do with a desire to make a contribution to the discipline in an area where more research was needed. Additionally, inherent interest or curiosity, fit with previous research, and pursuing a "hot" topic were mentioned by several respondents (see table 2–5). The prompted responses had over 80 percent mentioning publication opportunities as a reason for investing in an area. Moreover, curiosity, encouragement from academics, and encouragement from practitioners apparently influenced a high proportion of the respondents (see table 2–6).

The results also suggest that the researchers drew heavily from work in other disciplines in pursuing their projects. They did not find themselves building upon previous work in marketing as much as from work in psychology, economics, sociology, and organizational behavior (see table 2–7).

Table 2-3
Percent of Respondents Providing Unprompted Comments About Research Spark

	Mentioned At All	Mentioned 1st or 2nd	Mentioned First
Colleague encouragement/interaction	37.3	32.2	15.3
Extension/Fit with previous research	32.2	32.2	27.1
Desire to contribute to discipline	27.1	20.3	10.1
Encouraged/Attracted by funding	23.7	13.6	3.4
Work/Consulting experience	20.3	18.6	11.7
Serendipitious encounter	20.3	16.9	8.5
Student directed to project	18.6	15.3	13.6

Table 2-4
Percent of Respondents Providing Prompted Comments About Research Spark

Discussions with others	76.3
Previous research	59.3
Work/Consulting experience	57.6
Experience as citizen/consumer	32.2
Funding	32.2

Table 2-5
Percent of Respondents Providing Unprompted Comments About Research Investment

	Mentioned At All	Mentioned 1st or 2nd	Mentioned First
Desire to contribute to discipline	45.7	40.7	27.1
Inherent interest	30.5	27.1	15.3
Extension/Fit with previous research	16.9	15.3	13.6
Significance of area	16.9	16.9	8.5
Encouraged/Attracted by funding	13.6	11.9	8.5
Colleague encouragement/interaction	11.9	10.2	5.1
Teaching outgrowth	8.5	6.8	5.1

Table 2-6
Percent of Respondents Providing Prompted Comments About Research Investment

Publication opportunities	81.4
Just plain curiosity	72.9
Encouragement from academics	69.5
Encouragement from practitioners	62.7
Funding opportunities	44.1
Winning funding	35.6
Consulting opportunities	25.4

Table 2–7
Percent of Respondents Indicating Influence from Past Work in . . .

Other disciplines		83.1
Psychology	45.8	
Economics	27.1	
Sociology	20.3	
Organizational behavior	15.3	
Marketing		28.8

Table 2–8
Percent of Respondents Providing Unprompted Comments
About MSI's Role

	Mentioned At All	Mentioned 1st or 2nd	Mentioned First
Personnel generally helpful and encouraging	57.6	57.6	45.8
Member company people helpful	33.9	30.5	20.3
Organized a conference	18.6	15.3	6.8
Minimal	11.9	11.9	11.9
MSI people designed/did study	10.2	6.8	6.8

Respondents most frequently described the role MSI played in the knowledge-creation process as generally helpful and encouraging. They also appreciated the ability to make contact with member-company practitioners and obtain their advice and encouragement. Only a small proportion saw MSI as making a minimal or inconsequential contribution to their work (see table 2–8).

Overall, the responses from this exploratory study suggest that these researchers are typically motivated by a desire to make a contribution to the marketing discipline. They seek publications to help them make this contribution, not just for purposes of obtaining job security, financial rewards, or prestige. They are people who search widely for research ideas, both by reading outside the marketing discipline and by interacting frequently with colleagues and other researchers. Occasionally, they will have a serendipitous encounter that leads them to a research idea. They are also people who are cognizant of the helpfulness of funding and practitioner advice in doing research. In sum, these are *not* people who place their highest priorities on serving the needs of practitioners through providing useful research or giving consulting advice. Their goals and behavior tend to be oriented toward the academic world more than the practitioner world. However, they tend to see having an impact on the practitioner world as a pleasing by-product of their academic endeavors.

Perspectives on Knowledge Use

Knowledge development in marketing also includes the process by which newly created knowledge is transmitted to academics and practitioners to become part of their knowledge base or their way of thinking about marketing phenomena. This knowledge "use" process was of definite interest in the study, but it was given less priority than the knowledge-creation process because it is very difficult to examine. Identifying samples of academics or practitioners who have "used" a given research study is no easy matter.

Frankly, usage of academic research is low in many disciplines. Most scholarly articles are cited very infrequently, suggesting that even academics use only limited amounts of previously generated knowledge. For example, the number of citations received by the average 1981 and 1982 *Journal of Marketing* article during 1983 was 1.06, and the corresponding figure for the *Journal of Marketing Research* was 1.30 (*Journal Citation Reports*, 1984). Moreover, studies done on the use of social science research by policy makers suggest that usage is low (see Rich, 1977; Caplan, Morrison, and Stambaugh, 1975; and Weiss, 1980). In the marketing discipline, commentaries regularly appear lamenting the lack of "relevance" or usability of academic research. Perhaps the most telling statement of this type was issued by Myers, Massy, and Greyser (1980) at the conclusion of their work on the Effectiveness of Research and Development for Marketing Management Commission. They stated:

> The major and disturbing finding from these efforts is the discrepancy between the amount of new knowledge developed and available, and the amount being applied in day-to-day marketing management operations. A significant amount of marketing research effort, new-knowledge development, model building, and theorizing has had relatively little impact on improving marketing management practice over the period. (Myers, Massy, and Greyser, 1980, p. 279)

Despite the bleak picture about usage painted in previous assessments, it was decided that several notions from the literature on knowledge use were worth exploring in a marketing context. One particularly interesting notion comes out of work by Rich (1977), Caplan, Morrison, and Stambaugh (1975), Weiss (1980), and others. These people argue that the failure of previous studies to discover much usage of academic research could stem from how usage was defined. They concede that "instrumental" usage—or usage for making specific decisions—may indeed be rare. But they feel that "conceptual" usage of research for "general enlightenment" may be fairly commonplace. As Weiss states:

> Knowledge . . . is not often "utilized" in direct and instrumental fashion in the formulation of policy. Only occasionally does it supply an "answer" that policy actors employ to solve a policy problem. Instead, research knowledge usually affects the development and modification of policy in diffuse ways. It provides a background of empirical generalizations and ideas that *creep* into policy deliberations. Its influence is exercised in more subtle ways than the word "utilization"—with its overtone of tools and implements—can capture. (Weiss, 1980, p. 381)

Hence, academically generated marketing knowledge may be "creeping" into many organizations as practitioners are regularly exposed to articles, academic courses, and training seminars. Ways of thinking about marketing problems and strategies may have been gradually changed because of this exposure.

Another notion that was explored was that personal, oral communications can be valuable in diffusing knowledge (Garvey, 1979). The possibility is there that MSI facilitates knowledge use to as great an extent by providing a means for practitioners and academics to get together to discuss research as it does by publishing its working paper series. In fact, the oral and written communication may complement each other to allow each to be more effective than it would be by itself.

Method of Studying Knowledge Use

Multiple methods were employed to examine the usage and impact of MSI-supported research. First, questions about usage and impact were asked during the telephone interviews of MSI-supported researchers. Table 2-9 contains a listing of the relevant questions posed to this group. Second, the annotated resumes of forty-seven of these interviewees (84 percent), plus those of a few MSI researchers who were not interviewed, were examined to learn where their MSI-supported work—or outgrowths of it—had been published. The resumes contained comments from the researchers indicating which publications had come directly from an MSI-supported project and which had been indirect outgrowths of a project.

A third method that was employed was a telephone survey of ten former or current editors of the *Journal of Marketing, Journal of Marketing Research*, and *Journal of Consumer Research*. Since these journals have had a total of only seventeen editors since 1961, a few of whom are deceased, obtaining interviews with ten of them was considered a good response rate. Interestingly enough, while most of these people (there are two clear

Table 2–9
Questions on Knowledge Use Asked of Academic Researchers

1. What kinds of impacts do you think your work has had?

2. Are you aware of any recognition your MSI-sponsored work has received in academic circles? For example, has your work received favorable commentary in important review articles or books? Has it been reprinted anywhere?

3. Can you cite any examples of situations that you know about where companies have apparently made use of your MSI-sponsored research to solve specific marketing problems?

4. Can you cite any examples of situations that you know about where companies have apparently made use of your MSI-sponsored research for training and/or providing general enlightenment for their marketing personnel?

Table 2–10
Questions Asked of Journal Editors

1. Are you familiar with some of the research projects that MSI has supported over the years? What projects come to mind first?

2. Do you consider any of these projects "significant contributions" to the marketing discipline?
   Probe: If "significant contributions" are defined to be those that solve important problems and/or stimulate additional research, then would any (other) MSI-sponsored work qualify?

3. Could you please name two or three (other) research efforts in the marketing discipline that, in your opinion, belong under the heading of "significant contributions?"

4. I am going to read off a list of ten MSI-sponsored projects. Please tell me if you consider each work to be (1) a minor contribution, (2) an initial step or stimulator, (3) steady progress toward solving a problem, (4) a major contribution, or (5) some other description with which you feel comfortable.
   a. Green et al.'s work on scaling
   b. Buzzell et al.'s work on PIMS
   c. Churchill, Ford, and Walker's work in sales management
   d. Greyser's work on consumerism
   e. Webster's work on top management's views of marketing
   f. Lovelock et al.'s work on services
   g. Ray's work on involvement
   h. Wilkie's work on information processing.
   i. Curhan's work on shelf space and promotion
   j. Shapiro and Moriarty's work on national account management

5. Do you have any feelings or impressions about how much MSI-sponsored work has been utilized by practitioners?

6. How close has your affiliation with MSI been through the years?

7. If MSI had never existed, what would be different about the marketing discipline today?

8. Do you have any other feelings or comments you would like to express about the contributions MSI has made to marketing?

exceptions) have had limited involvement with MSI through the years, all seemed reasonably familiar with its operation. They were interviewed with the hope that they might be able to provide a more detached and objective (but expert) perspective on MSI's accomplishments. Since confidentiality was promised in order to encourage objectivity, editors' names are not revealed here.

The questions used in these in-depth interviews are listed in table 2–10. They include unprompted and prompted recall questions. A key question asked respondents' opinions about the contributions made by ten different MSI projects. The labels "minor contribution," "initial step," "steady progress," and "major contribution" were provided as descriptors

Table 2–11
Practitioners Who Were Interviewed

Name	Present or Former Company
David Allen	Whirlpool
Linda Alwitt	Leo Burnett
Stanley Atherton	IBM
Robert Bergen	Royal Bank of Canada
James Casey	Sears
William Cook	General Foods
Gloria Deragon	Lever Brothers
James Donovan	Xerox
Richard Elder	James River Dixie Northern
Paul Fruitt	Gillette
Larry Gibson	General Mills
Thomas Gillett	GTE
Stephan Haeckel	IBM
Philip Harding	CBS
Donald Hughes	Sears
Charles Jacobson	Nabisco
Herbert Krugman	General Electric
Philip Levine	Ogilvy and Mather
Michael McLoughlin	Chase Manhattan
Malcolm McNiven	Bank of America
Robert McNulty	IBM
George Mangold	General Electric
Claudia Marshall	Travelers
Gerald Mayfield	AT&T
Kent Mitchel	General Foods
William Moran	Lever Brothers
C.J. O'Sullivan	Shell
Joseph Plummer	Young and Rubicam
Robert Pratt	Avon
Alvin Riley	Campbell Soup
William Rossiter	Olin
Dudley Ruch	Quaker Oats
Harry Sunenshine	Kentucky Fried Chicken
Donn Tee	Goodyear
Martin Thomas	Ore-Ida
Sam Thurm	Lever Brothers and A.N.A.

to facilitate obtaining responses on a four-point scale. All of the interviews were conducted by a University of North Carolina marketing Ph.D. student using the procedures described for the interviews with the researchers.

Another task that was performed to examine usage and impact was to obtain MSI records on the sales of its working papers. It should be noted that these figures dramatically understate how widely disseminated and reprinted the MSI work has been. They do not reflect how many papers are disseminated for free to people on MSI's lengthy mailing list, which currently contains more than 500 names. Nor do these figures reflect how widely disseminated, reprinted, and cited an MSI paper has been when it has been published as a journal article or book. Of course, the inform-ation from the annotated resumes provided at least some indication on the extent of re-publication of MSI working papers.

A final method of examining the usage and impact of MSI-supported research was to conduct in-depth telephone interviews with thirty-six marketing practitioners who had at one time had a close connection with MSI or an MSI project. The names and affiliations of the practitioners who were interviewed are displayed in table 2-11. These people were selected by MSI's management to represent people who had diverse experiences with MSI, permitting them to comment on projects in the eight different topic areas covered in this volume. All the respondents were current or former trustees of MSI.

The questions presented in table 2-12 were asked by a Ph.D. student in marketing from the University of North Carolina. Unaided recall types

Table 2-12
Questions Asked of Practitioners

1. We are especially interested in your opinions about the research MSI has supported in the area of _____ . Do you have any particularly favorable or unfavorable comments to make about the MSI-supported research in this area?

2. Is there a specific project in this area that comes to mind which you feel was particularly successful? (Probe on what they liked about it.)

3. Can you cite some examples of how your company—or any other company with which you are familiar—has used or benefited from this research?

   Probe: Was this research used as . . .

   a. Background for a company study?
   b. Support for a marketing decision?
   c. Training material for internal company use?
   d. Material for speeches or similar uses?

4. Are there any other MSI projects that you recall in an especially favorable or unfavorable way?

5. How extensive has your personal involvement been with MSI through the years?

6. Would you like to say anything else about what MSI has meant to you or your company?

of questions were employed so as to focus the interviews on projects that
were most familiar to the respondents. Interviewing procedures were
similar to those used in the researcher interviews.

Summary of Results on Knowledge Use

The interviews with researchers, editors, and practitioners, plus the examination of annotated resumes and sales records, presented a reasonably
consistent message that MSI-supported research has received considerable usage. The assortment of data from this exploratory study seems to
indicate clearly that this body of research has made a difference to both
academics and practitioners.

 As can be seen by reading the quotes and summary statements in
the next eight chapters, the interviewed researchers generally offered
positive comments about how their work was received by academics and
practitioners. They often cited concrete examples of how others have
followed up their research or of how companies have utilized their thinking. Moreover, the interviewed practitioners generally confirmed the comments of the researchers, although in a few topic areas they were hard
pressed to cite useful research. The practitioners especially praised MSI
for providing the opportunity for personal interaction with academic
researchers. They also provided numerous examples of how MSI projects
had added to their "general enlightenment" (i.e., conceptual usage), and
they frequently mentioned specific decisions that had been influenced by
MSI work (i.e., instrumental usage). The pessimistic view about usage that
came out of the Myers, Massy, and Greyser (1980) study did not find
support in these responses. This difference in results might be explained
by the fact that Myers, Massy, and Greyser tended to focus on usage of
academically developed tools and techniques (e.g., conjoint measurement), whereas this study focused on usage of theories, models, and
frameworks (in addition to tools and techniques).

 Admittedly, the interviewed researchers and practitioners could be
considered part of the MSI "fan club," and their comments could have
been influenced by a desire to continue a friendly and rewarding
relationship with MSI. But even allowing for some overstatement, the
overall impression this author obtained about usage is positive. Nor is that
impression altered by the comments from the editors, who tended to
evaluate MSI in terms of its contributions to the growth of scholarly
research in marketing. This presumably more-objective group was not as
enthusiastic about the impact of MSI work when talking about it in general
terms. But when asked to provide unaided recall of specific projects or
to comment on ten specific bodies of work, they described a wide
assortment of MSI projects as valuable or significant contributions. A

summary of how they responded to the questions about ten specific projects is found in table 2–13. More details on their comments are presented in the next eight chapters.

The examination of the sales records of MSI papers and their publication history as revealed by the annotated resumes indicates that MSI research is fairly widely disseminated. The annotated resumes—which came from only a subset of MSI-supported researchers—revealed that more than thirty *Journal of Marketing Research* articles, more than fifteen *Journal of Marketing* articles, more than ten Harvard Business Review articles, more than five *Journal of Consumer Research* articles, and more than fifteen books have emerged directly from this subset of MSI-supported research. In addition, the sales records indicate that more than 33,000 working papers have been sold in the 1981–1985 period, with the top ten sellers being the following:

Table 2–13
Frequency Distributions of Editors' Responses to Prompted Questions About Specific Streams of Research

Research Stream	Response				
	Minor Contribution	Initial Step	Steady Progress	Major Contribution	No Answer
Buzzell and PIMS	1	1	2	5	1
Webster's Top Management	2	5	2		1
Churchill, Ford, Walker's Sales Management	1	3		5	1
Shapiro and Moriarty's National Account	1	3	1	1	4
Lovelock et al.'s Services	2	4	3		1
Wilkie's Information Processing		1	5	1	3
Ray's Involvement			8		2
Curhan's Shelf Space	1	3	2		4
Green's Scaling			4	5	1
Greyser's Consumerism	2	5	2		1

Shapiro and Moriarty (1982), "National Account Management: Emerging Insights"

Webster (1980), "Top Management Views of the Marketing Function"

Shapiro and Moriarty (1980), "National Account Management"

Greyser (1980), "Marketing Issues—Challenges for Marketing in the 1980s"

May, Ress, and Salmon (1985), "Future Trends in Retailing"

Shapiro and Moriarty (1984), "Support Systems for National Account Managment Programs: Promises Made, Promises Kept"

Taylor (1971), "Management Experience with Applications of Multidimensional Scaling Methods"

Pessemier (1975), "Managing Innovation and New Product Development"

Shapiro and Moriarty (1984), "Organizing the National Account Force"

Langeard, Bateson, Lovelock, and Eiglier (1981), "Services Marketing: New Insights from Consumers and Managers"

Format of the Remainder of the Book

The next eight chapters examine knowledge creation and knowledge use in eight different topic areas where MSI has had a significant involvement. These areas are:

1. Strategic Marketing Management
2. Industrial Marketing
3. Services Marketing
4. Consumer Behavior
5. Advertising and Mass Communications
6. Sales Promotion and Distribution Channels
7. Research Methodology and Model Building
8. Marketing and Public Policy

The most general, managerially oriented research is covered in chapter 3, followed in succession by material of most relevance to industrial (chapter 4), services (chapter 5), and consumer (chapters 6–8) marketers. Chapters 9 and 10 return to more general interest topics, reviewing research that could be relevant to a variety of organizations. In a few cases, somewhat arbitrary decisions were made in deciding where to discuss a particular research project. Thus, the reader should be alert to the possibility that a given project could be covered in several places. Where a project might just as well have been discussed in one chapter as another, an attempt has been made to note this in the text.

Each of the eight chapters follows an identical format. Each begins with a brief overview of how the whole marketing discipline has addressed a topic area. This is followed by a short synopsis of the issues within a topic area that MSI has focused upon during its twenty-five years. The first table in each chapter (except in chapter 9, where it is unnecessary) summarizes the questions explored in MSI-supported research. The tables assign the questions to four categories, namely those that essentially seek (1) description, (2) explanation, (3) prediction, or (4) control of marketing phenomena.

Each chapter next reviews the MSI-supported projects. Commentary—based primarily on the findings from the researcher interviews—about the origins and evolution of a significant proportion of the projects is included. This most lengthy section of each chapter is followed by a section summarizing what the findings from the researcher and editor interviews and the examination of the annotated resumes suggest about the impact of the body of work in the academic world. Finally, the findings from the researcher interviews, the examination of paper sales, and the practitioner interviews are summarized to provide evidence about the impact of the body of work in the practitioner world.

The final chapter of this book attempts to pull everything together and summarize, to a greater extent than has been done in this chapter, how much support was found for the integrated model and other theoretical notions that guided this investigation. In addition, a final assessment of the contributions of MSI is offered. Among other things, this assessment draws on the wide assortment of more general comments about MSI obtained during the interviews.

A Caveat

It seems only fair to warn the reader that the following eight chapters do not contain a completely exhaustive review of the research MSI has supported over the last twenty-five years. Although a very high proportion of this work is discussed, there are, regrettably, several excellent studies and reports that are not covered. A desire to keep this volume at a reasonable length contributed to the decision to leave some research out. Moreover, difficulty placing certain projects in one of the eight topic areas also led to some exclusions. Nevertheless, almost all the projects identified by the editors or practitioners as significant or useful are reviewed here, and for a high proportion of these projects, information is reported on their origins and evolution.

3
Strategic Marketing Management: A Search for Basic Strategies with General Applications

A portion of the research activity in the marketing discipline has always been concerned with developing general principles or theories about marketing that have application to a broad spectrum of organizations. Researchers have conceived and studied concepts such as market segmentation, product positioning, the marketing mix, and the product life cycle, all with an eye toward supporting the efforts of all marketers, not just those who operate in a particular industry or economic sector. This kind of thinking about marketing became especially prevalent in the 1950s, when scholars like Wroe Alderson—a consultant and Wharton professor whose writings on marketing theory were highly influential (see Alderson 1957, 1958; Alderson and Green, 1964)—strove to help marketing become more "scientific" and respectable as an academic discipline. Through the years, much of the research has focused on narrower areas like advertising, distribution channels, and sales promotion (see chapters 7 and 8). But there has consistently been a significant amount of research activity examining more basic aspects of marketing strategy formulation, looking at areas like market segmentation and new product introduction strategies.

During the last fifteen years, research on marketing strategy has been influenced by the growing amount of research in the relatively new field of *strategic management* (see Hofer and Schendel, 1978; Porter, 1980; Day, 1984). This interdisciplinary field—which has drawn heavily on thinking from marketing, organizational behavior, economics, and other fields—has been concerned with how an organization develops and maintains a viable fit between its objectives and resources and its external environment. A key issue for researchers in strategic management has been: "How should a company decide what businesses it should be in?" The complementary issue of concern to researchers in marketing strategy has been: "For the businesses the company selects to be in, what long-run courses of action are most likely to achieve the desired responses from target markets?" Thus, marketing strategy researchers have been examining market entry and exit strategies, competitive response strategies, life-cycle extension strategies, and similar basic aspects of formulating a marketing program.

MSI Research on Strategic Marketing: Origins and Evolution

In the early 1970s, MSI launched and managed the Profit Impact of Market Strategies (PIMS) project. It was a collaborative effort of many firms to establish a huge data base that could be analyzed to learn how various basic strategies had worked in the past for a cross-section of similar businesses. Although this activity was spun off by MSI in 1975 to form the (unrelated) Strategic Planning Institute, the research done with the data base while it was still under MSI auspices has proven to be important in both marketing and strategic management. The background and findings of this PIMS research are reviewed first, followed by a review of other MSI-supported marketing strategy projects that tended to build, to some extent, on the PIMS work. Next, two more narrowly focused strategy topics are addressed: (1) determining product-market boundaries and (2) introducing new products. Both areas have received considerable attention from MSI. Finally, a few MSI projects are reviewed that dealt with how to organize and manage the marketing function in a large company. An overview of the marketing strategy issues that have been addressed in MSI-supported research is presented in table 3–1.

Table 3–1
Questions About Strategic Marketing Management Addressed by MSI Researchers

Description	Explanation	Prediction	Control

1. Do "experience curves" exist?
 	
2. How can the boundaries of markets be identified?
	1. What basic strategies are related to profitable performance?
	
	2. What is the relationship between market share and profitability?
	
	3. What factors are related to adoption of strategic planning systems?
			1. How can more effective *basic* marketing strategies be *formulated*?
			  a. . . . in new product development?
			  b. . . . at other stages of the product life cycle?
			  c. . . . when defending a market position?
			
			2. How can more effective *basic* marketing strategies be *implemented*?
			
			3. What are the most effective ways of *organizing* the overall marketing effort?

The PIMS Project

PIMS got its start at the General Electric Company, where Dr. Sidney Schoeffler and others put together and analyzed a data base containing information on strategies and profit and loss statistics over ten years for the company's many businesses. After five years of intensive research and testing, GE's Project PROM (i.e., Profitability Optimization Model) produced a computer-based model that captured in one complex equation the major factors that explained a great deal of the variability in the return on investment achieved by eighty diverse product-line businesses within GE. But the data reflected only the experience at GE, and Schoeffler had an interest in extending the data base to include more companies. The opportunity came through MSI, which at the time (early 1970s) was looking for a major project to give it increased visibility and impact. Harvard's Robert Buzzell, MSI's Executive Director, approached Shoeffler about forming a collaborative venture after learning about PROM during a chance conversation with colleague Ralph Sultan, who had recently seen Schoeffler make a presentation about his project. As Buzzell recalls:

> It was kind of serendipity. It wasn't any kind of academic process. It was happenstance, I suppose, as much as anything else, that we just discovered somebody who was doing something that fit. MSI was doing a lot of little things, but they weren't very much connected and they didn't have nearly enough cumulative impact. So I saw this as something we could build around and really do a lot of work that tied to it.

Spurred by the enthusiasm of the people from GE and the other companies that joined the project, Buzzell led a multi-phase effort that first sought to resolve issues like obtaining uniformity and maintaining confidentiality of the data. Then the project team sought to explain variation in return on investment across hundreds of business units from dozens of companies. Variables and specifications for the econometric models that were developed were drawn primarily from the literature in industrial organization economics. An early working paper from the project (Schoeffler, Buzzell, and Heany, 1973) gave the following conclusions, based on a model that explained 84 percent of the variance in the profits of the business units studied:

- Larger market share is strongly linked to larger profits.
- Product quality is also very positively related to profits.
- When product quality is low, it does not pay to have high marketing expenditures.

- High research and development spending hurts profitability when market position is weak, but increases it when market share is high.

Another early paper (Buzzell, Gale, and Sultan, 1974) focused on explaining why market share is such a key factor in explaining profitability. The conclusions reached were:

> PIMS data indicate that both turnover on investment and margin on sales are sources of increased profitability for high-share businesses. The greater investment turnover of high-share businesses reflects, in part, typical inventory economies of scale. Two important sources of increased profit margins for high-share businesses are lower costs of purchased material and components and lower marketing costs per dollar of sales. (Buzzell, Gale, and Sultan, 1974, p. 26)

The authors cautioned that the importance of market share varied considerably across industries and types of market situations, with the relationship between market share and profitability being greatest for infrequently purchased products and services that have sales distributed among many small customers. Choosing among "building," "harvesting," and "holding" strategies was seen as something that requires careful analysis of the given situation.

Follow-up Research with PIMS. Buzzell's involvement with PIMS has continued, and over time he has guided many of his Harvard doctoral students toward doing dissertations that make use of the PIMS data. MSI has supported some of these research projects, even though it no longer has a formal affiliation with the PIMS program. One such project was conducted by Ralph Biggadike (now at the University of Virginia). Using PIMS data on the strategies and performance of forty businesses during their first two years—and twenty-eight of them for their second two years—Biggadike (1977) was able to evaluate what strategies seemed to work most effectively for entering new markets. In general, he found that new entrants performed rather poorly, but that under certain circumstances a few strategies could be effective. Perhaps his most noteworthy finding was that "entry on a large scale is necessary for eventual success in rapid growth markets" (Biggadike, 1977, p. 49). Stated more specifically, he claims "incurring larger financial losses in the first two years in order to obtain higher relative share is likely to be a better long-run bargain than smaller losses and lower relative share" (Biggadike, 1977, p. 50). Additional insights formed about entering markets included:

- Established firms with a distinctive competence in technology are best suited to an incrementally innovative and early entry.

- Established firms with a marketing competence may be best suited to an imitative and later entry and should concentrate on customer services and product design tailored to customer needs.
- The gains in relative share achieved by substantially lower prices were not significant.
- Strategies employing substantially higher relative product quality did not do significantly better than those with moderately higher quality. (Biggadike, 1977, p. 51)

George Yip also used the PIMS data base for his dissertation research at Harvard. After completing this dissertation and joining the Harvard faculty (he is now with the Management Analysis Center), Yip wanted to pursue additional analysis of PIMS data in conjunction with extensive interviews of managers. His previous research and teaching experiences had made him especially interested in the issue of how extensively consumer products companies used strategic planning. Yip worked with MSI as a way of gaining access to the practitioners he sought. An MSI mini-conference was organized and the practitioners in attendance helped, according to Yip, guide him "from a general area to a set of hypotheses and a research design."

Yip proposed that the degree to which a company adopts a formal strategic planning system is determined by the factors found in figure 3–1. Through interviews with managers from eleven consumer products companies and two industrial products companies, Yip found support for his hypothesis that the less intense use of strategic planning by consumer companies tended to be associated with structural factors such as having less complex markets, lower market growth rates, or lower environmental threats. An analysis of the PIMS data also tended to support his thinking, since consumer companies were found to differ from industrial ones on measures of structural features that could influence interest in strategic planning.

Other Marketing Strategy Research

An assortment of MSI projects have looked at marketing strategy issues without utilizing the PIMS data base. Work has been done on life cycles, integrated planning, experience curves, and defensive strategy.

Life Cycle Research. MSI has been involved with research on the product life cycle throughout its history. For instance, an early project done by Rolando Polli and Victor Cook (1969)—who were research associates of MSI during the Philadelphia days—found that the familiar life-cycle curve was found in several markets. This particular project was, according to

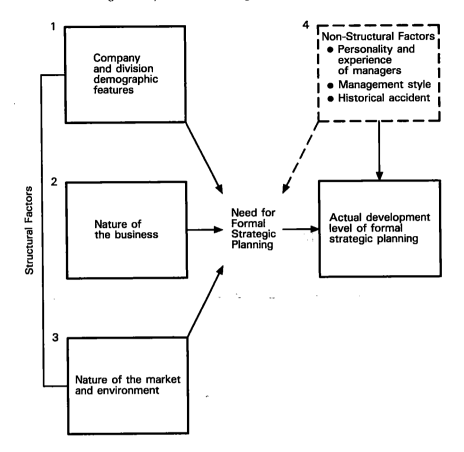

Source: Reprinted with permission from George S. Yip, "The Role of Strategic Planning in Consumer-Marketing Businesses," Report No. 84-103, Marketing Science Institute, Cambridge, Massachusetts, p. 10.

Figure 3-1. Factors Affecting Need for Strategic Planning

Cook, an outgrowth of a larger project describing brand policy determination (Cook and Schutte, 1967) which concluded, among other things, that verification of the life-cycle curve was needed.

Cook had originally come to MSI and worked on the brand policy project while still a doctoral student at Michigan. His advisor, Maynard Phelps—one of MSI's original academic trustees—had attended a trustees meeting and discovered that Thomas McCabe, Sr., MSI's chief founder, wanted such a project done. With Phelps' recommendation, Cook got the job of heading up the brand policy project and eventually stayed on to be part of the MSI staff for five years. Cook, who is now on the faculty at Tulane, recalls his years at MSI fondly, saying:

> The exposure was intense. MSI trustees and talented academics were always around. I considered taking a position at McKinsey and Company about the third year of the MSI work. But I decided what I was learning within MSI was as real and as lively an environment as I could find in an official consulting capacity. Besides that, it was much more far-reaching and stimulating. It was incredible. It was one of the great educational experiences of my life.

The early MSI-supported work on the product life cycle has been followed up by a number of projects that have examined what strategies tend to work better at different stages of the life cycle. One such project was completed by Derek Abell (then at Harvard), who wrote a paper on competitive marketing strategy based on case studies. He was concerned with framing the major strategic choices facing the manager at each life-cycle stage. Abell's major conclusions were:

- In the initial stages, the choices are primarily with what force to enter the market and whether to target a relatively narrow segment of customers or a much broader customer group.
- In the growth stage, the choices appear to be to what extent to fortify and consolidate previously established market positions or to develop new primary demand. In the latter case this may be accomplished by a variety of means, including the development of new applications, geographic extension, trading down to previously untapped consumer groups, or the addition of related products.
- In the late growth and early maturity stages, the choices lie among the various alternatives for achieving a larger share of the existing market. This may involve product improvement, product line extension, finer positioning of the product line, a shift to in-depth focus rather than breadth of offering, invading the market of a competitor who has invaded your own market, or cutting out some of the "frills" associated with the product to appeal better to certain classes of customers.
- In the mature stages, market positions have become established and the primary emphasis is on nose-to-nose competition in the various segments of the market. This may take the form of price competition, minor feature competition, or promotional competition. (Abell, 1975, p. 24)

Another MSI-supported project that examined strategies for different life-cycle stages was completed by Frederik Wiersema while he was a Harvard doctoral candidate and teaching at Simmons College. Wiersema (1982) argued that the life cycle should not be viewed as merely reflecting a market growth rate. Instead, forces which affect market growth—

demand maturation, technical maturation, and competitive maturation—
should be monitored, and different strategies should be adopted based
on the extent of each of these forms of maturation. Wiersema concluded
by stating:

> The potential benefit of this broader application of the PLC concept
> could be considerable: a sound understanding of market evolution
> would diminish the uncertainty inherent in strategic decision making,
> and could solidify the contribution of marketing to corporate planning
> in the 1980s. (Wiersema, 1982, p. 23)

Integrated Planning. Several MSI-supported projects have emphasized
the need to merge thinking from marketing and strategic management.
For example, John McCann (then at Cornell) and David Reibstein (then
at Harvard) worked on a project that highlighted the limited use of
marketing thinking in corporate planning models. As they put it: "The
role of the marketing department in the planning process frequently is
limited to providing a sales forecast which serves as an input to the
financial and production planning" (McCann and Reibstein, 1978, p. 1).
The authors stressed the need to build models that explicitly relate sales
to both external variables *and* marketing decision variables, and they
offered the example of a planning model used by Delta Airlines to show
how this could be done.

According to Reibstein, this project came out of some of his consulting
experiences, where he had observed a lack of integration between
marketers and strategic planners. A similar experience is reported by
George Day of the University of Toronto, who has worked on several MSI
projects in the marketing strategy area, all of which put an emphasis on
integrating marketing thinking and strategic management thinking. Day
credits his consulting with companies like General Electric with helping
to spark his interest in this kind of research. However, his interest in doing
integrative research also was stimulated by his doctoral work in the mid-
1960s at Columbia, where he majored in business policy (i.e., strategic
management) with a specialization in marketing. In Day's words:

> I have always flipped back and forth between marketing issues—tactical
> issues and analysis of consumer behavior—and strategic topics. I've
> always had a mixed approach to it, not being totally in marketing. I feel
> that you have to have depth in one functional area to bring a distinctive
> perspective to general management issues. It's only been in the last four
> or five years that strategic management has evolved into its own
> distinctive body of concepts, methodologies, and so forth.

Day has drawn on his multi-disciplinary background and his considerable
consulting experience to help him identify gaps in knowledge about

marketing strategy. Working with MSI has been especially attractive to him because of the access it has provided to even more practitioners.

In a conceptual paper written for MSI, Day (1980) essentially contrasted the strategic management and marketing approaches to analyzing markets. Labeling the two approaches as, respectively, "top-down" and "bottom-up," he stressed that they possessed the differences highlighted in table 3–2. He recommended that firms take an integrated approach to market analysis that balances the production and cost-oriented "top-down" approach with the customer-oriented "bottom-up" approach, avoiding the blind spots inherent in using the approaches by themselves. According to Day, "the pay-off will be clearer thinking and faster response to emerging threats and opportunities" (Day, 1980, p. 23).

Day more recently worked on a project with Robin Wensley of the London Business School that, again, sought to examine the differences between strategic management and marketing perspectives. Day and Wensley (1983) were critical of the traditional outlook or paradigm that marketing academics have adopted in approaching marketing, seeing it as one that has emphasized the marketing concept and the functions of the marketing mix. They did not view this as meshing well with the reality of what practitioners regularly face, stating:

Table 3–2
The View from the Top-Down Versus the Bottom-Up

Issue	Top-Down View	Bottom-Up View
1. Defintion of market	Markets are arenas of competition where corporate resources can be profitably employed.	Markets are shifting patterns of customer requirements and needs which can be served in many ways.
2. Orientation to market environment	Strengths and weaknesses relative to competition • cost position • ability to transfer experience • market coverage.	Customer perceptions of competitive alternatives • match of product features and cutomer needs • positioning.
3. Identification of market segments	Looks for cost discontinuities.	Emphasizes similarity of buyer responses to market efforts.
4. Identification of market niches to serve	Exploit new technologies, cost advantages, and competitor's weaknesses.	Find unsatisfied needs, unresolved problems, or changes in customer requirements and capabilities
5. Time frame	2 to 5 years	1 to 3 years

Source: Reprinted with permission from George S. Day, "Strategic Market Analysis: Top-Down and Bottom-Up Approaches," Report No. 80–105, Marketing Science Institute, Cambridge, Massachusetts, p. 10.

- The implicit one-way, or stimulus-response, model of an exchange transaction is clearly at odds with contemporary dyadic exchange theory and research.
- The dominant orientation toward customers has deflected attention from the pursuit of competitive advantage.
- There is no recognition of the role of marketing as an innovating and adaptive force in the organization. The four P's are misleading in the sense that they imply static distinctions.
- The marketing concept relies on inappropriate neoclassical economic premises and should be grounded in a more relevant constituency-based theory of the firm. (Day and Wensley, 1983, p. 6)

As an alternative, they proposed an integrative paradigm for marketing that views the marketing function as something that "initiates, negotiates, and manages acceptable exchange relationships with key interest groups, or constituencies, in the pursuit of sustainable competitive advantages, within specific markets, on the basis of long-run consumer and channel franchises" (Day and Wensley, 1983, p. 10).

Experience Curves. Day's most recent MSI-supported project looked at the phenomenon of "experience curves." Completed in collaboration with Stanford professor David Montgomery, the project examined the problems associated with applying the commonly-held belief that "unit costs and unit prices decline systematically in real terms as cumulative volume increases" (Montgomery and Day, 1985, p. 1). This belief has frequently been offered as a rationale for strategies seeking high growth and/or high market shares. In their review of previous research, Montgomery and Day found some empirical support for the existence of experience curves, but cautioned against placing too much faith in these findings. They stressed that empirical research on experience curves is plagued by problems with aggregation, errors in variables, specification of correct functional form, and measurement. They concluded by calling for additional research attempting to resolve these issues.

Defensive Strategy. A recent paper issued by MSI is concerned with how a firm should respond to the entry of a new competitor to a market that has previously been highly profitable. John Hauser of M.I.T., a management scientist, has been working on this issue for quite some time, and the paper he wrote for MSI summarizes his findings (Hauser, 1985). Using an analytical model—which contains assumptions about consumer behavior and the effects of price, advertising, product quality, and distribution that are grounded in previous empirical research—Hauser has been able to draw the following strategy recommendations for defending a market position profitably:

- Reduce spending on distribution and "awareness" advertising.
- Reduce prices.
- Make product improvements along the defending brand's relative strengths.
- Increase spending on "repositioning" advertising that emphasizes the defending brand's relative strengths.

The last three recommendations are conditional on there being a uniform distribution of consumer tastes. If this is not the case, then other recommendations would be in order, such as increasing prices for certain segments (Hauser, 1985). In general, Hauser has found his thinking has held up during consulting assignments with several companies.

Product-Market Boundaries

A research area in which MSI has had an especially heavy involvement is in how to determine product-market boundaries. This research had its roots in some consulting George Day did for General Electric and other companies, where he regularly observed people having difficulty identifying their competitors. Day mentioned this issue during a visiting seminar he gave at the University of Pittsburgh, and Allan Shocker, who was on the faculty there at the time, suggested that they start working together to address the problem. Shocker's consulting experience with a local bank had uncovered the same issue of "Who is the competition?" and he felt that his previous research on perceptual mapping would be applicable. Working with MSI, according to Shocker, "certainly impacted what we could do. The release time enabled us to move faster and broaden the scope."

Day and Shocker's research first produced a review paper that (1) covered the reasons why interest in identifying product-market boundaries had increased and (2) critiqued nine different methods of defining product-market boundaries. The methods examined ranged from calculating cross-elasticity of demand, to constructing perceptual maps, to obtaining direct customer judgments of substitutability. Among their major conclusions were:

- The suitability of different empirical methods is strongly influenced by the character of the market environment, including purchase frequency, stage of product life cycle, relative importance of subjective and objective characteristics, buyer decision-making process, ease of entry of competition, nature of distribution, and the type of market data which is commonly available.
- Empirical methods which can be used to *identify* the brands or products in a competitive set are normally inappropriate for *measuring* the degree

> of substitutability between members of the set—and vice versa. (Day
> and Shocker, 1976, p. 42)

Day and Shocker understandably endorsed the notion of using multiple
methods in trying to reach a consensus about market boundaries.

Day and Shocker went on from this project to write another paper
with William Massy of Stanford on how the different methods of
determining product-market boundaries might be useful to public policy
makers when defining "relevant markets" in antitrust deliberations (Day,
Massy, and Shocker, 1978). Moreover, Shocker proceeded to chair and co-
chair two MSI-sponsored conferences in this general area (Shocker, 1979;
Srivastava and Shocker, 1982).

Edgar Pessemier of the University of Virginia was involved with both
of Shocker's conferences, and his work using direct consumer judgments
of substitutability has been important to the study of product-market
boundaries. Pessemier (while at Purdue University and as MSI's Visiting
Research Professor in 1974-75) conducted several projects on "market
structure analysis" that not only pointed the way toward methods for
identifying market competitors, but also suggested how these methods
could be built upon to design more effective communications and new-
product introduction strategies (Pessemier, 1976, 1979a, 1979b). For
example, the diagram found in figure 3-2 reflects Pessemier's thinking
about the sequence of steps a manager could take to utilize market
structure analysis and his "STRATOP" simulation model to test out
different communication and new-product design strategies (Pessemier,
1976).

MSI's most recent involvement in the product-market boundary area
has been through the work of Leigh McAlister of the University of Texas
at Austin (then at M.I.T.) and James Lattin of Stanford. These authors were
particularly interested in the problem of defining boundaries in markets
where consumers naturally seek variety. They argued:

> Several traditional techniques for partitioning a product market assume
> that if consumers switch back and forth between two brands, those
> brands must be close substitutes. However, in some product categories,
> consumers who are looking for change/variety may switch back and forth
> between brands not because they are close substitutes but because they
> are different (complements). For such categories, the technique proposed
> in this paper reveals not only which brands substitute for one another
> but also which brands are chosen as complements to jointly satisfy the
> consumer's desire for variety. (McAlister and Lattin, 1984, p. vi)

When they tested their "cross consumption response measure" on data
about the soft drink consumption of thirty-six students, they found their
approach labeled colas and noncolas as complementary drinks rather than
substitutes for one another, as the more traditional techniques seemed

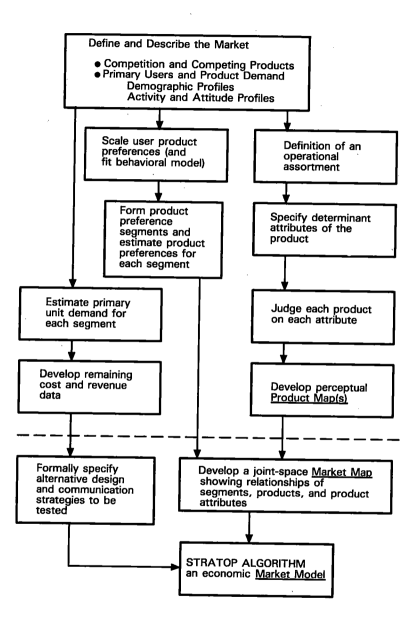

Source: Reprinted with permission from Edgar A. Pessemier, "Market Structure Analysis of New Product, Market, and Communication Opportunities," Report No. 76-106, Marketing Science Institute, Cambridge, Massachusetts, p. 33.

Figure 3–2. The Sequence of Analysis in Finding and Testing the Economic Effects of Alternative Design and Communication

to do. In addition, their approach identified other subtle interrelationships among the drinks that the more traditional approaches overlooked.

New Product Introductions

In addition to the work discussed earlier, Edgar Pessemier and Leigh McAlister have done MSI-supported research on the marketing of new products. In fact, Pessemier's writing on market structure analysis developed from his MSI-supported research on new product marketing, undertaken during his year as Visiting Research Professor at MSI (1984–85). The project was a direct outgrowth of the first "research priorities" program organized by MSI, where the trustees called for research on how to create an environment conducive to new product development.

More than fifty personal interviews were completed with researchers, analysts, and managers who had new product introduction responsibilities in ten major companies. The companies were selected to represent organizations that had experienced either very good or very poor results with new product introductions. From these interviews, Pessemier was able to identify many issues that practitioners found troublesome about new product marketing. Some had to do with how to organize and staff new-product functions; others had to do with how to fund and support the generation of new ideas. Throughout his report on the study, Pessemier (1975) offered recommendations on how to deal with the cited problems. Some examples of his thoughts follow:

- A planner or coordinator should be assigned to each important new-product project. (Pessemier, 1975, p. 23)
- Management should create an administrative atmosphere in which *constructive* contention is considered the normal mode of dealing with product proposals and new-product development projects. (Pessemier, 1975, p. 23)
- Large organizations should encourage the development of new *types* of businesses that can be handled within the corporate structure. A procedure should also be provided for spinning off the people and technologies that will flourish best outside the existing corporate organization. (Pessemier, 1975, p. 48)
- Adequate user tests and test marketing should be positively encouraged as a risk-reducing, project-improving activity. Inconvenience or modest extra costs should not be criteria for rejecting the approach. (Pessemier, 1975, p. 49)

One of the many projects Pessemier has pursued to follow up his interest in new product marketing was done with Leigh McAlister. This project materialized during a summer visit Pessemier was making to

Seattle, where McAlister was teaching at the time (at the University of Washington). As McAlister recalls:

> Pessemier had gotten into variety seeking through his new product work, and he had seen my dissertation on this subject. We were just sitting around in Seattle trying to do something productive with our summers, and we came up with this joint project on variety seeking.

They obtained support from MSI and then pursued a project that (1) developed a quantitative model of variety-seeking behavior and (2) found support for that model in data obtained from a mail survey of 450 respondents.

Although their project was focused more on developing and testing theory than on finding managerial implications for new product development, McAlister credits personnel from MSI member companies with pushing them in the direction of addressing more important, interesting, and relevant problems. Thus, among their conclusions were the following practical insights:

- Buyers' needs for information and stimulation determine the rate and type of new product introductions that should be made in product classes dominated by direct, *intrapersonal* variety motives.
- Buyers' needs for socially relevant independence and identification determine the types of new products and the rate with which they should be introduced in product classes dominated by *interpersonal* motives. Not only must the behavior of buyers be monitored but also the behavior of relevant social influentials must be understood.
- Since variety segments may be effectively developed, product positioning efforts and marketing communications should exploit the homogeneity of each segment and the between-segment differences. (Pessemier and McAlister, 1982, pp. 26–27)

The authors concede, however, that much additional research is needed before these thoughts can be treated as more than tentative suggestions.

Other work that suggested segmentation possibilities for improving the effectiveness of new product introductions was completed by Eric von Hippel of M.I.T. Drawing on his extensive background in researching the technological innovation process, von Hippel (1984) recommended targeting "lead" users and "high-benefit" users when doing research for new product ideas and when launching new product marketing efforts. "Lead" users were defined as "individuals or firms who have needs which are not now prevalent among users of a given product, but which can be predicted to become general and to constitute a commercially interesting market in the future" (von Hippel, 1984, p. 8). "High-benefit" users were defined as "individuals or firms who have a significantly stronger *unmet* need for a given novel or familiar product attribute or product concept than does the average user" (von Hippel, 1984, p. 12). Not surprisingly, von Hippel warns that finding users with these characteristics "calls for judgment and ingenuity on the part of the market analyst" (von Hippel, 1984, p. 10).

Organizing for Marketing

Over the years, MSI has supported a number of projects on how companies should organize themselves for effective marketing. For example, an early monograph by MSI staffers Victor Cook and Thomas Schutte (1967) looked, in part, at how brand management systems were employed by selected companies. Similarly, an early MSI paper titled "The Corporate Marketing Staff: Its Role and Effectiveness in Multi-Division Companies"—written by two practitioners (Snyder and Gray, 1971)—described how corporate marketing staffs operated in several major companies. It also provided suggestions as to how these staffs might improve their consulting assistance to division management.

A more recent project that addressed an organizational issue was completed by Frederick Webster of Dartmouth. Webster (1980) was concerned with how marketing is viewed by the chief executives of major corporations—and with the implications of their viewpoints for designing better-functioning marketing organizations. He became interested in this specific topic as the result of a discussion with Harvard professor Stephen Greyser (then MSI's Executive Director). Webster recollects:

> I was trying to think of issues at the interface of marketing and corporate strategy, and when I talked to Steve Greyser about what I had in the back of my mind—very roughly—and about how I was looking forward to a sabbatical, we came up with the ideas that led to that particular piece of research.

Since the topic seemed consistent with the direction his teaching responsibilities were moving (i.e., away from industrial marketing toward marketing strategy), and since he saw interviewing executives as an enjoyable and interesting endeavor, he pursued the project.

Webster personally conducted twenty-one interviews, and MSI trustees volunteered their services to conduct another nine interviews, all with chief executive officers or chief operating officers of major corporations. The provocative comments of these people led Webster to draw the following major conclusions:

> This sample . . . is virtually unanimous in feeling that marketing is the critical strategic function in their business. They also share a fundamental perception that their markets are becoming more competitive and the market environment more uncertain. They are not entirely confident that today's marketing managers are ready for these future challenges. Marketers are seen to be risk-avoiders, short-term in their orientation, and lacking in innovative and entrepreneurial outlook. (Webster, 1980, p. 27)

Additional insights were offered about (1) the need for top management to provide clear signals about priorities and objectives for marketing, (2) the need for organizational structures that properly integrate marketing and sales and relate marketing to other parts of the business, and (3) the need for MBAs who enter marketing to have received a good general management orientation as well as solid training in financial management and analytical techniques (Webster, 1980).

The problem of getting more innovation and entrepreneurial thinking out of marketing personnel, identified in Webster's research, was examined more directly in two other recent MSI papers. One of them reported a study by Tyzoon Tyebjee, Albert Bruno, and Shelby McIntyre (1983) of the University of Santa Clara. These researchers interviewed managers of several successful, rapidly growing, high-technology firms to learn what they were doing well in marketing. They found these firms tended to pass through four evolutionary stages, which they characterized as the entrepreneurial, opportunistic, responsive, and diversified marketing stages. The companies' success in building an effective marketing organization was in large part attributable to their ability to plan for subsequent stages, not their haphazard responses to new situations created by growth.

The other MSI paper on innovation was written by University of Minnesota management professor Andrew Van de Ven. In a review of the literature from his discipline, Van de Ven (1985) delineated four basic problems in managing innovation within a company. He labeled these:

- the human problem of managing attention;
- the process problem of managing new ideas into currency;
- the structural problem of managing part-whole relationships; and
- the strategic problem of institutional leadership.

A few suggestions were offered on how to deal with these problems, but a need for additional research on them was also emphasized.

The most recent MSI-supported project on organizational issues was completed by three other University of Minnesota marketing professors. Robert Ruekert, Orville Walker, and Kenneth Roering (1985) developed a contingency theory that sought to explain how the organization of marketing tasks affects marketing performance. They proposed that no single organizational structure will do equally well on all performance dimensions. Instead, that the appropriate structure will depend on factors like the product-market life cycle and the competitive strategy being employed.

MSI Research on Strategic Marketing Management: Impact and Utilization

The PIMS project and several of the other research efforts discussed in this chapter have clearly affected both marketing academics and practitioners. This body of research has facilitated the cross-fertilization of ideas between the marketing and strategic management disciplines, and it has also helped marketing managers and corporate planners work together more effectively.

Impact in the Academic World

Although the PIMS project is not without its detractors in the academic community (see, for example, Anderson and Paine, 1978; Naylor, 1978; Ramanujam and Venkatraman, 1984), it would be hard to deny that it has stimulated a large amount of academic research and thinking. A recent bibliography prepared by Robert Buzzell (1985) identified more than seventy journal articles and fifteen doctoral dissertations that either drew on the PIMS data base or critiqued PIMS findings. PIMS has also received considerable attention in several textbooks on marketing strategy and/ or strategic management. As Buzzell claims: "This is simply the source of a lot of empirical generalizations that people cite."

Another project that seemed to stimulate considerable follow-up research was Day and Shocker's product-market boundaries research. Day comments:

> The work on product-market boundaries has been very productive in terms of triggering research. Several dissertations have been written on the topic and it continues to spawn related articles. It has identified and focused a major area of research activity.

MSI has also helped to stimulate this research activity by sponsoring two conferences in this area and publishing the proceedings.

An impressive list of publications has come out of the research reviewed in this chapter. The highlights include the following:

- Buzzell's work on PIMS led directly to a *Journal of Marketing* article, two *Harvard Business Review* articles, and several proceedings papers, and it led indirectly to two *Journal of Marketing* articles, two *Harvard Business Review* articles, a *Management Science* article, and a *Strategic Management Journal* article.
- Yip's study of strategic planning produced an article for the *Journal of Business Strategy*.
- Cook's product life-cycle research appeared in the *Journal of Business*.
- Day's strategic management research with Wensley produced a *Journal of Marketing* article, and his work with Shocker on product-market boundaries led to articles in the *Journal of Marketing, Strategic Management Journal,* and several conference proceedings. The Day and Shocker work also led indirectly to articles Shocker had published in the *Journal of Marketing* (twice) and the *Journal of Consumer Research,* one of which won the Alpha Kappa Psi award as the *Journal of Marketing* article that contributed the most to the practice of marketing during 1984.
- Pessemier's MSI-supported work on new product marketing and market structure analysis led to a book published by John Wiley and articles in the *Journal of Consumer Research* and the *Journal of Contemporary Business*. His work on variety-seeking with McAlister also produced a *Journal of Consumer Research* article.
- Webster's piece on the views of top management was also published in the *Journal of Marketing*.
- Tyebjee, Bruno, and McIntyre's work produced a *Harvard Business Review* article.
- Van de Ven's MSI paper was also published in *Management Science*.
- Ruekert, Walker, and Roering had their work on marketing organization published in the *Journal of Marketing*.

The interviews with the editors revealed several interesting insights about the academic impact and contribution of some of the work discussed in this chapter. Without prompting, three of the editors labeled the Day and Shocker work on product-market boundaries as significant, and two of them gave this label to the PIMS research. When asked specifically about the PIMS research, five out of nine who commented chose to call it a "major contribution," and only one saw it as a "minor contribution." This latter person did comment, however, that the work Buzzell had been involved with had been better than the rest. Positive comments about PIMS from two editors included the following statements:

> I think PIMS was very significant. Its importance may have been exaggerated for a time, but, over the years, it has provided a lot of insights into strategy.
>
> PIMS was just a terribly important project. Only an MSI-type of organization could do that. There are many projects that lots of people can do, but there are certain projects that only certain organizations can do. It's important that an organization do those things that it is uniquely qualified to do.

As could be expected from individuals who have been involved with very rigorous empirical and theoretical research, editors expressed a less-positive opinion about Webster's research on top management views. Of those who responded to a prompt about this work, two saw it as a "minor contribution," four as an "initial step," and one as "steady progress."

Impact in the Practitioner World

Researcher Interviews. Researchers sensed that their work in the strategic marketing management area had been well received and frequently utilized by practitioners. Many of the projects were covered by the business press, and a few enjoyed above-average distribution as MSI working papers. Much consulting, speaking, and seminar leading seemed to materialize from this exposure.

The PIMS project has probably received the most publicity and utilization. According to Buzzell, many major companies have made use of the PIMS findings. He points out that executives from several companies have been making public speeches about the value of PIMS, including one from a company in Sweden who claims it is "the greatest thing since marinated herring." Buzzell also cites the situation at DuPont, where PIMS findings are regularly reported in an in-house newsletter.

Other reports of practitioner utilization from the interviewed researchers include the following:

- Yip indicates that several of the companies that participated in his strategic planning research are now his clients and use the results.
- Cook recalls doing a large number of seminars on the product life cycle and brand management for major companies during his tenure at MSI.
- Day and Shocker report that they have been called into many companies to help identify competitors. Among the companies were a major telecommunications firm and two major financial institutions.
- Webster reports an incredible response to a *Wall Street Journal* article about his "top management" findings, since a flood of phone calls and requests for copies of the paper occurred. He also feels, based on

, follow-up conversations, that many of the interviewees were
stimulated by the interview experience to "focus on issues and take
actions that they wouldn't have taken otherwise."

It should be noted that some of the MSI papers discussed in this
chapter have achieved modest, though substantial, distribution through
direct sales. For example, more than 1,700 copies of Webster's (1980)
working paper were sold between 1981 and 1984.

Practitioner Interviews. The interviewed practitioners provided unprompted, favorable comments about several projects. For example,
George Mangold, a retired General Electric executive, said "a vindication
of some sort came out of the MSI work" for all the effort the company
had put into developing many strategic planning and strategic marketing
concepts. Also commenting on PIMS were Robert Pratt (Avon), who sees
it as "standing out," and William Moran (formerly with Lever Brothers),
who sees it as "widely used." Moran recalls:

> Lever Brothers used PIMS to reassure businessmen that general economic
> principles did work in the everyday business world. For the most part,
> businessmen have considered that general economic principles just did
> not apply in the micro world of business. I think the most astonishing
> thing to the operating officers of Lever Brothers was the fact that these
> empirically derived relationships were just what they had learned in
> school in Economics 101. That came as an enormous surprise, and led
> to more serious strategic thinking in general economic terms about the
> effects of various economic activities.

Kent Mitchel (formerly with General Foods, now MSI's President) offers
this perspective on PIMS:

> I think the PIMS work is a classic example of what MSI can do. It's a good
> example of an excellent use of MSI for data gathering to prove out some
> particularly splendid academic work. It demonstrated the chicken and
> egg issues. Did you have big advertising because you had big share or
> vice versa? It cast some light on some of that. Moreover, some of the light
> it cast would give the Federal Trade Commission indigestion.

Other projects that received favorable comments from practitioners
included: (1) Day's strategy work, viewed as "relevant" by Robert Pratt
(Avon); (2) the early brand policy work by Cook and Schutte, which Donn
Tee (Goodyear) describes as a "classic" that he references periodically;
(3) the recent organizational work of Reukert, Walker, and Roering, which
Dudley Ruch (retired from Quaker) finds "impressive"; and (4) the new
product introduction work of Pessemier, which George Mangold

(retired from General Electric) and William Rossiter (retired from Olin) both appreciate. Commenting on the mini-conferences that were a part of the Pessemier project, Rossiter recalls that his firm "sent people from our new business activity, who by working with people from other companies got a lot of benefit out of it."

Finally, two interesting comments about the impact of Webster's work on top management views can be reported. First, Donald Hughes (Sears) states:

> I thought it was a very honest study, and it pointed out some of the problems with the interface of marketing and top management. I thought it was good and I shared it with my staff. However, I couldn't point to any particular action that we took or a specific benefit.

And Kent Mitchel finds this study "pretty illuminating." He claims it was used "to remind a lot of people in the marketing department about what they really ought to be focusing on."

4

Industrial Marketing: Gradually Recognizing the Differences in Selling to Organizations

The marketing problems of organizations that sell products primarily to other organizations have not been the focus of a substantial amount of academic research. Considerably more scholarly research has been devoted to the marketing of consumer products. Nevertheless, since the mid-1960s, a relatively small, but steady, stream of research on industrial marketing has emerged from academia, and this research has gradually helped clarify approaches to managing more effective marketing programs in the industrial sector.

Researchers have recognized that differences exist in marketing industrial products versus marketing consumer products, and that finding ways to cope with these differences requires attention to different kinds. of theories and research methods than one tends to use in studying consumer marketing. Thus, thinking from organizational behavior and industrial psychology has had a major influence on industrial marketing researchers. This thinking showed up in several early models of the industrial buying process that were proposed (Robinson, Faris, and Wind, 1967; Webster and Wind, 1972; Sheth, 1973). Additionally, it has permeated less comprehensive efforts to examine aspects of how buyers, purchasing agents, or "buying centers" make purchasing decisions. Organizational behavior ideas have also influenced research on the other side of the buyer-seller "dyad," since people who have studied industrial sales management have paid considerable attention to factors such as role strain, motivation, leadership, and performance evaluation (Churchill, Ford, and Walker, 1983; Bagozzi, 1979).

To date, the bulk of the research in industrial marketing has remained in the areas of organizational buying behavior and sales management. However, there has been some attention paid to industrial pricing (Farley, Hulbert, and Weinstein, 1980), industrial channels of distribution (Matthews, 1972), and industrial communications decisions (Galper, 1979). Additional research on these latter topics may come as researchers become interested in the more sophisticated marketing approaches that many industrial marketers are adopting.

MSI Research on Industrial Marketing: Origins and Evolution

MSI has had a close connection with much of the important research on industrial marketing. It supported some of the early work on models of organizational buying behavior and, through the years, it has been involved with several significant studies seeking to explain industrial purchasing behavior. It also has supported some work on market segmentation and other aspects of industrial marketing management. In addition, MSI has supported several research programs on various aspects of sales management. This work has been concerned with explaining good sales-force performance, predicting good salespersons, and several other issues (see table 4–1).

Organizational Buying Behavior

One of the first projects MSI supported during its Philadelphia days was an in-depth examination of industrial buying behavior in a few major companies. Out of this research came the book by Patrick Robinson (then MSI's Director of Management Studies), Charles Faris (Boston Consulting Group), and Jerry Wind (Wharton) titled *Industrial Buying and Creative Marketing*. Among other things, the book proposed the "Buygrid Analytic Framework for Industrial Buying Situations" presented in table 4–2. This

Table 4–1
Questions About Industrial Marketing Addressed by MSI Researchers

Description	*Explanation*	*Prediction*	*Control*
1. How do organizational buyers search for information?	1. Why do organizational buyers behave the way they do?	1. Is there a way of predicting who will be a good sales-person?	1. How can more effective *industrial* marketing strategies be *formulated*?
2. Can more effective ways of segmenting industrial markets be formulated?	2. How is sales-force performance influenced by: a. . . . organizational climate? b. . . . motivation? c. . . . territory characteristics?		2. How can more effective *industrial* marketing strategies be *implemented*? 3. What are the most effective methods of managing and organizing a sales force?

framework suggested eight "buyphases" or stages in the industrial buying process that may or may not occur depending on the "buyclass" (i.e., new task, modified rebuy, and straight rebuy) of the buying situation. Robinson, Faris, and Wind's (1967) framework served as a seminal work in the field, and numerous other authors have built upon it to help describe organizational buying behavior.

A decade later, MSI supported Thomas Bonoma (then at the University of Pittsburgh), Gerald Zaltman (Pittsburgh), and Wesley Johnston (then a Pittsburgh doctoral candidate) in writing an extensive literature review of previous research in industrial buying behavior. Bonoma states that this project was stimulated, in part, by his experiences

Table 4–2
The Buygrid Analytic Framework for Industrial Buying Situations

		Buyclasses		
		New Task	Modified Rebuy	Straight Rebuy
B	1. Anticipation or Recognition of a Problem (Need) and a General Solution			
U	2. Determination of Characteristics and Quantity of Needed Item			
Y	3. Description of Characteristics and Quantity of Needed Item			
P	4. Search for and Qualification of Potential Sources			
H	5. Acquisition and Analysis of Proposals			
A	6. Evaluation of Proposals and Selection of Supplier(s)			
S	7. Selection of an Order Routine			
E	8. Performance Feedback and Evaluation			
S				

Source: Reprinted with permission from Patrick Robinson, Charles W. Faris, and Yoram Wind, *Industrial Buying and Creative Marketing*, (Boston: Allyn and Bacon, 1967), p. 14.

Notes:
1. The most complex buying situations occur in the upper left portion of the BUYGRID matrix, when the largest number of decision makers and buying influences are involved. Thus, a New Task in its initial phase of problem recognition generally represents the greatest difficulty for management.
2. Clearly, a New Task may entail policy questions and special studies, whereas a Modified Rebuy may be more routine, and a Straight Rebuy essentially automatic.
3. As Buyphases are completed, moving from phase 1 through phase 8, the process of "creeping commitment" occurs, and there is diminishing likelihood of new vendors gaining access to the buying situation.

as a consultant to several industrial goods companies. Moreover, his background in social psychology, where he had studied group processes, contributed to his interest. Bonoma acknowledges that MSI played an important role in helping him decide to pursue this particular project. As he comments:

> The ability to do a mini-conference where it was possible to assess that there was significant corporate interest in this topic—plus the ability to do a funded literature review that enabled us to organize past knowledge and go beyond it a little bit—all of those were major influences in putting my time into this topic rather than another.

Bonoma, Zaltman, and Johnston (1977) contrasted the prevailing research paradigm of the time, which they labeled the "unit" paradigm, with a "dyadic" paradigm, which they felt had more explanatory power. As highlighted in table 4–3, they were disturbed by the focus on the individual buyer in previous research, and they felt much could be learned by looking at dyadic behaviors (or the relationships between buyers and sellers). After reviewing theoretical thinking and empirical results from research that had taken a more "dyadic" perspective, they offered eighty-five provocative propositions about industrial buying behavior that could be tested in future research. They concluded their review by stating:

1. Industrial buying behavior is a social phenomenon, and must be studied with theoretical constructs and empirical tools pitched at a social level.
2. We currently know most about the individual purchasing agent within the firm, i.e., one of the nonsocial aspects of purchasing. We know least about the interactional or social aspects of purchasing.
3. All other questions aside, it appears that much of the "legwork" in industrial buying behavior remains to be done.
4. Marketings's disciplinary colleagues, the other social sciences, appear to have much to offer the study of industrial buying behavior, both theoretically and methodologically.
5. Regardless of which theoretical approach is taken, serious methodological difficulties are encountered in the study of industrial buying behavior. (Bonoma, Zaltman, and Johnston, 1977, pp. 77–79)

Another review of the industrial buying literature was conducted for MSI by Rowland Moriarty and Morton Galper (both were then Harvard doctoral candidates). This review also stressed the need to look at industrial buying more broadly. After summarizing some of the major work in this area, Moriarty and Galper (1978) concluded:

> Organizational buying was originally thought to be a rational economic process quite different from consumer buying. As more and more

Table 4–3
Two Fundamental Paradigms in Industrial Buying Behavior

Feature	Unit Paradigm	Dyadic Paradigm
Structure	*Learning Model* S ——►O ——►R	*Social Model* A ◄——►B
Major Process	Exogenous influence.	Reciprocal influence, mutual problem solving.
Explanatory Mechanisms	Stimulus-Response.	Interpendence.
Typical Models or Premodels	Sheth's organization buying model. Attitude and multi-attribute information processing models.	Ammer's "Realistic Reciprocity." Bagozzi's exchange model.
Typical Foci	Reactivity. Closed systems. Prediction. Control.	Social exchange. Power/influence relations. Bargaining and negotiation. Conflict, cooperation, competition. Other social relationships. Explanation and understanding.
Typical shortcomings	Reductionistic. Mechanistic. Violates *social* character of marketing. Neglects the meaning of products, actions, etc., in mediating behavior (e.g., through symbols. Fails to account for purposeful behavior.	Most approaches have been applied only to customer-salesman situations. A majority of models have represented only a limit set of social processes.

Source: Reprinted with permission from Thomas Bonoma, Gerald Zaltman, and Wesley J. Johnston, "Industrial Buying Behavior," Report No. 77–117, Marketing Science Institute, Cambridge, Massachusetts, p. 22.

progress is made in understanding industrial buying, the similarities to consumer buying become more apparent. For example, the adoption process seems to be relevant in both situations. Likewise, the concept of perceived risk is equally applicable. Even the three classes of industrial buying situations seem to parallel the three classes of consumer purchases (shopping goods, specialty goods, and convenience goods). There are, however, two major influences in industrial buying behavior that are not present in consumer behavior—the organization and the interpersonal dynamics of the decision-making unit. To date, very little research has been conducted to understand how these two factors influence buying behavior. (Moriarty and Galper, 1978, p. 30)

MSI responded to the calls for further research coming out of these reviews by supporting two empirical research projects on organizational buying behavior. One was conducted by Raymond Corey of the Harvard Business School, who had been writing about and teaching industrial marketing for quite some time. Corey became interested in industrial *buying* when a colleague teaching an industrial procurement course asked to team up with him and combine courses. The colleague was retiring and did not want to see his procurement course disappear. As Corey puts it:

> I found I needed new teaching materials on industrial procurement, but I really didn't know very much about the subject. It was a blind spot in my own knowledge. So as a way of educating myself about procurement, I started that project. When I got through with it, having looked at it from the other side of the table, I found that I didn't know as much about industrial marketing as I thought I knew.

Corey's (1978) project consisted of in-depth case studies of the procurement practices of six large companies, including several MSI members. He wanted to obtain an accurate description of these practices and identify factors that might explain the strong trend toward centralized procurement that had been occurring for several years. His major conclusions were:

1. Industrial buying behavior ought clearly to be understood as a group-behavior process in which the dynamics of individual interactions shape the outcomes.
2. The position of procurement activities within the organizational structure will greatly influence the shaping of the firm's supplier complex in the long run.
3. The involvement of other functional areas (i.e., engineering, production, marketing, and finance) and the relative influence of each will vary significantly depending on the type of purchase decision to be made.
4. A powerful factor shaping the outcome of buying decisions which involve new products and/or new suppliers is the performance measures to which managers in different functional areas respond. Often these measures lead to goal incongruency, which introduces a high degree of dissonance in the purchasing process. (Corey, 1978, p. 3)

Rowland Moriarty (after he joined the faculty at Harvard) and Robert Spekman (then at Maryland) conducted another MSI-supported empirical study. The project originated, according to Spekman, in a discussion the two had at an American Marketing Association conference in 1978, when Moriarty was exploring job opportunities at Maryland. Spekman became interested in data Moriarty had collected for his dissertation, and wanted to use it to test some notions about the use of various forms of information in organizational buying. He was particularly interested in exploding "the myth that buyers in organizations are only interested in information made available to them by salespeople." Spekman had worked as a buyer before entering academia and had done considerable research on organizational buying.

Spekman kept in touch with Moriarty, and they eventually collaborated on a study using data from 489 persons representing 319 companies—all of whom had recently purchased nonintelligent data terminals. They used the data to identify five major classes of information used by buyers, and then to explore the factors that influenced use of each form of information. Among their conclusions was the following:

> The findings of the present study suggest that decision participants seek published information from the manufacturer (e.g., direct mail pieces, catalogs) and information from trade sources at other than the earliest stages of the decision process and often use these two sources of information in buying situations which embody high levels of decision conflict and/or perceived risk. As the costs associated with a personal sales effort continue to escalate, the relative importance of these other commercial information sources warrants greater scrutiny by industrial marketers than earlier research implies. (Moriarty and Spekman, 1983, p. 24)

In general, the findings led them to recommend that industrial marketers should use comprehensive communications plans employing all the information sources they identified.

Industrial Market Segmentation

Another study using Moriarty's data base was conducted by Moriarty and David Reibstein (Wharton). It looked less at organizational buying behavior and more at the strictly managerial issue of finding a better way to segment industrial markets. Moriarty and Reibstein (1982) found that service, reliability, manufacturer stability, and software support were the most important attributes to those who bought terminals. Additionally, the priority given to these four attributes varied across four relatively distinct segments. Unfortunately, they also found that these four segments had no good identifying characteristics other than the benefits they sought. The segments did not really differ significantly by size of company or industry, SIC code, respondent's level and function within the organization, characteristics of the purchase, or characteristics of individual respondents. The results therefore suggested that it would be difficult to segment this market efficiently and effectively.

Thomas Bonoma and Benson Shapiro (both from Harvard) prepared a monograph presenting a more general examination of the problem of segmenting industrial markets. MSI supported them to provide a managerially oriented review that would reflect what was known about industrial market segmentation and provide guidance on implementing and controlling a segmentation scheme (Bonoma and Shapiro, 1983). The project came about as the result of a discussion between colleagues. As Bonoma recalls:

> We got to chatting one day and decided that we could do something in segmentation that would be more powerful than anything either of us could do alone. The driving force was complementarity of interests between two people who came at a topic very differently: Shapiro looked at things much more in the aggregate—he was very managerially oriented. I was very micro or industrial buyer behavior oriented. We tried to tie together the selling and the buying notions.

Shapiro had previously worked with MSI on a managerially oriented piece titled "Industrial Product Policy: Managing the Existing Product Line" (Shapiro, 1977), and Bonoma had worked with MSI on the industrial buying review discussed earlier (Bonoma, Zaltman, and Johnston, 1977). So they approached MSI about supporting and publishing this new segmentation work. Bonoma claims that they were especially interested in obtaining the editorial support and publication dissemination that MSI could provide. In their monograph, Bonoma and Shapiro (1983) recommended a "nested" approach to industrial market segmentation. They urged consideration of the five segmentation bases presented in figure 4-1 as part of a systematic approach where the marketer would move "from the outer nests containing the more general, easily observable potential segmentation bases to the inner nests with the more specific and subtle ones" (Bonoma and Shapiro, 1983, p. 8). After describing each segmentation base in detail and suggesting potential ways of using each, they concluded by stating: "Perhaps the strongest advantage of the 'nested' approach to segmentation is that it encourages clear and meticulous thinking by naming and ordering the various bases which managers can use to think about their markets" (Bonoma and Shapiro, 1983, p. 113).

Personal Selling and Sales Management

MSI has had a deep involvement in research on selling and sales management throughout its existence. It has (1) sponsored several conferences on selling (e.g., Bagozzi, 1979), (2) supported original empirical research on selling (discussed below), and (3) regularly published or

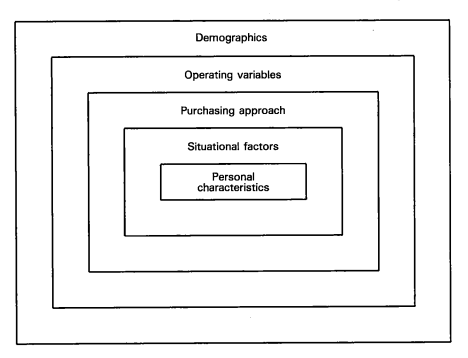

Source: Reprinted with permission from Thomas V. Bonoma and Benson P. Shapiro, "Industrial Market Segmentation: A Nested Approach," Report No. 83-100, Marketing Science Institute, Cambaridge, Massachusetts, p. 9.

Figure 4–1. A Nested Approach

facilitated publication of literature reviews on work in this area (e.g., Robinson and Stidsen, 1967; Weinberg and Ryans, 1981). The most recent of these reviews was completed by James Comer of the University of Cincinnati and Alan Dubinsky of the University of Minnesota. This review reached the following major conclusions about the two areas of research that were focused upon: (1) the predictors of sales success and (2) the management of sales personnel:

- The physical characteristics, mental abilities, personality characteristics, and experience/background factors investigated in previous empirical work apparently are unrelated to success in industrial sales. The lack of substantiated relationships between predictors and sales success may suggest that a "good" industrial salesperson must possess a blend of several important qualities necessary for success rather than one or a few qualities.
- The traditional sales management belief that job performance increases as salesperson motivation increases is supported by research. This

> enhancement of performance through motivation can be attained by designing sales jobs so that salespeople perform a variety of tasks, complete entire assignments, have job latitude, and feel that they make important contributions to the firm. Furthermore, managers who allow sales personnel to participate in relevant decision making and who show genuine concern and awareness for the sales personnel should have better-performing salespeople. Finally, when role conflict and ambiguity are decreased, job performance of salespeople tends to increase. (Comer and Dubinsky, 1985, pp. 59–61)

These conclusions were drawn after examining a large number of diverse studies, only a small portion of which were funded by MSI. The origins and findings of the MSI-supported research in this area are reviewed below, using the same categorization system as Comer and Dubinsky. That is, work that examined the predictors of sales success is reviewed first, followed by work on the management of sales personnel. In the latter category, research is reviewed that examined creating a better organizational climate for selling, motivating the sales force, determining sales force territories, and utilizing national account management systems.

Predictors of Sales Success. Barton Weitz of the University of Florida (and previously at UCLA and Wharton) has done research on personal selling with steady support from MSI. Weitz began his research while pursuing a doctorate at Stanford. He had an inherent interest in the subject that developed during an eight-year stint as a salesperson and marketer for a small electronics company. As he states:

> I have an undergraduate degree from M.I.T., and when I originally started at Stanford, they thought I was a quantitative person. But it turned out that I realized to be a quantitative person you really need a Ph.D. in mathematics to be successful. So I looked at an area where my capabilities and my interests could make a contribution over what other people could do.

Weitz applied for and received funding from MSI to support his dissertation research, and under the direction of his advisor, Peter Wright, pursued a project that explored how a salesperson's insights about his or her customers can affect performance. Drawing on social psychology research on impression formation, Weitz and Wright (1978) proposed a model of the sales process that emphasized how learning more about one's customers allows a salesperson to project a better impression and formulate more persuasive message strategies (see figure 4–2). To test their thinking, Weitz and Wright surveyed samples of both salespersons and customers for oscilloscopes. They found that salespersons who had more accurate impressions of the attributes that were important to customers— as well as more accurate impressions of where customers perceived various brands stood on those attributes—were more successful.

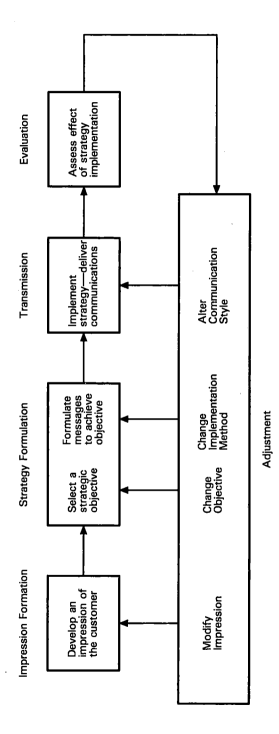

Figure 4–2. ISTEA Sales Process Model

Source: Reprinted with permission from Barton A. Weitz and Peter Wright, "The Salesperson as a Marketing Strategist: The Relationship Between Field Sales Performance and Insight About One's Customers," Report No. 78–120, Marketing Science Institute, Cambridge, Massachusetts, p. 3.

Weitz undertook another MSI-supported project in collaboration with one of his students at UCLA, Robert Saxe. This project extended Weitz's exploration of how selling performance is impacted by the way salespersons think about their customers. In this study, Saxe and Weitz (1982) developed a "SOCO" scale, which measured how Sales-Oriented or Consumer-Oriented a salesperson might be. They were reasonably successful at developing a scale with acceptable validity and reliability, and they found moderate support for the notion that greater customer-orientation—as measured by agreement with items like "A good salesperson has to have the customer's best interest in mind"—produces greater selling performance (in certain situations).

Organizational Climate for Selling. MSI has had a long-standing association with Gilbert Churchill (Wisconsin), Neil Ford (Wisconsin), and Orville Walker (Minnesota) on a wide variety of sales management research projects. The collaboration among these researchers began when Walker was a marketing doctoral student at the University of Wisconsin, under Churchill and Ford, during the late 1960s. Walker had previously earned a master's degree in social psychology at Ohio State, and had written a thesis about role conflict among industrial salespersons. He had moved in another direction for his doctoral studies and dissertation, but he had not forgotten his earlier thesis. According to Walker:

> One day toward the end of my program, I was sitting around with Gil and Neil and said: "You know I did this master's thesis and it was kind of fun, but I never really carried through on it." And they got interested and said: "Why don't we fool around a little bit with this as an area of joint research?"

Ford adds:

> To be very candid, we felt that our chances for success would probably be a lot higher in an area where, first of all, there was very little activity at the time. And we also felt that our chances for success would be a lot higher since this is an area of such extreme importance to most marketing companies.

They began their research activity before ever approaching MSI, but eventually found a need for greater funding. As Ford recalls:

> We got to a point where we sort of said, "Hey look, we have to get some support because we've been operating on a shoestring long enough." And, fortunately, MSI came through, especially in Phase I of our research. I know, pretty certain, that they underwrote quite a bit of the expense themselves because they, too, had a belief that the area deserved a lot of attention and that we could probably pull it off.

The vast amount of research Churchill, Ford, and Walker have conducted on sales management—most of it with at least some MSI connection—has filled numerous papers and articles and several books (see Ford, Walker, and Churchill, 1983 for a collection of many of the papers). Therefore, only a sampling will be presented here. One of their most extensive studies (Churchill, Ford, and Walker, 1976) surveyed 265 salespersons from ten companies to determine the relationship between organizational climate and job satisfaction. Scales utilized in the questionnaire had been thoroughly tested for their validity and reliability in previous studies (Churchill, Ford, and Walker, 1974). They found that more than 40 percent of the variation in total job satisfaction was explained by the seven climate variables they examined. This occurred even when the effects of time on the job were excluded. Churchill, Ford, and Walker (1976) concluded that salespersons tend to be more satisfied when they perceive that:

- their immediate supervisor closely directs and monitors their activities;
- management provides them with adequate assistance and support;
- they are an active participant in determining company policies and standards that affect them;
- role ambiguity and role conflict are not extensive.

Of course, these findings were incorporated into the previously cited conclusions of Comer and Dubinsky (1985).

Salesforce Motivation. Churchill, Ford, and Walker's research on organizational climate led them naturally into an interest in how to motivate salespersons to perform better, and they conducted several studies that focused on how various rewards could be used to do so. For example, in one survey of 202 salespersons for two major companies, they looked at the valence or value the respondents seemed to place on pay/financial compensation, job security, promotion, recognition, liking and respect, personal growth and development, and feelings of worthwhile accomplishment (Churchill, Ford, and Walker, 1976). Their findings led them to conclude:

- Salesmen like money, but they want self-fulfillment, too.
- Some rewards that are important to workers in other occupations do not seem to be very highly valued by salesmen. Security and the social rewards of recognition and respect all received relatively low valence ratings.
- As salesmen reach a satisfactory pay level, they are not as strongly motivated by opportunities to earn more pay.

- The attractiveness of high-level rewards, such as promotion and opportunities for accomplishment and growth, does not decline as salesmen become more satisfied with their attainment of such rewards.
- Salesmen's personal characteristics influence their valences for different kinds of rewards. The most surprising finding here is the strong desire of older and more tenured salesman for additional pay. (Churchill, Ford, and Walker, 1976, pp. 51–55)

A later replication of this study (Ford, Walker, and Churchill, 1981) with a different sample of salespersons reached very similar conclusions.

Salesperson motivation has drawn the attention of several other MSI-supported researchers. For instance, Harish Sujan (Penn State) and Barton Weitz (Florida) conducted a study that explored the factors that influence the degree to which salespersons work "hard" and work "smart" (Sujan and Weitz, 1985). According to the authors, salespeople can "work harder by putting in longer hours at work or by working more intensely during these hours" and they can "work smarter by altering their selling approach to match the particular sales situation encountered" (Sujan and Weitz, 1985, p. 1). The factors that the authors thought might influence working harder and/or smarter included salespersons' self-attributions when experiencing failure, their reward orientations (intrinsic or extrinsic), and certain characteristics of their organizations. A survey of 1,283 salespersons from 123 companies revealed that:

- salespeople who attributed their failures to insufficient effort were motivated to work harder without changing the direction of their effort;
- salespeople who attributed failures to poor strategies were motivated to change the direction of their work without altering the amount of effort they expend;
- an extrinsic reward orientation influenced salespeople to attribute failures to lack of effort;
- unexpectedly, an intrinsic reward orientation related negatively to making either strategy attributions or effort attributions for failure;
- "Type A" cultures, simple task environments, contingent money rewards, and the presence of feedback all led to extrinsic orientations.

A more direct examination of the influence of money rewards was completed by Anne Coughlan (Northwestern) and Subrata Sen (Yale). This project began when both, as faculty members at the University of Rochester, attended a one-day conference sponsored by Eastman Kodak on industrial marketing. According to Sen:

One thing that seemed to come up repeatedly during the conference was that people didn't seem to know what kinds of sales compensation schemes would be successful under what circumstances. At that time, my understanding—based on manuscripts I had seen as editor of *Marketing Science*—was that people had done scattered kinds of work on sales compensation, but nobody had tried to put it all together to come up with a general framework. So Ann and I thought we could contribute something that would be meaningful both to practitioners and academics by writing what we originally envisioned as a review paper that would put together the different literatures. It turned out that we did not only a review paper, but also some empirical work to try to test some of the ideas that had been presented in the literature.

Sen also acknowledges that a review of the research priorities of MSI encouraged them to pursue the project and apply for MSI funding.

Coughlan and Sen (1986) found that the conclusions of previous management science research on salesforce compensation were highly sensitive to the assumptions made in formulating the analytical models. They recommended having assumptions changed in the models that would allow (1) uncertainty in the sales response function (for selling effort), (2) interdependence among the cost and demand functions for multiple products sold by a salesforce, and (3) interactions between selling effort and other marketing mix variables. But in spite of the shortcomings they saw in previous work, they were able to generate twenty hypotheses about salesforce compensation that appeared worthy of careful testing. These included provocative ideas such as:

- When there is a finite degree of uncertainty and the salesperson is risk-averse, the optimal compensation plan typically includes both nonincentive (salary) and incentive (commission) components.
- The greater the risk tolerance of the salesperson, the greater should be the rate of increase in commission rate as sales increase.
- The sales effort level is lower for a risk-averse salesperson paid with a straight commission than for a risk-neutral salesperson paid in the same way.

Coughlan and Sen were able to test some of their hypotheses using archival data obtained from four different data sources. They claimed:

The hypotheses are by and large supported. However, the variable measures are very rough. (Coughlan and Sen, 1986, p. 51)

They concluded with a call for more extensive analytical and empirical research on the salesforce compensation issue.

Territorial Effects. Another collaborative effort that drew on management science thinking to address sales management problems was conducted by Adrian Ryans (University of Western Ontario) and Charles Weinberg (University of British Columbia). Both were on the faculty at Stanford when their joint work began, and both had developed some interest in sales management through previous consulting and work experiences. Ryans was also teaching the sales management course at Stanford. He claims they pursued this work because "there was not much attention being paid to the sales management area." Or as Weinberg recollects:

> It really comes back to the fact that I sort of like to work in areas in which I don't think much research is being done, and areas that I also think are of significant importance to marketing management. If you can find areas where not much work is being done, there is more room to make a contribution.

Ryans and Weinberg (1979) examined the determinants of salesforce performance, giving particular attention to the role of territory characteristics. Using data from three major companies, they ran several regressions to see how the variation in dollar sales of individual salespersons was explained by factors such as closeness of supervision, salesperson experience, competitor strength, and territory potential, concentration, and dispersion. They concluded that territory potential is an especially important determinant, and that it deserves more attention from sales managers.

National Account Management. Benson Shapiro of Harvard and his former doctoral student and current Harvard colleague, Rowland Moriarty carried out a major research program on national account management. According to Moriarty, "the genesis of this project came from a number of points, but the key one was from MSI." Apparently, MSI came to the two of them suggesting that several companies were willing to provide financial support and ample cooperation for a project on this subject. Since both of them had considerable consulting and work experience with national account management, and since they both had written extensively on industrial marketing and sales management, they were natural candidates for the project. They became excited about working on something beyond Moriarty's dissertation topic, and they particularly liked all the practitioner enthusiasm they saw. As Shapiro recalls: "Here was a very relevant topic with a lot of companies saying, 'Hey, we're interested!'"

The project was designed to explore the problems of managing large, complex accounts in major industrial companies. Specifically, Shapiro and Moriarty (1980) set out to address the following issues:

1. What criteria should management use to select accounts for treatment as national accounts?

2. How should one service and sell to national accounts?
3. How should national account managers be recruited, trained, supervised, compensated, and promoted?
4. What organizational structure should be used to manage national accounts?

A literature review, extensive interviews with managers from nineteen companies, and several case studies have been conducted as part of the project. In addition, several workshops and conferences have been held where personnel from the companies have made presentations and shared their experiences. The papers that have been published have looked at how national account programs have developed historically (Shapiro and Moriarty, 1982), how national account systems can be organized most effectively (Shapiro and Moriarty, 1984a), and how support systems can be set up for national account programs (Shapiro and Moriarty, 1984b). Among their conclusions have been the following:

- Most companies go through the same general life cycle in developing a national account program. The four stages of this life cycle are: (1) problem recognition, (2) the honeymoon, (3) growth and regression, and (4) equilibrium.
- Factors which encourage developing a national account program include: (1) increased complexity of personal selling, (2) intensified competition, and (3) heightened emphasis on salesforce efficiency and performance.
- There is no one best solution among the alternative organizational structures available for guiding a national account program. It depends on the situation and can change over time. Some deciding factors are customer overlap among divisions or groups and the strength of a company's customer versus product orientation.
- Of all the specific support activities that can supplement the work of the national account manager, information services present, perhaps, the greatest opportunity.
- Top management involvement and direction is the most important organizational factor necessary to develop a strong account orientation.

MSI Research on Industrial Marketing: Impact and Utilization

Organizational buying behavior and sales management have received relatively less research attention than many other areas in the marketing discipline. So the MSI-supported work reviewed in this chapter is a significant portion of the academic research that has been done. It has had a substantial impact. Moreover, industrial marketing practitioners have generally appreciated the insights provided by this research stream. In terms of its impact on academics and practitioners, the work discussed in this chapter has probably been as influential as any other material covered in this volume.

Impact in the Academic World

Authors who had done work in industrial buying behavior consistently indicated that their MSI projects had stimulated much additional research. For example, Bonoma states:

> If you judge by citations and reprints, then you'd have to say our work has opened up a new area in the study of buyer behavior with emphasis on transactional, relational, or other group measures as an appropriate focus. If you look at the whole stream of work that was MSI generated—and that would include a lot of pieces that don't appear under the MSI logo—then we'd have to throw in that there is a doctoral dissertation or two, a theory of buyer behavior, and five to ten publications that seem to be influential in the discipline. A significant ripple effect developed from that small investment.

Similarly, Corey claims:

> I think it's had a significant impact in the academic world because the book is still selling modestly, but steadily. I get a lot of correspondence from the U.S. and outside asking about cases and ideas.

Further, Spekman relates that "our paper has only been out a year, but we've gotten some very positive feedback on it."

Certainly, the MSI-supported work on organizational buying has helped to generate an impressive publication list. Here are some highlights:

- Bonoma, Zaltman, and Johnston's work on industrial buying led directly or indirectly to articles in the *Journal of Marketing, Industrial Marketing Management* (three times), and the *Harvard Business Review*. Bonoma and Zaltman also edited a book on organizational buying published by the American Marketing Association.

- Moriarty's industrial buying research produced a book published by Lexington Books and two articles (one with Spekman) in the *Journal of Marketing Research*.

- Corey's work led to a book published by CBI Publishing.

- Bonoma and Shapiro's work on industrial market segmentation led to a *Harvard Business Review* article, an *Industrial Marketing Management* article, and a book published by Lexington Books.

Commenting on his segmentation book, Bonoma states, "a book that we expected to sell 2,500 copies has gone into its fourth printing and has sold 15,000 to 20,000 copies."

An equally upbeat picture was painted by the authors who were interviewed about their MSI-supported work on sales management. Weitz, for example, feels his work has been cited frequently and has been reprinted in several anthologies. He thinks that "over time it will change the orientation that people have to incorporating sounder theoretical principles, based on psychology, into studies of personal selling." A similar theme comes from Ford:

> Broadly speaking, I think that we've helped to contribute to the respectability of research in the sales-force management and sales-force performance areas. We have seen a rather decided increase in the number of articles that deal with these topics. Prior to our involvement, you could probably count on one hand the number of articles that had appeared in the *Journal of Marketing* or *Journal of Marketing Research* that dealt with salesforce performance—in what you could maybe classify as an acceptable or solid empirical manner, with some sort of a conceptual model already developed. So, I think that we have provided the framework, especially in the article that appeared in the 1977 *Journal of Marketing Research*, that's allowed many other researchers, both at the doctoral level and at the faculty level, a chance to plug into various boxes of our model—much like the Howard-Sheth model provided a framework for a lot of other consumer researchers.

Weinberg provides still another comment on a similar theme:

> One of the things that we learned when we looked at previous work was that there was really very little that was done that was statistically sound. We did statistically sound work that set a standard for others. In addition, we gave an overall structure for how you look at sales-force management problems that has been picked up in a number of textbooks.

Walker emphasizes how his work with Churchill and Ford added some intellectual respectability to the area and helped bring back sales management courses into the curriculum. He comments that "there is a conceptual framework and some empirical support to talk about, rather than just leafing through trade magazines and giving war stories."

Here are some examples of publications that have emerged from the MSI-supported research on selling and sales management:

- Weitz's work led to two *Journal of Marketing Research* articles, one *Journal of Marketing* article, and several proceedings papers.

- Churchill, Ford, and Walker's research led directly or indirectly to five *Journal of Marketing Research* articles, two *Journal of Marketing* articles, three *Journal of Business Research* articles, numerous proceedings papers, a textbook published by Richard D. Irwin, and a monograph published by Lexington Books. In addition, these authors won the William O'Dell award for their 1976 *Journal of Marketing Research* article and were finalists for this award on three other occasions.

- Ryans and Weinberg's work led to a *Journal of Marketing Research* article, a *California Management Review* article, and three proceedings papers.

- Comer and Dubinsky's review was published as a monograph by Lexington Books.

Editors held generally positive views about the impact of the work discussed in this chapter. Without prompting, three editors called Weitz's selling work "significant," two gave this label to Churchill, Ford, and Walker's work, and one gave it to Shapiro and Moriarity's national account research. One editor also commented that the whole stream of MSI-supported research on organizational buying has had a "major impact." When asked specifically about the Churchill, Ford, and Walker research, five out of the nine who responded selected the label "major contribution," while three chose "initial step," and only one chose "minor contribution." Less enthusiasm was displayed for the Shapiro and Moriarty work on national account management. Only one editor chose to describe this as a "major contribution," and only one saw it as "steady progress" (perhaps because this work has not appeared in the form of journal articles).

Impact in the Practitioner World

Researcher Interviews. Authors unanimously viewed their work as very helpful to practitioners. Many of the projects required the authors to form close relationships with specific companies to collect data and insights, and through these contacts, they were able to observe their research ideas being put to use. All of the authors have also been heavily involved in teaching management development seminars, and have therefore had a chance to disseminate their thinking to practitioners at many other companies. Finally, this body of work has received considerable coverage in the trade press, leading to many inquiries and requests for reprints.

Among the more interesting researcher comments about practitioner usage are the following:

- Bonoma states that their work on industrial buying received coverage in *Financial Times, Sales and Marketing Management,* and several high tech journals. Many phone calls from practitioners were received and much consulting emerged. For example, a large project for a major tele-communications vendor—involving the revamping of their selling practices—came out of one of these contacts.

- Corey's research led to a heavy involvement in training programs with the National Association of Purchasing Managers. His derivative consulting work has included an effort to develop computer programs for doing procurement with a major high tech company.

- Ford recalls specific instances where companies made major policy changes because of their research findings. One company had a major problem with its compensation system that they had not recognized until the researchers pointed it out. Another company thought its contests and recognition programs were well-liked by its salesforce, until the research results showed otherwise.

- Weinberg relates that a presentation he and Ryans made to the sales manager of a major company led to a reassessment of its methods of judging sales-force performance.

- Shapiro and Moriarty both report an overwhelming response to their research, not only from the companies involved but from as many as forty or fifty other *Fortune* 500 companies.

It should also be noted that the Shapiro and Moriarty national account papers (1980, 1982, 1984a, 1984b) have consistently sold extremely well, breaking the 200 mark for single-year sales five times, the 300 mark three times, and the 400 mark twice. Other papers that have sold more than 100 copies in a single year include Moriarty and Galper (1978), Moriarty and Reibstein (1982), Bonoma and Shapiro (1983), Corey (1978), and Churchill, Ford, and Walker (1983).

Practitioner Interviews. The interviews revealed that practitioners generally appreciated the studies. A strong sense emerged that this research had been used in making specific decisions—not only for adding to the general enlightenment of managers. For example, Gerald Mayfield (formerly with AT&T) states that Moriarty's organizational buying work "broke new ground and helped quantify and clarify some things that some of us thought intuitively were correct." He claims that AT&T replicated some of Moriarty's methods in a smaller study and that the material was used in sales training programs and as documentation to support marketing and sales strategy decisions.

Another example comes from Stephan Haeckel (IBM), who has this to say about the Churchill, Ford, and Walker research:

It provided us with useful information about how other companies are addressing the same kinds of problems. It enabled us to compare ourselves with other companies that are comparable in the aggregate. It gave us another source of information upon which to test our assumptions and hypotheses. We used this work for background for our own company study.

By far the most appreciated research from the practitioners' perspective was Shapiro and Moriarty's work on national account management. Six practitioners provided unprompted recall of positive features and contributions of this research program. Included in this group were C.J. O'Sullivan (Shell), George Mangold (retired from G.E.), James Donovan (formerly with Xerox), Robert McNulty (formerly with AT&T), Stanley Atherton (IBM), and William Rossiter (retired from Olin). Reflecting the feelings of the others, Atherton states:

> The national account program project was very successful and has opened doors in many companies, and has assisted them in improving their marketing programs. I think the pattern that they developed and the four stages that they identified in developing a national account program were of particular value. A company could understand and follow what they did. We improved our pattern of operation somewhat after this.

And Rossiter recalls how Shapiro and Moriarty were invited to make a presentation, which then led to some decisions that "had a large impact on the bottom line of the corporation."

5

Services Marketing: Gaining Ground After a Slow Start

S cholarly research about the marketing problems of service organizations was rare prior to the 1970s. A few articles and texts called attention to the growth of the service sector and the need to recognize certain differences about services marketing (Rathmell, 1966; Stanton, 1967), but little else was written on the subject. However, in 1969, Kotler and Levy wrote their seminal article "Broadening the Concept of Marketing" in the *Journal of Marketing.* It encouraged using marketing concepts and tools in new settings, especially in nonprofit, social cause, and political organizations. And, indeed, the article seemed to stimulate people to study and write about social cause marketing (Kotler and Zaltman, 1971), health care marketing (Zaltman and Vertinsky, 1971), political marketing (Rothschild, 1974), transit marketing (Lovelock, 1973), and other forms of nonprofit marketing. As the interests of marketing academics "broadened," increased attention was paid to both nonprofit and profit-making *service* organizations.

What was happening in the marketing discipline reflected what was happening in the world at large. Government agencies, transportation systems, charities, associations, hospitals, universities, banks, insurance companies, airlines, hotels, fast-food chains, and health spas began to employ a rapidly increasing proportion of the world's workforce. Marketing became a problem to many service organizations, especially those operating in industries where deregulation had stimulated intense competition (for example, banking, air travel, trucking, and health care). The marketing problems of these organizations began to attract an increasing proportion of the research "work" of marketing academics. Starting with a trickle of articles and papers in the early 1970s, the stream of publications on services marketing has become a flood in recent years. A services marketing bibliography published by the American Marketing Association (Fisk and Silpakit, 1985) lists 1,262 relevant publications that appeared between 1975 and 1985. This contrasts with only 137 articles in the previous decade (Fisk, Silpakit, and Hromas, 1985).

Much of the early academic writing on services marketing could be viewed as "sales pitches" for marketing. Basic marketing concepts and tools that had been successfully employed in other settings were described and promoted for use in a particular kind of service industry. But it was quickly recognized that some distinctive marketing problems in the service sector make it difficult to apply marketing approaches that succeed with tangible products (George and Barksdale, 1974; Sasser, 1976; Shostack, 1977). Thus, a considerable body of work focused on identifying what, in general, makes services marketing *different*. Only now is empirical research beginning to follow up this typically descriptive and conceptual work as researchers seek to understand more general ways of overcoming the marketing problems confronting service organizations. Until recently, the bulk of the empirical work throughout the discipline has tended to be rather applied and has not typically produced results that can be generalized beyond a specific service industry.

MSI Research on Services:
Origins and Evolution

Much of the work on services marketing supported by MSI has tended to fall in the "What makes services marketing different?" category. However, support has also been provided for research on how consumers react to participation in the service production process and how consumers form quality perceptions for services. In addition, most of the supported research has indirectly or directly addressed how to formulate and implement more effective service marketing strategies (see table 5-1).

The Differences in Services Marketing

As mentioned earlier, a steady stream of writing about the differences in services marketing appeared in the mid-1970s. Among those who had taken the lead in addressing this subject was Christopher Lovelock, who was then an assistant professor at the Harvard Business School. Lovelock was building on a long-standing interest in the service sector. Members of his family had worked in banking and transportation, and he had worked for an advertising agency prior to studying for his doctorate. His doctoral work at Stanford had deepened his interest in services. While there, he wrote a dissertation on transit marketing and developed a close working relationship with a new assistant professor, Charles Weinberg, who was teaching a new course on public sector marketing. When Lovelock arrived at Harvard in 1973, he too began to organize a new course with a services emphasis, partly in reaction to comments he received from

Table 5–1
Questions About Services Marketing Addressed by MSI Researchers

Description	Explanation	Prediction	Control
1. What makes services marketing different?	1. How do consumers respond to participation in the service production process?		1. How can more effective *services* marketing strategies be *formulated*?
	2. What determines consumer satisfaction with service quality?		2. How can more effective *services* marketing strategies be *implemented*?

MBA students who were disappointed with the lack of services content in the first-year marketing course. He began to write services cases (e.g., Southwest Airlines, Federal Express) and scholarly papers (Lovelock and Weinberg, 1975; Lovelock, 1975).

While attending a conference in France, Lovelock encountered Pierre Eiglier and Eric Langeard, two European marketing professors who suggested that they all work together on a joint project. MSI was seen as the logical place to go for support, and a proposal was put together for a research program in consumer services. It was designed to uncover new, general insights into the differences in services marketing and the strategic implications of those differences. John Bateson became involved with the project, essentially by being in the right place at the right time. He was a first-year doctoral student taking a seminar from Lovelock, and he was also working part-time as a research assistant at MSI. A term paper he had just written on services marketing for Lovelock's course—which he claims to have pursued because "in true doctoral student fashion, I was looking for an area that had no papers in it so that I could do a quick review"—made him a logical candidate to be a research assistant on the project.

The consumer services research program commenced with the production of what Lovelock terms a "think piece" titled *Marketing Consumer Services: New Insights* (Eiglier et al., 1977). The work provided some new conceptualizations of what makes services marketing different, building on (1) previous writings, (2) some exploratory interviews conducted in France by Eiglier and Langeard, and (3) discussions held between the researchers and personnel from MSI member companies. Lovelock credits the MSI staff with making a strong contribution by allowing everyone to interact with one another more often than they would have otherwise. He further credits this experience as being helpful in his course development activities. As he puts it: "It was the key ingredient in my doing the service marketing course, because it gave me the opportunity to bat ideas off other people—to talk to practitioners through MSI."

Among the "new insights" presented in the five papers of this first monograph were the following:

1. Bateson offered the idea that *intangibility* is the driving force behind all the structural differences between services and product marketing that have been identified by other authors. He claimed that services are "doubly intangible"; they are both impalpable and difficult to grasp mentally. As suggested in figure 5–1, he argued that impalpability leads to simultaneous production and consumption which, in turn, leads to a variety of problems having to do with inseparability. In addition to the problems noted in the figure, inseparability was also seen as creating (*a*) no inventories, (*b*) short or nonexistent channels of distribution, and (*c*) the need for convenient, widespread, service operations facilities. Bateson viewed the difficulty of grasping a service mentally as making it harder to research what clients are seeking or how they define quality. He argued that this further contributed to problems of (*a*) differentiating offerings from competitors, (*b*) managing how employees interface with clients, and (*c*) maintaining quality control.

2. Eiglier and Langeard emphasized several additional differences. They suggested that determining prices is more difficult for services, both because costs are hard to measure and because unusual psychological reactions to service prices may exist. They also argued that word-of-mouth is likely to play a bigger role in services marketing, as consumers are inclined to turn to others to make them feel more comfortable in choosing providers. Another point they emphasized was that obtaining consistent, client-pleasing behavior from diverse employees is frequently a serious problem.

3. Lovelock and Young described several cases where productivity had been increased by having consumers become more involved with the service production process. Getting consumers to use postal zip codes and long-distance direct-dialing were among the examples cited.

Another MSI work that focused on the differences between services and product marketing is the monograph by Christian Gronroos (1983) of the Swedish School of Economics and Business Administration. This work built on some of the ideas presented in Eiglier et al. (1977). Among his major conclusions were the following:

1. Consumers' perceptions of service quality and their consequent future behavior are influenced by many resources and activities that are outside the arena of traditional marketing mix activities but which have a marketing impact.

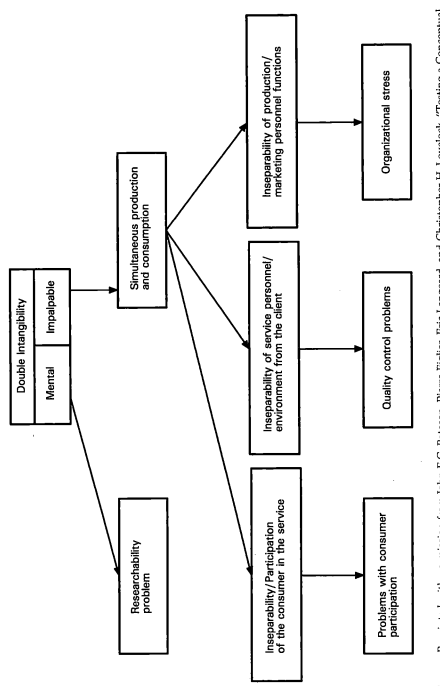

Figure 5–1. The Development of Key Problems or Issues

Source: Reprinted with permission from John E.G. Bateson, Pierre Eiglier, Eric Langeard, and Christopher H. Lovelock, "Testing a Conceptual Framework for Consumer Service Marketing," Report No. 78–112, Marketing Science Institute, Cambridge, Massachusetts, p. 21.

2. Service businesses may easily fall into a "strategic management trap" if they fail to recognize that strategic decisions about production, administration, and marketing all have an impact on the efficiency with which the firm performs externally as well as internally.

Additional (more managerial) conclusions from this work are cited later in this chapter.

Consumer Response to "Servuction"

As mentioned earlier, Eiglier et al. (1977) discovered considerable interest among services marketing practitioners in achieving greater productivity through getting consumers more involved with service production. Thus, a major portion of their followup work to their "think piece" was devoted to finding out how consumers respond to doing what the authors labeled "servuction" (i.e., service production). Do consumers like automatic tellers, self-service gasoline pumps, and self-service restaurants? They hoped to discover that favorability toward participation in production would provide a useful basis for segmenting markets.

The researchers surveyed two large samples of customers of financial institutions (Langeard et al., 1981). They sought reactions to a variety of self-service practices from the hotel, travel, banking, gasoline, and restaurant industries. Respondents were classified into five groups, based on their willingness to participate in different service production experiences. The authors found that "nonparticipators" were very concerned that something might go wrong if they participated, and they also expressed concern about the amount of effort required of them. Low participators, on the other hand, exhibited less concern about these issues and were attracted most by the prospect of saving time and achieving greater efficiency. Medium, high, and maximum participators were also attracted by time savings and efficiency, but were even more enticed by the ability to exert greater control over the situation. Based on these findings, the authors concluded that willingness to participate is likely to be a useful segmentation variable.

The Determinants of Satisfaction with Service Quality

The survey research conducted by Langeard et al. (1981) also provided data on the attributes that consumers find important in deciding on banking services. The researchers compared these data to information obtained from bank field managers and found that, overall, the managers had a poor understanding of customers' needs and expectations. They tended to underestimate the proportion of customers who believed a particular attribute was "very" or "extremely" important in choosing between banks in the same location. The attributes included:

- simple banking procedures,
- paperwork that is easy to complete,
- accuracy in handling customers' accounts,
- a full range of services,
- competitive interest rates and bank charges,
- routine banking that is not a hassle.

On the other hand, the managers were reasonably accurate in assessing the high degree of importance consumers give to "quick check cashing" and "knowledgeable employees."

These results provide a beginning for understanding what a service provider can do to satisfy customers. But the results may not be generalizable to other industries. An attempt to obtain a deeper understanding of how consumers, in general, form quality perceptions is taking place in an MSI research program being conducted by A. Parasuraman (Texas A&M), Valarie Zeithaml (Duke), and Leonard Berry (Texas A&M). This is another research program that has matched MSI with researchers who have had a long-standing interest in an area. These three academics have done extensive writing on services marketing and had discussed pursuing a project on service quality even before contacting MSI. But MSI probably had an influence on *when* they pursued this project. As Zeithaml explains:

> MSI's willingness to participate and give us access to the companies was an important factor. They put us in touch with four companies. We got to talk to all the important people that deal with services quality. That had a lot to do with our choosing to deal with that topic at that time.

A goal of this research program has been to develop a general set of questions or scales that service companies can use to measure how much quality they are providing to consumers. In an initial phase, exploratory, focus-group research (Parasuraman, Zeithaml, and Berry, 1984) has identified ten dimensions along which consumers tend to evaluate service quality in a variety of industries. These dimensions are presented in table 5-2. The authors proposed a model that suggests a consumer's overall judgment of quality of a service will be determined by how well a service is perceived to have performed on these dimensions, as compared to what was expected for performance.

The second phase of this research program developed the "SERVQUAL" scale, a multiple item scale for measuring customer perceptions

Table 5–2
Dimensions of Service Quality

Reliability involves consistency of performance and dependability.
It means that the firm performs the service right the first time.
It also means that the firm honors its promises. Specifically, it involves:
—accuracy in billing,
—keeping records correctly,
—performing the service at the designated time.

Responsiveness concerns the willingness or readiness of employees to provide service. It involves timeliness of service:
—mailing a transaction slip immediately,
—calling the customer back quickly,
—giving prompt service (e.g., setting up appointments quickly).

Competence means possession of the required skills and knowledge to perform the service. It involves:
—knowledge and skill of the contact personnel,
—knowledge and skill of operational support personnel,
—research capability of the organization, e.g., securities brokerage firm.

Access involves approachability and ease of contact. It means:
—the service is easily accessible by telephone (lines are not busy and they don't put you on hold),
—waiting time to receive service (e.g., at a bank) is not extensive,
—convenient hours of operation,
—convenient location of service facility.

Courtesy involves politeness, respect, consideration, and friendliness of contact personnel (including receptionists, telephone operators, etc.) It includes:
—consideration for the consumer's property (e.g., no muddy shoes on the carpet),
—clean and neat appearance of public contact personnel.

Communication means keeping customers informed in language they can understand and listening to customers. It may mean that the company has to adjust its language for different consumers—increasing the level of sophistication with a well-educated customer and speaking simply and plainly with a novice. It involves:
—explaining the service itself,
—explaining how much the service will cost,
—explaining the tradeoffs between service and cost,
—assuring the consumer that a problem will be handled.

Credibility includes trustworthiness, believability, honesty. It involves having the customer's best interests at heart. Contributing to credibility are:
—company name,
—company reputation,
—personal characteristics of the contact personnel,
—the degree of hard sell involved in interactions with the customer.

Security is the freedom from danger, risk, or doubt. It involves:
—physical safety (will I get mugged at the automatic teller machine?),
—financial security (does the company know where my stock certificate is?),
—confidentiality (are my dealings with the company private?).

Understanding/Knowing the Customer means making the effort to understand the customer's needs. It involves:
—learning the customer's specific requirements,
—providing individualized attention,
—recognizing the regular customer.

Table 5-2 continued

Tangibles include the physical evidence of the service:
  —physical facilities,
  —appearance of personnel,
  —tools or equipment used to provide the service,
  —physical representations of the service, such as a plastic credit card or a bank statement,
  —other customers in the service facility.

Source: Reprinted with permission from A. Parasuraman, Valarie A. Zeithaml, and Leonard L. Berry, "A Conceptual Model of Service Quality and its Implications for Future Research," Report No. 84-106, Marketing Science Institute, Cambridge, Massachusetts, pp. 13-14.

of service quality (Parasuraman, Zeithaml, and Berry, 1986). Rigorous procedures were followed to develop a scale with desirable psychometric properties. An initial set of ninety-seven items was put through two phases of scale purification using data obtained from 1,000 respondents. A final 26-item instrument emerged that can be used to measure how a service provider is perceived to have performed on five different dimensions of service quality. The ten quality dimensions listed in table 5-2 were "boiled down" to the following five dimensions as a result of the scale purification steps:

1. *tangibles*—physical facilities, equipment, and appearance of personnel;

2. *reliability*—ability to perform the promised service dependably and accurately;

3. *responsiveness*—willingness to help customers and provide prompt service;

4. *assurance*—knowledge and courtesy of employees and their ability to convey trust and confidence; and

5. *empathy*—caring, individualized attention the firm provides its customers.

The authors point out that this scale can be used to help a service firm decide whether it needs to take actions that would improve certain quality perceptions, modify unreasonable customer expectations, or both.

Strategy Formulation and Implementation

All of the works discussed thus far contain sections offering explicit ideas for strategy formulation and implementation. Several of these ideas have been cited already, such as Langeard et al.'s notion of segmenting by willingness to participate in the service production process. Some of the other ideas include:

1. professionalize the client/contact person relationship (Eiglier et al., 1977);

2. use the environment in which the contact takes place to create confidence, pleasure, and desired behavior (Eiglier et al., 1977);

3. directly involve senior management in the marketing orientation of the business, being careful to delegate marketing responsibility (Gronroos, 1983);

4. Urge top management to develop an integrated functional perspective instead of a single functional view of the firm's business (Eiglier et al., 1977);

5. pursue "internal marketing" (Berry, 1981),(i.e., an active, marketing-like approach designed to shape employees' attitudes and behavior toward their jobs, the customers, and the internal environment) so that service firms ensure the all-important customer-service interaction is satisfactory (Gronroos, 1983).

Implementing ideas such as these in a service organization presents many obstacles. One MSI study that addressed these problems (and other issues) was conducted by John Czepiel of New York University (1980). Once again, the research was an outgrowth of previous research by the author, but in this case the work had not been done on services. Czepiel had been working in the area of measuring consumer satisfaction. He was concerned about the relevance of his work to practitioners, especially to those who market products. While attending a conference in France during 1978, he heard a presentation on services marketing that helped him realize the service sector was an opportune setting for trying out his ideas. As he puts it: "I thought a lot could be done in this area—that the payoffs in managerial practice would be rather rapid even though the work could be done at a fairly decent theoretical level."

Encouragement and financial support from MSI helped reinforce his thinking about the potential of providing "added value" in the services area. He therefore embarked on a study designed to develop and test a model of the management process in a service firm. The prescriptive model he conceived is presented in figure 5-2.

Czepiel's model highlights the importance of ideas suggested in other research, such as having top management leadership, integrating marketing and operations, doing research to learn more about what determines consumer satisfaction with service quality, and doing internal marketing. A pilot study with three large firms—a domestic airline, a retail banking firm, and a national fast food operation—provided evidence of the model's usefulness. However, the study also identified a strong need for further research on (1) the sources of customer satisfaction, (2) the organizational forms that are most effective for service businesses, and (3) the best systems for monitoring consumer satisfaction.

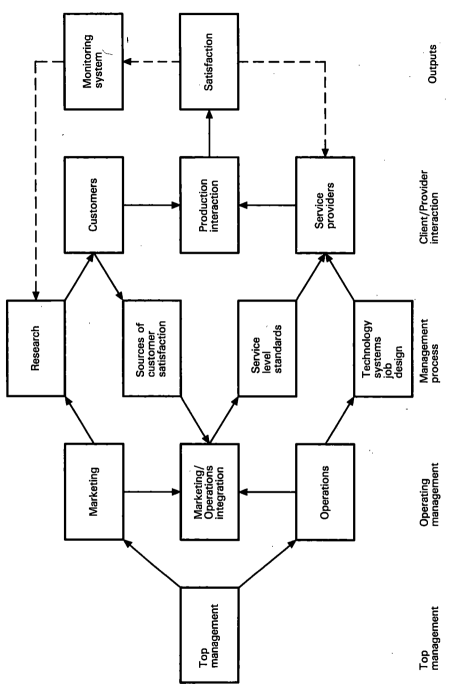

Source: Reprinted with permission from John A. Czepiel, "Managing Customer Satisfaction in Consumer Service Buisnesses," Report No. 80–109, Marketing Science Institute, Cambridge, Massachusetts, p. 7.

Figure 5–2. The Management Process in Consumer Service Businesses

MSI Research on Services:
Impact and Utilization

MSI-sponsored research on services marketing—as with most of the research in this area—is still relatively young. Nevertheless, there is evidence that the thinking in this field is drawing attention in both the academic and practitioner worlds.

Impact in the Academic World

There has been an explosion of publications on services marketing during the last ten years (Fisk, Silpakit, and Hromas, 1985). Although it is impossible to determine exactly how much credit the MSI work deserves for stimulating this explosion, it seems fair to say that it helped significantly. For one thing, Lovelock, Bateson, and Czepiel maintain that the work has been cited frequently. (But this claim cannot be readily checked because the *Social Science Citation Index* does not list citations to MSI working papers.) In addition, there is the following praise:

1. Bateson's paper from Eiglier et al. (1977) received an award as the best paper at the first American Marketing Association Services Conference in 1981.
2. A revised version of Parasuraman, Zeithaml, and Berry's first MSI paper was published in the *Journal of Marketing*.
3. An article by Lovelock, that he views as an outgrowth of his MSI work, received the prestigious Alpha Kappa Psi award as the *Journal of Marketing* article judged to have contributed the most to marketing practice during 1983. He has also published a textbook on services marketing with Prentice-Hall that draws on his MSI work.
4. An article co-authored by Czepiel, that he views as an outgrowth of his MSI work, appeared in the *Journal of Marketing*. He also co-edited a book, the product of a workshop co-sponsored by MSI, that has been published by Lexington Books.

Finally, MSI-supported researchers have played a major role in organizing the increasingly popular Annual American Marketing Association Services Conference. Zeithaml, Czepiel, and Diane Schmalensee (MSI's Vice President, Research Operations) have all chaired or co-chaired this event in the last few years.

Despite these accomplishments, it is not clear that the services marketing area has attained a position of strong "academic respectability." For instance, the work of Lovelock et al. was one of the lowest rated among the ten bodies of MSI work evaluated by the journal editors, none of whom gave unprompted comments about services research. As Bateson laments: "The real problem is to prove that 'scholarly research' can be done in this area." But as research moves beyond descriptive efforts into the realm of trying to uncover explanations for phenomena that occur frequently, but not solely, in the service sector, perhaps more respectability will come.

Impact in the Practitioner World

Researcher Interviews. Practitioners have exhibited keen interest in new thinking about services marketing. They have supported the American Marketing Association's conferences and activities on services, and they have been receptive to MSI's initiatives in the area. Researchers generally felt that personnel from MSI member companies had welcomed their ideas during meetings arranged through MSI. Moreover, all of these researchers had been invited to conduct seminars about their MSI research. Several very positive reactions were reported, including Czepiel's comment that one major company has "duplicated" his model. And Zeithaml reports that a large marketing research firm reacted to one of her presentations by breaking up its managers into ten focus groups and having each group brainstorm about one of the quality dimensions Zeithaml and her co-authors had identified.

Practitioner Interviews. The practitioners who were asked to comment on MSI's research on services were generally complimentary of the initiatives that had been made in this area. Thomas Gillett (GTE) captures the feelings of most in saying:

> I think MSI has been instrumental in being on the leading edge of encouraging research into this area. Services marketing is something we were all doing. We've all been in the services business. But we didn't know it was different from being in the product business. I think that because an organization like MSI exists to encourage thought into this area, we've all realized, "Gee, we have to be more sophisticated than just dealing with it the way we deal with the product side. I think they've played an instrumental role by encouraging academicians to help us by increasing the knowledge base in services marketing.

And Paul Fruitt (Gillette) offers a somewhat similar perspective:

> It's a field that did not have much work. For many companies that are not primarily services companies but are now getting into that area in one way or another, it has been useful work in helping them to understand the differences and similarities in services marketing and product marketing. In our company, it has been instrumental in helping

people to understand the services business a little better from a theoretical standpoint. There have been several pieces that have been helpful. In fact, the whole stream has been helpful—you just don't see it much elsewhere.

More specific comments were offered about the Langeard et al. work and the Parasuraman, Zeithaml, and Berry work. Harry Sunenshine (Kentucky Fried Chicken) claims the former work was beneficial to him and his company for "framing people's thinking and getting them on a different track." Five people gave unprompted recall and praise to the latter work: Donald Hughes (Sears), Al Riley (Campbell Soup), Michael McLaughlin (Chase Manhattan), Malcolm McNiven (Bank of America), and Claudia Marshall (Travelers Insurance). In fact, McNiven claims that the results of this work have led Bank of America "to change its whole approach to setting quality standards." Marshall's use of this work has been to adopt it "for talking points and for considering issues related to quality in our company."

6
Consumer Behavior: Addressing More Basic Questions

Marketers have always been interested in understanding consumer behavior. But it was not until the 1950s when the "marketing concept" came to prominence with its emphasis on a consumer orientation—that research into consumer behavior became a significant area of academic inquiry. At first, the research tended to focus on understanding consumer motives (using projective techniques) and on describing the characteristics of various consumer segments (using survey research). But during the 1960s, marketing academics began to look seriously at what the behavioral sciences had to offer to help understand consumer behavior. Several books came out that introduced theories from psychology, sociology, and other disciplines in the marketing field (Bliss, 1963; Zaltman, 1965; Kassarjian and Robertson, 1968), and many studies began to appear testing notions about personality, cognitive dissonance, perceived risk, diffusion of innovations, interpersonal influence, family decision making, and attitudes.

In the late 1960s, comprehensive models of consumer behavior were proposed by several authors (Howard and Sheth, 1969; Engel, Kollat, and Blackwell, 1968; Andreasen, 1965; Nicosia, 1966), who tried to show the complex nature of the processes and factors that determine consumer behavior. While these models could not be tested very effectively in their entirety, they served as a focal point for discussion and research. Additionally, these models, and the books in which they were presented, became vehicles around which courses in consumer behavior were developed at many schools. The increased research and teaching created a base of support for the formation of the Association for Consumer Research in 1970. This association has held annual meetings (with published proceedings) every year, and it has published the highly regarded *Journal of Consumer Research* since 1974.

While the topic of attitudes has received sustained, heavy attention throughout the last three decades, most of the topics that aroused substantial interest in the 1960s have faded. The 1970s and 1980s have witnessed the emergence of extensive research programs studying topics such as information processing, decision making and choice, attribution and self-perception theory, and consumer socialization. Most of this research has been very *basic* and very narrow in terms of the issues addressed. The emphasis has been on obtaining a detailed understanding of what happens to consumer thoughts, attitudes, and behaviors under various conditions. The research has typically been done to add to a body of knowledge about consumer behavior. Serving marketing practitioners has usually been, at best, a secondary objective. This orientation may, according to one leading researcher in the field (Sheth, 1979), eventually contribute to consumer behavior becoming a distinct, separate discipline of its own.

MSI Research on Consumer Behavior: Origins and Evolution

Consumer behavior has been a concern of a large number of MSI-supported studies. Many research projects discussed in this volume have explored aspects of consumer behavior. But the research covered in this chapter differs from this other work. It tends to be more basic, with less direct emphasis on being immediately useful to decision makers. It places more emphasis on explaining why consumers are the way they are. Yet, this research is not nearly so distant from practical marketing problems as is much of the non-MSI work in consumer research. As will be shown, the MSI-supported research tends to have very strong connections to real-world marketing problems.

The major questions addressed in MSI-supported research on consumer behavior are presented in table 6–1. The work falls primarily into three overlapping areas: (1) consumer socialization, (2) attitude theory and (3) consumer information processing.

Consumer Socialization

The consumer movement that emerged during the 1960s raised many questions about marketing practices, including the heavily debated practice of television advertising to children. Consumer advocates argued that it was unfair and deceptive to subject children to a barrage of persuasive messages they had limited ability to defend themselves against.

When controversy over children's advertising surfaced around 1970, Scott Ward was completing a Ph.D. in communications at the University of Wisconsin and taking a job at the Harvard Business School in the marketing area. Eager to begin a stream of research that could draw on

Table 6-1
Questions About Consumer Behavior Addressed by MSI Researchers

Description	Explanation	Prediction	Control
1. How do consumers actually behave in the marketplace?	1. Why do *consumers* behave the way they do?		1. How should information be presented to consumers in labels, advertising, and elsewhere to facilitate usage?
2. How does the consumer socialization process work?	2. How does television advertising affect children?		
3. How do consumers acquire and process information? a. . . . on consumer durables? b. . . . on nutrition?	3. What leads consumers to develop certain thoughts, attitudes, and behaviors?		
4. How do consumers spend their time?			

his doctoral training in family communications and produce results that would have rather immediate relevance to practitioners, Ward was attracted to the area of children's advertising. He discovered that the National Institute of Mental Health was funding research on the social effects of television on children, and he applied to them for money to begin looking at questions about how television advertising affects children.

Thus began a long series of studies involving numerous researchers and several different funding agencies. Prominent among the collaborating researchers were Daniel Wackman—who had gone through the doctoral program at Wisconsin with Ward and later joined the communications faculty at the University of Minnesota—and Thomas Robertson, a Harvard colleague of Ward's at the time (who also now works with him at Wharton).

The combination of an inherently interesting topic, good colleague interaction, and ample funding seemed to keep this research going. Robertson "found it to be a rich area that put us in touch with other academicians. It actually allowed us to get out of the business school and talk to people in education and child development, which we found interesting." Wackman comments: "It was interesting. I like working with kids. That's really fun research to do." He also states: "Once you start getting grants and you get grad students working with you, then they're kind of dependent on you, so you have to continue getting funding." Ward points out: "I probably would have continued trying to do research in the area in the absence of support, but frankly, the kind of research that it was proved costly. It was survey research and diaries, and whenever you're going out and talking to people, it costs money."

The presence of ample funding from other sources placed MSI in a slightly different role with respect to this research than it had been in with respect to most of the other projects discussed in this volume. At least in the early 1970s, MSI served more as an institutional home and focal point for the research activity than as a source of funding, contacts, and support. Scott Ward served as a Research Associate of MSI throughout this period, and Daniel Wackman spent a summer as a visiting researcher, but they used MSI more as "a neighborhood watering hole" where they could enjoy the company of stimulating people than as a formal research operation. These researchers feel grateful to MSI for providing such an atmosphere. Ward and Wackman also appreciate how MSI left them free to reach independent conclusions about sensitive issues. Ward comments: "There was never any pressure to do anything that I wouldn't want to do as a professional researcher." And Wackman recalls: "There was never any interference from MSI to try to get us . . . to say anything, or modify what we said." Ward summarizes his feelings this way:

> I think the ultimate validity of the research program that we did and the thing that I am most proud of and happy with in the whole research program was the following scenario. When we testified before the "Kid Vid" hearings, before Reagan was elected and all this stuff went down the tubes, we had offers from the FTC to pay our way there, to consult for the FTC. And we had offers from industry to consult for industry. And we did neither. We paid our own way. So, we didn't take any lucre from either side. And also, the other wonderful part of it was that at the end of our testimony, neither side liked it.

It is extremely difficult to summarize the vast amount of research that these people conducted. However, there appear to be at least three segments of their research that had MSI connections:

1. the work done by Ward, Wackman, Robertson, and others stemming from the original NIMH grant;

2. the work done by Ward, Wackman, and Wartella (who was a University of Minnesota graduate student, and later a communications professor at Ohio State) stemming from a major grant provided by the Office of Child Development of the U.S. Department of Health, Education, and Welfare (the book *How Children Learn to Buy* (Ward, Wackman, and Wartella, 1977) came out of this activity); and

3. the work done by Ward and several Harvard graduate students stemming from a grant provided by CBS, Inc., a member company of MSI.

The original NIMH grant was provided to conduct exploratory research that would generate hypotheses about the effects of television advertising on children and teenagers. Given the lack of previous research in the area, Ward and his associates were chiefly interested in determining whether the variables and relationships presented in figure 6-1 seemed worthy of further study.

The researchers conducted three surveys and one clinical investigation. The first survey was conducted with 1,094 junior and senior high school students in Maryland. The second survey was conducted in the Boston area and involved having 134 mothers of five- to twelve-year-olds observe their children watching television for six to ten hours during a ten-day period. The third survey involved the same 134 mothers and sought to obtain their perceptions of a variety of issues, including how frequently their children attempted to influence purchases and the extent of parental yielding to those attempts. Finally, the clinical examination included group interviews with four sets of five children from kindergarten, second, fourth, and sixth grades.

Ward summarized the results of their early studies by offering the following hypotheses:

1. Young children's reactions to television advertising reflect stages in cognitive development. Children progress from confused perceptions of commercials, i.e., not discriminating between program and commercials, nor between advertisements and products—to beginnings of cynicism about advertising and perceptions of the intent of advertising by second and fourth grade.
2. "Selectivity" in viewing commercials increases with age, but processes of commercial watching are highly complex.
3. Mothers perceive that television advertising influences their children, and they estimate commercials' effects by the frequency with which their children attempt to influence purchases.
4. Adolescents hold negative attitudes toward television advertising, and there are only slight differences between black and white adolescents in attitudes.
5. Adolescents acquire consumer attitudes and skills from television advertising. Such consumer learning occurs as a function of the quality of advertising use, more than the quantity of media use. (Ward, 1971, pp. 28-31)

Ward and his colleagues broadened their research mission after these first studies and became concerned with understanding the entire consumer socialization process, not just advertising's influence in the process. Consumer socialization was viewed as "the processes by which young people acquire skills, knowledge, and attitudes relevant to their

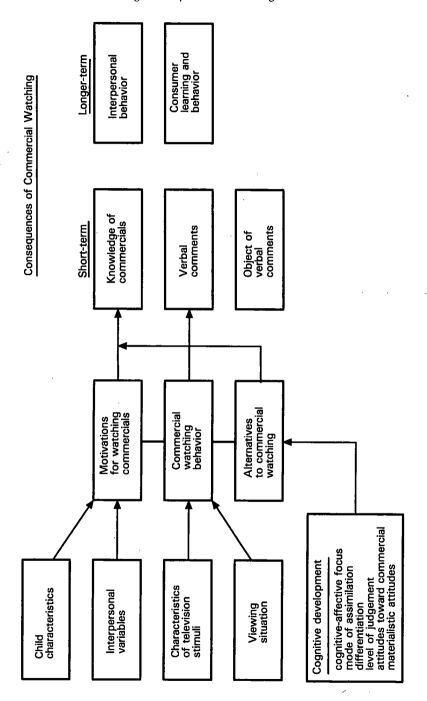

Source: Reprinted with permission from Scott Ward, "Effects of Television Advertising on Children," Report No. 71-114, Marketing Science Institute, Cambridge, Massachusetts, p. 4.

Figure 6-1. Major Variables in Studies of Effects of Television Advertising on Youth

functioning as consumers in the marketplace" (Ward, 1974, p. 2). Of particular interest to the researchers was how information processing skills develop. They used the funding from the Office of Child Development grant to conduct more than 600 personal interviews in Boston and Minneapolis with six- to twelve-year-olds and their parents. The intent was to examine the variables and processes identified in figure 6–2.

Among the conclusions the researchers offered were the following:

- Across various consumer behavior situations involving information processing of television advertising and product information in purchase decision making, there are consistent age-related changes in the kinds of information children attend to, select, and use to describe and conceptualize the consumer environment. This change appears to reflect basic developmental growth in children's cognitive capabilities toward increased awareness and use of more abstract, functional kinds of information in consumer information processing. (Ward, Wackman, and Wartella, 1977, p. 79)
- Children display some understanding of money use norms regardless of age; however, only sixth-graders exhibit any consistency between money norms and behavior, although the relationship is a slight one. (Ward, Wackman, and Wartella, 1977, p. 178)

Independent Variables	Child's Information Processing		Behaviors
Cognitive Development			
	Initial Processing	Central Processing	
Family context			
			Money use
● Parent's own consumer behavior	Information search	Interpretation and comprehension	Spending
	Attention		Saving
● Parent-child interaction	Information selection	Structuring of information evaluation	Purchase requests
● Children's independent consumer opportunities		Use of information	
Television Advertising			

Source: Reprinted with permission from Scott Ward, Daniel B. Wackman, and Ellen Wartella, *How Children Learn to Buy*, (Beverly Hills, California: Sage Publications, 1977), p. 29.

Figure 6–2. Research Model: Children's Consumer Socialization

- No significant differences were found in the frequency with which children of varying ages make requests to their parents to buy products except in the case of "child-relevant" products. Older children were more likely to request these kinds of products (record albums, clothing) than were younger children. (Ward, Wackman, and Wartella, 1977, p. 178)

- Interaction with the child about consumption increases as the mother's social status increases. On the other hand, lower-status parents appear to give their children more opportunities to operate as independent consumers by providing higher income levels and more power in making purchases. (Ward, Wackman, and Wartella, 1977, p. 144)

- Mothers of older children are much more likely to negotiate with their child about purchases, whereas mothers of younger children are much more likely to refuse their child's purchase request but explain their reasons for doing so. (Ward, Wackman, and Wartella, 1977, p. 144)

- Kindergarten children learn consumer skills more easily as a function of direct, purposive parental teaching than through the observation of parental behaviors. The data certainly suggest that even these young children can learn basic consumer skills through such interaction. On the other hand, older children seem to learn best by modeling parental consumer behaviors. (Ward, Wackman, and Wartella, 1977, p. 181)

The authors concluded by offering ideas about the implications of their findings for public policy makers, consumer educators, and marketing practitioners. However, they were unable to offer any simple prescriptions for anyone to implement.

The CBS-supported studies focused on the issue of purchase requests by children. Opponents of children's television advertising have argued that such requests are stimulated by advertising and that this, in turn, can lead to dysfunctional parent-child conflict. While Ward and his colleagues recognized that it would be extremely difficult to isolate the effect of advertising on purchase requests and conflict—versus the effects of factors like seeing a friend's toy—they set out to find what evidence they could through analyzing data obtained from diaries kept by 255 families in the Boston area. A variety of children's age ranges and socioeconomic backgrounds were represented in the sample.

In a first pass at analyzing the data, Isler, Popper, and Ward (1979) reached several descriptive conclusions, including:

- The number of requests for products and services decreased with age. This differed from the Ward, Wackman, and Wartella (1977) finding, but was consistent with other research they reviewed.

- The most frequent "request strategy" by children was "just asking," rather than pleading or bargaining.
- Reports of mothers' refusals (to accede) leading to conflict were rare.
- The citing of television as a main influence on children's requests decreased with age.

They summarized their results by saying "mothers generally accede to children's requests, and the amount of conflict caused by requests appears to be quite low." (Isler, Popper, and Ward, 1979, p. 24)

In a second pass at analyzing the same data, multivariate analysis techniques (i.e., two-stage least-squares regression analysis) were employed to examine how the number of purchase requests and parental yielding to those requests were related to several variables, including the amount of television viewing. Henderson, et al. (1980) found that a child's age was the strongest predictor of the number of requests, followed by mother's yielding behavior and amount of TV viewing. Although the amount of TV viewing per se was associated with a higher number of requests, there was little evidence that exposure to commercials for a particular product led to a request for that product. Further, younger children generally requested more products but did not appear to be any more susceptible to advertising persuasion than older children.

At the same time, Henderson et al. (1980) found that the most important variable explaining mothers' yielding behavior was one of the situational aspects of the request: A mother's perception that requests were motivated by friends, siblings, or seeing a product at the store rather than by TV advertising was associated with greater yielding. Aspects of overall parent-child interaction were also significantly related to yielding behavior. In sum, they concluded that "a causal link between viewing commercials and product requests is not necessarily confirmed in this study." (Henderson et al., 1980, p. 23)

Attitude Theory

Consumer attitudes have been examined in a large number of MSI-supported studies. Much of this work was concerned with attitude measurement (see chapter 9), and other work dealt with attitude change in response to persuasive communications (see chapter 7). MSI also gave partial support to work done by Edgar Pessemier (then at Purdue University) and William Wilkie (then at Purdue) to critique the marketing discipline's use of multi-attribute models for understanding the composition and determinants of attitudes. These models viewed a person's attitude toward a brand as the sum of (1) the person's beliefs about the extent to which certain attributes are offered by a brand, weighted by (2) the importance the person attaches to each attribute.

Forty-two empirical studies were examined to reach conclusions about strengths and weaknesses of previous research.

While Pessemier and Wilkie's research did not produce the volume of papers generated by other MSI projects, it produced an extremely important and widely cited review article (Wilkie and Pessemier, 1973). It also provided a stepping stone for more lengthy streams of MSI-supported work by Wilkie and others on consumer information processing (discussed later in this chapter) and by Pessemier on new product development (see chapter 3).

According to Pessemier, he first became interested in attitude research because of a visit he made to the BBD&O advertising agency, where he learned of work being done with data on consumer attitudes, interests, and opinions. With financial support from BBD&O and, to a lesser degree, MSI, Pessemier and a group of Purdue doctoral students extended this early work. They developed analysis approaches for using these kinds of data for doing psychographic and other types of market segmentation. They also used the data to explore the predictive validity of multi-attribute attitude models. Persuaded by this early research of the need for more well-developed attitude theory—and stating this in a review of the group's early work published by MSI (Hustad and Pessemier, 1971)—Pessemier began working with Wilkie on an extensive review of marketing studies that had used multi-attribute attitude models.

Wilkie and Pessemier (1973) offered a lengthy list of issues to be concerned about when using multi-attribute models. Among the questions they raised were:

1. How should one specify the attributes included in the model? Should they be independent from one another? How many attributes should be included?

2. Should the beliefs represent only people's cognitions, or should they reflect both the cognitive and affective aspects of how someone perceives a brand?

3. Should beliefs be measured using bipolar scales, probabilistic scales, scales with "ideal points," or other approaches? What techniques do the best job of limiting "halo effects," where people rate a brand positively or negatively on all attributes?

4. Should the weight assigned to each belief reflect importance of the attribute, value of the attribute, or something else? What scales are best for determining these weights? Should these weights be normalized in doing cross-sectional analysis?

5. Does the typically used linear compensatory or summative model provide the best explanation of overall attitude, or does some alternative way (e.g., lexicographic, conjunctive) of combining beliefs and importance weights do better?

Wilkie and Pessemier reviewed how different researchers addressed these issues, but did not take any strong stances of their own on how the issues should be resolved. Nevertheless, their article set an agenda for future research on attitudes that had considerable impact.

Information Processing

The work Wilkie did on multi-attribute models provided a natural lead into information processing. Research on information processing held the promise of gaining insights into how beliefs are formed in the first place. Wilkie was also attracted to the subject because of his experiences as a resident consultant at the Federal Trade Commission during 1972–73. The FTC and other government regulatory agencies were introducing new information disclosure requirements (e.g., corrective advertising, care labeling, energy labeling), and people were interested in understanding the conditions under which consumers would process and use all this information. Thus, when Wilkie arrived at MSI to spend the 1973–74 academic year as a Visiting Research Professor, he was attracted to the idea of working on a review of research on information processing for the National Science Foundation, an agency that MSI had already made contact with. Wilkie describes the situation this way:

> It is an important research area, and at that time it was a new research area, making it small enough so that you could try to do an overview of it. There were interesting theoretical questions, and at the same time it was obvious that it had important implications for public policy and marketing. Moreover, there was funding available.

The review Wilkie conducted for NSF led to a long stream of publications. The initial publications were review pieces that focused on providing insights for public policy makers, especially for making decisions about deceptive advertising and product labeling (Wilkie, 1975). However, funding from the American Association of Advertising Agencies (through MSI) also stimulated him—and Paul Farris (then on the faculty at Harvard)—to explore what the information processing literature had to say to advertising practitioners (Wilkie and Farris, 1976). Later, when Wilkie joined the faculty at the University of Florida, MSI supported him to conduct a series of empirical studies on information processing in collaboration with several doctoral students.

Wilkie's initial reviews stressed how little *consumer* information processing research had been done up to that time. Most of the information processing research that had been done in psychology had not examined consumer buying situations, which Wilkie felt to have some distinctive properties. Wilkie was therefore willing to offer only the following generalizations about consumer information processing:

1. It is heavily dependent on the individual, his situational setting, and the nature of his problems (i.e., consumer information processing is "adaptive" in nature);

2. long-term memory plays a crucial role in consumer information processing;

3. there are finite limits to the amount of consumer information processing that can occur during a period of time (i.e., capacity constraints on processing); and

4. consumers tend to proceed in stages rather than all at once— "subproblem" processing is the rule rather than the exception. (Wilkie and Farris, 1976, p. 7)

Wilkie (1975) pointed to five problem areas that he felt were particularly deserving of further research. These were (1) motivational factors, (2) system capacities, (3) existing knowledge and predispositions, (4) system invariance, and (5) individual differences. He argued that additional research on these and other topics would serve both public policy makers and marketing practitioners by helping them to design information programs that consumers would be motivated and able to use effectively.

Information Processing for Consumer Durables. Wilkie also received NSF money (through MSI) to write a review of the behavioral science literature—with an emphasis on information processing research—that was relevant for explaining how consumers buy household durables. He collaborated with Peter Dickson, a doctoral student at Florida who was eager to pursue attitude and information processing research with a focus on something more important to consumers than toothpaste or soda. The review they wrote drew on a variety of sources, including some data they were able to obtain from the U.S. Census Bureau on the relationship between household moves and appliance purchases. Dickson relates the following story about how they obtained these data:

> I was employed as a research assistant on Wilkie's NSF grant and I accompanied him to a meeting in Washington with Alden Clayton from MSI and several government officials. We were all sitting around the table talking about appliances, energy labeling, and so forth. I happened to be sitting beside a guy from the Census Bureau. I can't remember how it came up, but I asked him if he could get me some information about appliance shopping behavior other than just the basic reporting of annual purchasing information. I don't know why, but I asked if he could produce some crosstabs relating residential moving and appliance shopping. He

said he could and the data went into our monograph. It was the genesis of my interest in trying to find out if situational purchase circumstances influenced shopping and search.

The review written by Dickson and Wilkie (1978) generated the hypothesized model of the acquisition of consumer durables presented in figure 6–3. They ·offered six propositions drawn from the model for future research:

1. Deliberate and highly involved search behavior, however short, is either precipitated by an unexpected event or is triggered by an expected event which converts priorities or stalled plans into action.
2. Casual acquisition of product information may occur over an extensive time before a precipitating or catalytic event occurs. This knowledge is obtained under very different conditions of interest, concern, and product involvement from what will be found at stages of deliberate and intensive search.
3. The search for and choice of the purchase outlet frequently may precede the consideration of specific brands and, consequently, clearly influences the composition of the evoked choice set. Store loyalty can be a more important concept than brand loyalty.
4. The expertise and interactive skills of the store personnel are significant in the purchasing of major durables.
5. After sufficient search, immediate purchase may be abandoned or postponed and the process may lie dormant until activated by a future event. Abandonment will have an impact on acquisition priorities for other products.
6. The decision process is under the pervasive influence of a number of cultural and economic factors. (Dickson and Wilkie, 1978, p. 149)

Wilkie and Dickson (who is now at·Ohio State) followed up their review with an extensive survey that obtained responses from 433 households that had recently purchased a refrigerator, freezer, clothes washer, or clothes dryer. Some of their major findings (Wilkie and Dickson, 1985) were:

• A wide distribution was found in the amount of time people spent gathering information. One- third spent less than a week, while one-fourth spent more than three months.
• High variability was also found in number of stores visited and brands considered. Around one-third visited only one store and considered only one brand; but one-fourth visited four or more stores and one-sixth considered four or more brands.

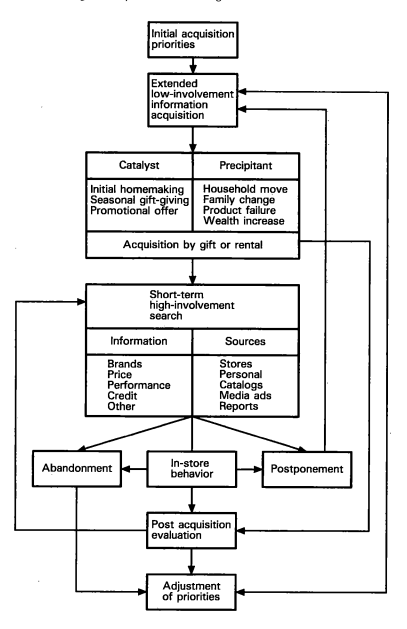

Source: Reprinted with permission from Peter R. Dickson and William L. Wilkie, "The Consumption of Household Durables: A Behavioral Review," Report No. 78–117, Marketing Science Institute, Cambridge, Massachusetts, p. 10.

Figure 6–3. A Model of the Acquisition of Major Durables

- The majority did not report consulting independent sources of information like *Consumer Reports*.
- Almost half indicated that they had spent less than two hours in total shopping for their appliance.
- Once consumers are in a given store, their shopping appears to be focused on a single brand rather than on comparisons of competing brands.
- Salespersons were the dominant information source used by consumers—over advertising, catalogs, friends, magazines, etc.
- Less than one in three purchases is likely to be a "brand loyal" purchase.
- Consumers generally seemed rather satisfied with their purchases.

The results provided a picture that was somewhat surprising to the authors, since their review had led them to expect a somewhat more extended and complicated decision process. They concluded by proposing a new, simpler model of the search process presented in figure 6–4. This model places special emphasis on the role of the salesperson, in-store evaluations, and cost-benefit assessments of the value of further search.

Wilkie also worked with two other Florida doctoral students, Bruce Hutton and Dennis McNeill (both of whom later joined the faculty at the University of Denver), on projects stemming from the NSF/MSI grant. Hutton and Wilkie (1980) examined the effectiveness of offering consumers "life cycle cost" information versus yearly energy cost information versus only purchase prices of refrigerator/freezers. The "life cycle cost" represented the total energy, service, and purchase cost of an item over a fourteen-year period. In a laboratory experiment, they found that the life cycle cost information led people to favor and choose more energy-efficient models.

McNeill (and William Swinyard) worked on a study evaluating the effectiveness of presenting consumers with comparative product information—or informing them about (1) how the average brand in the product category performed on an attribute and (2) what the range of performance across all brands was on an attribute. They compared how this information was used in evaluating microwave ovens and toothpaste. In a laboratory experiment, they found that comparative product information led people to acquire fewer information dimensions and to spend more time with each dimension. They were also more satisfied with their choices. In addition, consumers took longer and used more information to evaluate microwaves than to evaluate toothpaste (McNeill and Swinyard, 1980).

Nutrition Information. Since the mid-1970s, MSI has been involved with several studies to examine how consumers search for food products (e.g.,

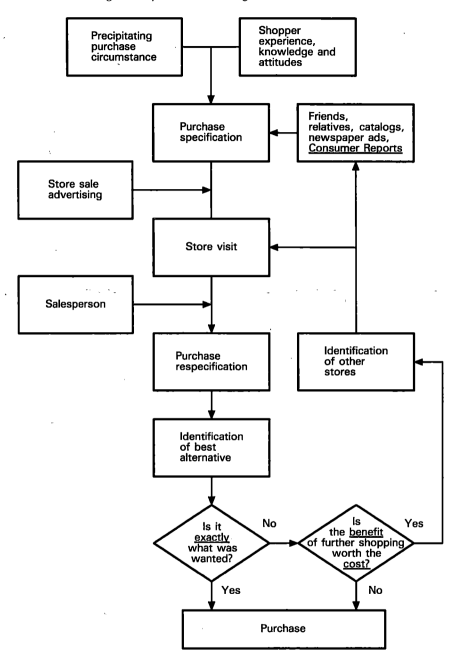

Source: Reprinted with permission from William L. Wilkie and Peter R. Dickson, "Shopping for Appliances: Consumers' Strategies and Patterns of Information Search," Report No. 85-108, Marketing Science Institute, Cambridge, Massachusetts, p. 36.

Figure 6–4. A Dynamic-Adaptive Model of Shopping Behavior

Quelch, 1978). In particular, these studies have looked at how consumers process nutrition information. In one study by a team of MSI staff members, nutrition experts, and Harvard graduate students (Schmalensee, 1982)—which was funded by the Department of Agriculture—national surveys were done in two phases to evaluate determinants of food consumption. The major conclusions reached were:

- Food likes and dislikes were probably the most important determinant of what consumers eat, followed by the cost of food and concerns about weight and dieting.
- On the average, respondents showed a limited knowledge of nutrition. In contrast, most were satisfied with their nutritional knowledge and performance.
- Respondents tended to be confused by or skeptical of available nutrition information. They did want to learn about ingredients that may be dangerous to their health and about the nutritional value of certain foods.

In another study, conducted by J. Edward Russo (Cornell), Richard Staelin (Duke), Gary Russell (Berkeley), and Barbara Metcalf, a field experiment was run for a thirty-four-week period in fourteen supermarkets. Large signs displaying one of three different nutrition information formats were set up along supermarket aisles in six different product categories. The formats were: (1) a "Matrix" format that listed calories and U.S. RDAs of eight nutrients for all the brands in a product category, (2) a "Summary" format that combined all the Matrix information into an overall rating of nutritional quality for each brand in a product category, and (3) a "Complete" format that included both of the previous formats.

Contrary to expectations, the displays did not have a significant effect on purchases. Facilitating information processing by providing the displays did not lead people to buy more nutritious foods. However, the displays did seem to affect people's knowledge and attitudes about nutrition, with the Matrix format (in spite of being more complex) creating more knowledge and more favorable attitudes than the other formats (Russo et al., 1985).

Consumers' Time Expenditures

MSI recently has begun to play a role in helping to support consumer behavior research in some new and underexplored areas. One such study was done on consumers' time expenditures by Philip Hendrix (Emory University), Thomas Kinnear (University of Michigan), and James Taylor (University of Michigan). Using data collected during a study supported by the National Science Foundation and conducted by Michigan's

Institute for Social Research, they sought descriptions and explanations of how much time consumers spend in meal preparation, housework, and shopping. This study got started, according to Kinnear, by discussions among students and faculty at Michigan. He claims they decided to pursue the project because "it had consequences that were important to somebody. The work wasn't trivial; it went beyond narrow-minded journals to the way the world works."

Hendrix, Kinnear, and Taylor (1983) extracted the following results from a data base containing time diaries obtained from 1,519 respondents:

- Women spent three to five times more time on meal preparation and housework than men. The larger the household, the more time women spent at these activities, while the amount of time men devoted to these activities was unaffected by household size.
- Enjoyment of an activity increased the amount of time devoted to it, except that women spent the same amount of time at housework whether they enjoyed it or not.
- Employment reduced the time devoted to the three activities (housework, meal preparation, and shopping).
- Older people spent more time on meal preparation and housework and less time on shopping.
- Higher income increased women's meal preparation time and all respondents' shopping time.

In general, the researchers found support for their proposed model of time allocation.

The Consumer Behavior Odyssey

Another new research direction supported by MSI (and several other organizations) has been labeled the "Consumer Behavior Odyssey." A group of academics from different universities spent the summer of 1986 traveling around the United States together, observing consumers in a variety of buying situations. Drawing on research approaches from anthropology, sociology, and phenomenology, these researchers interviewed, filmed, and tape recorded consumers as they participated in "swap meets," bought tourist offerings, and made other purchases. Specific hypotheses about consumer behavior were not tested, since the researchers entered the experience with few preconceived notions or biases. They hoped that this unconventional approach to studying consumer behavior would produce fresh ideas and lead researchers in new and productive directions in their quest to understand consumers better.

MSI Research on Consumer Behavior:
Impact and Utilization

The research MSI has supported in consumer behavior has been somewhat limited in its coverage relative to the wide-ranging exploration that has characterized the field of consumer research in recent years. Nevertheless, the MSI-supported work in consumer socialization and information processing has been rather influential among both academics and practitioners.

Impact in the Academic World

The MSI-supported research in consumer socialization by Ward and his colleagues and in information processing by Wilkie and his colleagues has generated a large number of publications by these authors. The consumer socialization research has produced the following:

1. articles (by Ward and others), that came directly from MSI-supported work, appearing in the *Journal of Consumer Research, Journal of Marketing Research, American Behavioral Scientist, Journal of Communication,* and *Advances in Consumer Research* (several times);
2. the book *How Children Learn to Buy,* published by Sage Publications;
3. articles (by Robertson and others), that indirectly followed the MSI-supported work, appearing in the *Journal of Consumer Research* (twice), *Journal of Marketing Research, Journal of Communication* (three times), *Communication Research, Public Opinion Quarterly,* and *Advances in Consumer Research;*
4. books (by Robertson and others) with indirect connections to MSI-supported work that were titled *The Effects of Television Advertising on Children* (Lexington Books) and *Televised Medicine Advertising and Children* (Praeger Publishers).

Moreover, a substantial amount of research by other investigators followed this initial work, most of it with roots in the MSI-supported research. As Wackman comments:

> We showed what kinds of questions needed to be asked, what kinds of interpretations seemed to make sense if you took a developmental point of view. Since that time, most studies of children have at least paid lip service to the notion that much of what happens when children respond to an advertisement or move into a consumption decision depends on how they think about it due to their phase of psychological life.

The MSI-supported work on information processing by Wilkie and his colleagues has appeared in the *Journal of Consumer Research* on three different occasions and in several other places. In addition, Wilkie and Dickson report that articles that were direct or indirect descendents of their MSI work have appeared in the *Journal of Marketing* (twice), *Advances in Consumer Research* (twice), *Communication Research,* and several other outlets. Moreover, the monographs published by MSI were apparently widely distributed and can fairly be said to have helped spark the enormous interest that has developed in consumer information processing.

It should also be noted that the Wilkie and Pessemier (1973) *Journal of Marketing Research* article on multi-attribute attitude models was recognized as a citation classic by the *Social Science Citation Index* and was also found to be the most frequently cited article in the marketing literature during the 1970s.

The work discussed in this chapter did not make an especially strong impression on the editors. The only research streams they cited in an unprompted fashion were the ones by Ward et al. (once) and Wilkie et al. (twice). However, five editors did answer the prompted question about Wilkie's information processing work with the answer "steady progress," and one chose the label "major contribution." The only other answer selected was "initial step."

Impact in the Practitioner World

Researcher Interviews. The work on consumer socialization is viewed as having had a substantial impact on public policy makers and marketing practitioners by the researchers who were interviewed. For a while in the 1970s, this research received regular coverage in the business press—especially *Advertising Age*—and the researchers delivered testimony to the Federal Trade Commission on several occasions. Companies and advertising agencies with an interest in children's advertising gave the research special attention. For instance, Ward reports that General Foods (an MSI member company) had them write a "white paper" on the children's advertising issues. Ward further comments:

> I know that some companies are using many of the research approaches and methodologies we used and developed in order to pretest ads with kids and look for potential problems with miscomprehension and so forth.

In addition, both Ward and Robertson are now actively involved in helping several European companies change their approach to children's advertising, in response to activist pressures.

On the other hand, Wilkie and Dickson are less able to point to examples of how their information processing research has affected policy makers or marketers. While Wilkie's thinking has certainly had an impact on how the FTC implements its affirmative disclosure and corrective advertising programs—he was a consultant there for a long time—he finds it hard to judge exactly what that impact has been. As for the work done on consumer durables, Dickson feels that the results have not been disseminated long enough to assess their impact.

Practitioner Interviews. The practitioners revealed some disappointment over the amount and quality of research MSI has sponsored on consumer behavior—although in fairness to MSI it should be noted that these people would probably be disappointed with how the entire field of consumer behavior has progressed in recent years. For example, Dudley Ruch (retired from Quaker)—who otherwise had very favorable comments to make about MSI—feels that MSI "hasn't done anything very interesting in consumer behavior since Bill Wilkie and some of the information processing stuff." Another critic of the research in this area, and related work in advertising, is Larry Gibson (retired from General Mills). However, Gibson does acknowledge the usefulness to his company of the children's work by Ward and his colleagues when he states:

> In terms of technical merit, the work on children in advertising was uneven—some good, some not so good. But the reality is so distant from what the critics of a few years ago used to assert about how advertising perverted those marvelous little minds and psyches. The critics were so wrong that even uneven research did much to redress the balance. My company gained a great deal in that the studies brought some rationality back to the discussion.

Philip Harding (CBS) also appreciates the influence the Ward et al. work had on toning down the debate over advertising to children. In addition, Harding speaks favorably of the impact in Washington of Wilkie's information processing work, saying:

> The FTC had come up with outrageous suggestions for loading up TV commercials with all kinds of disclosure material. Nobody had looked at the amounts of information a TV commercial could carry without becoming counterproductive. Wilkie did a lot. We were very pleased.

Another Wilkie admirer is Jim Casey (retired from Sears), who worked with him and Dickson on the consumer durables project. Casey claims:

> My company benefited indirectly in that I benefited. It gave me some ideas so that when a subject that needed research came up I could say: "Ah—that MSI study."

Finally, in discussing the same Wilkie and Dickson project, David Allen (Whirlpool) provides evidence of direct industry usage in stating that it led his company "to change how we present information from the point-of-sale on back."

7

Advertising and
Mass Communications:
Integrating Several
Research Traditions

U nderstanding how advertising works has been a major interest of marketing academics for many years. Moreover, research on advertising has also been done in great abundance by practitioners, who have frequently published their findings in places like the *Journal of Advertising Research*. Much of the pre-1970 research on advertising was influenced heavily by the long-standing research tradition in the field of communications, where the focus has been on understanding: "Who says What to Whom through which Channels with what Effect?" (Lasswell, 1948) Thus, researchers examined how effective advertising was when it employed various spokespersons (e.g., high-credibility sources), message content (e.g., fear appeals, humor appeals), or distribution channels (e.g., print, outdoor, television). Moreover, early research frequently examined the manner in which the demographic, attitudinal, and personality characteristics of audiences moderated the effects of advertising.

Another noteworthy research stream from the pre-1970 era was work that was more mathematical in nature. Model-builders became intrigued with problems such as media selection and advertising budgeting, and developed simulation and analytical models to help managers deal with these problems. At the same time, more statistically oriented researchers sought ways to quantify the relationship between advertising and sales, using regression and econometric techniques.

These research traditions continue today, but the theories and methods have become much more sophisticated. The last fifteen years have seen thinking from communications blended with thinking from social and cognitive psychology—especially work on attitude change and information processing—to help enrich our understanding of how consumers respond to advertising. In particular, interest has steadily grown in examining how consumer *involvement* mediates responses to advertising. Along with this growth, more revealing experimental methods and measurement tools have been developed (e.g., brain-wave and eye-movement monitoring), and more powerful statistical tests

have been refined (e.g., time series, structural-equations, meta-analysis).
The manner in which advertising works is steadily becoming less
mysterious.

MSI Research on Advertising:
Origins and Evolution

A large portion of MSI-supported research has touched on some aspect
of advertising. The focus in this chapter is on the MSI research that has
tended to build on the research traditions from communications and
psychology. This includes work that has sought to understand how
advertising affects the thoughts, attitudes, and behavior of consumers—
and how involvement, media clutter, repetition, message content, and
other factors moderate advertising's effects (see table 7–1). MSI-supported
work on how to measure the relationship between advertising and sales
is covered in the review of model-building research (chapter 9); and the

Table 7–1
Questions About Advertising Addressed by MSI Researchers

Description	Explanation	Prediction	Control
1. How can brain-wave measurement be used in studying the effects of adver-tising?	1. How does advertising affect a. . . . sales? (See chapter 9) b. . . . children? (See chapter 6) c. . . . competition? (See chapter 10) 2. How does advertising affect thoughts, atti-tudes, and behaviors? 3. How does involve-ment mediate the effects of advertising? 4. How does media clut-ter moderate the effects of advertising? 5. How does repetition influence the effects of advertising? 6. How do various mes-sage strategies and exe-cutional factors influ-ence the effects of advertising?		1. How can more effec-tive *advertising* strategies be *formulated*?

work on advertising's effects on children and on the economic effects of advertising are covered in the chapters on consumer behavior (chapter 6) and public policy (chapter 10) respectively.

The research that is reviewed here owes much to the thinking of Professor Michael Ray of Stanford University. Ray was instrumental in bringing ideas from communications and psychology into the marketing discipline. Moreover, empirical research he has conducted in collaboration with a steady stream of doctoral students has added to his contributions. In the following section, the thoughts of Ray and others on how to conceptualize the way advertising works are reviewed. Subsequent sections cover empirical research on the effects of media clutter, repetition, executional factors, and several other subjects.

Conceptualizing the Persuasion Process

Prior to the late 1960's, it was relatively common to view advertising as something that attempted to guide consumers through a "hierarchy of effects" process. Advertising and other forms of persuasive communications were seen as producing a "stair-step" set of sequential steps, as consumers proceeded through cognitive (e.g., awareness, knowledge, comprehension), affective (e.g., interest, conviction, feeling), and conative (e.g., trial, action, adoption) stages. This model of consumer response to communications was grounded in psychological learning theory, and it guided much of advertising practice. The popularity of the DAGMAR concept ("Defining Advertising Goals for Measured Advertising Results") (Colley, 1961), with its emphasis on seeking communication goals rather than sales goals for advertising, reflected an underlying faith in the hierarchy of effects model. Advertisers often believed that it was necessary to pull people through the cognitive and affective stages in order for the conative stage to occur.

A Three-Orders Model. A number of scholars began to raise questions about the hierarchy of effects model, including a team of researchers from MSI and the Wharton School who published an early MSI monograph on "advertising measurement and decision making" (Robinson et al, 1968). Prominent among those who questioned the model was Professor Ray, whose experiments with his Stanford doctoral students beginning in the late 1960s led him to feel that persuasion can occur via other routes. Influenced by the thinking and writing of MSI trustee Herbert Krugman (then with General Electric) on *low-involvement* responses to mass communications (Krugman, 1965), Ray (1973) conceptualized what he labeled as a "Three-Orders" model which explicitly proposed three alternative hierarchies a consumer could pass through. He saw the traditional *learning* hierarchy (i.e., cognitive-affective-conative) as one that would occur when (1) the audience is highly involved in the topic of the message and (2) clear differences exist between alternatives. In such a situation, mass media communications can definitely be effective in pushing people through the hierarchy.

However, where (1) the audience is highly involved, (2) alternatives are indistinguishable, and (3) non-media or personal communication encourages action without first providing opportunities for thinking, then a *dissonance-attribution hierarchy* is likely to occur. This hierarchy proceeds from conative to affective to cognitive, as people will act first, change attitude to bolster the action, and then obtain information and knowledge in a selective manner to be consistent with their behavior and attitudes.

A third hierarchy proposed by Ray—with appropriate acknowledge-ment to Krugman (1965)—would exist in situations of (1) low involvement and (2) minimal differences between alternatives. This *low-involvement* hierarchy would proceed from cognitive to conative to affective. People would form some thoughts about an advertised product, such as recollecting a brand name, because they would not put up any perceptual defenses against processing information about something with which they had little involvement. These thoughts would be retrieved when encountering a buying situation, such as an in-store display, and trial of the product would follow. Attitudes would then be formed later, based on the experience with using the product.

As mentioned earlier, Ray formulated this three-orders model (portrayed in figure 7-1) drawing on his previous research experiences. Ray had been involved with the advertising industry in some form or another "since he was thirteen years old." He had studied journalism as an undergraduate, done research for a major advertising agency following this, and pursued a variety of advertising research projects as a doctoral student in social psychology at Northwestern University and as a young marketing professor at Stanford. Noteworthy among his early Stanford efforts was work he did with Alan Sawyer (1971), Roger Heeler (1972), and Michael Rothschild (1974) on the effects of repeating various types of advertisements.

All of these studies reinforced Ray's notions about the importance of involvement in understanding advertising's effects, and this perspective was prominent in his mind when he came to MSI for the 1972–73 academic year as Visiting Research Professor. While at MSI, Ray refined his conceptualization of the three-orders model and prepared several papers that discussed it, including one that he presented at a seminal 1972 workshop—supported in part by MSI—on "buyer/consumer information processing" co-chaired by G. David Hughes of the University of North Carolina and Ray himself. Other work he did during his visiting year

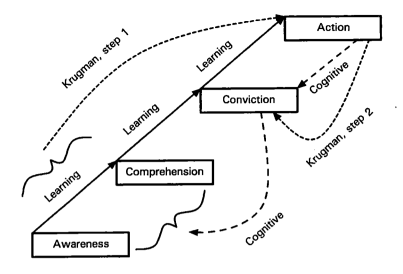

The standard "learning" hierarchy is represented by the solid arrows, the reverse "cognitive" hierarchy by the dashed arrows, and Krugman's "low involvement learning" by the dotted arrows.

Source: Reprinted with permission from Michael L. Ray, "Consumer Initial Processing: Definitions, Issues, and Applications," in G. David Hughes and Michael L. Ray (Eds.), *Buyer/ Consumer Information Processing*, (Chapel Hill: The University of North Carolina Press, 1974), p. 149. Copyright by The University of North Carolina.

Figure 7–1. Three Views of the "Hierarchy" in Initial Processing of Communication Response

included a study with Scott Ward (then at Harvard) on preparing effective anti-drug campaigns (Ray, Ward, and Lesser, 1973). Since public service announcements find clutter to be a particular problem, this study helped stimulate his interest in the subject. The research Ray conducted on clutter with his student, Peter Webb, is reviewed later.

Ray's early research was not funded by MSI. The American Association of Advertising Agencies' (4A's) Educational Foundation was his major source of funding. But MSI helped in connecting Ray with the 4A's and later with the Association of National Advertisers and the National Institute of Mental Health (for the drug abuse study with Ward). MSI also provided funding for his clutter and repetition research. Ray describes MSI's role in his research as that of a "facilitator" or "broker." He further credits MSI with helping supply practitioner encouragement and ideas. As he puts it: "The nice thing about MSI is that they pull in some practitioners who have real vision and understand how the research process works."

Carry-Over Effects in Advertising. Another MSI-supported work that focused on conceptualizing the persuasion process was a paper on carry-over effects in advertising written by two former collaborators of Michael Ray's—Alan Sawyer (then at the University of Massachusetts) and Scott Ward (then at Harvard) (Sawyer and Ward, 1976). This paper apparently was an outgrowth of Darral Clarke's quantitative work on measuring the effects of advertising, which is discussed in chapter 9. According to Sawyer, Clarke was working with MSI to prepare a session for an AMA conference and a monograph treating the subject of carry-over effects. He wanted someone to look at what the behavioral science literature had to say about the subject, and so he asked his Harvard colleague at the time, Scott Ward, to contribute a literature review. Ward was apparently overcommitted and, in turn, asked Sawyer to help him out. As Sawyer recollects:

> It was a better idea than the other ideas I had at the time. I get stimulated by going to libraries, and that's what the project involved. It was also summer, and the library was cooler than the outdoors. I really liked doing it.

Sawyer and Ward developed "an information-processing model of factors involved in carry-over effects of advertising," which is presented in figure 7–2. Moving from the right side of this model to the left, they reviewed what the psychology and communications literature had to say about how the variables and processes identified in the model impact the duration of advertising's effects on thoughts, attitudes, and behaviors. Since much of the research they reviewed had not been performed in an advertising context, they were unable to reach any firm conclusions about how advertising works. However, they were able to offer twenty-five provocative propositions designed to stimulate additional research. A few of their more interesting ideas are:

- Learning decays in a negatively accelerated fashion with most of the decay occurring relatively shortly after last exposure.
- Unlike learning, attitudes may actually increase (i.e., become more salient or favorable) over time.
- High levels of repetition are very effective in preventing decay of both initial learning and attitude change.
- For a given number of advertising exposures, persistence in learning over a given time period is greater for a spread schedule of advertising exposures than for a concentrated schedule.

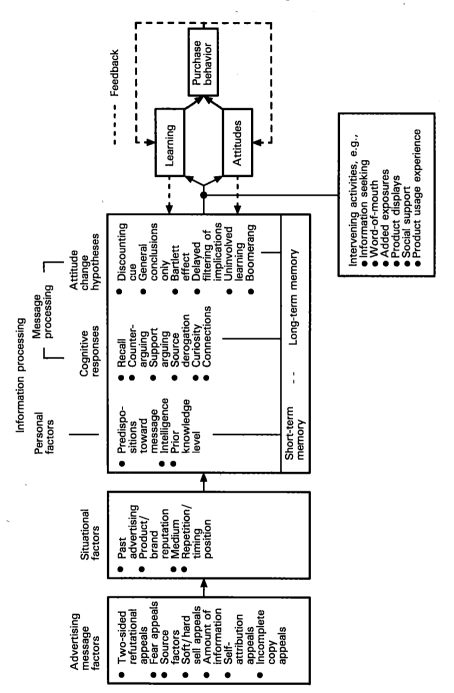

Figure 7–2. An Information-Processing Model of Factors Involved in Carry-Overs Effect of Advertising

Source: Reprinted with permission from Alan G. Sawyer and Scott Ward, "Carry-Over Effects in Advertising Communication: Evidence and Hypotheses from Behaviorial Science," Report No. 76–122, Marketing Science Institute, Cambridge, Massachusetts.

- Because of the opportunity for reexposure, and the potential for active audience involvement, print media are likely to produce greater persistence effects than broadcast media.
- Advertising generating high levels of fear produces greater persistence effects than a message generating low amounts of fear.
- Soft-sell advertising appeals produce greater persistence effects than hard-sell advertising.
- Advertising that includes several product benefits results in greater persistence of attitudes than advertising presenting fewer product benefits.
- Once consumers learn product information, persistence effects will be greater if advertising appeals are changed than if identical brand information advertising is continued.

Affective Reactions to Advertising. Recognition that advertising may not persuade consumers in a straightforward, hierarchy-of-effects manner has led to increased interest in affective reactions to advertising, which in some cases, may occur prior to cognitive reactions. An early MSI-supported effort that touched on this subject was a paper written by Alvin Silk of M.I.T. and Terry Vavra of the National Broadcasting Company. This paper was originally presented at the 1972 Hughes and Ray workshop on buyer/consumer information processing discussed earlier. Silk and Vavra (1974) suggested that two basic schools of thought existed on affective reactions to advertising. The "law of extremes" view hypothesizes the more that people like *or* dislike a commercial message, the greater its impact. On the other hand, the "superiority-of-the-pleasant" view holds that advertising that evokes "pleasant" or favorable reactions is more effective than advertising that "irritates" or elicits unpleasant feelings. Silk and Vavra concluded that there is no overwhelming evidence to support either viewpoint. However, they did report on a study of their own in which they found (1) a "hard-sell" radio commercial to be more persuasive than a "soft-sell" one after one exposure and (2) the persuasiveness of the soft-sell message to increase, and that of the hard-sell message to decrease, after a second exposure. They interpret this as giving some support to the notion that positive feelings generated by advertising can become associated with the product as message repetition occurs.

A more recent paper by Fred van Raaij (1984) of Erasmus University, which was published by MSI, took a stronger stance on how affective reactions to advertising tend to work. Van Raaij argued that affective reactions typically precede any cognitive reactions to advertising, and that this "primary" affective reaction can have a substantial influence on persuasion. Drawing on the work of former MSI trustee Herbert Krugman

(1977) and psychologists such as Zajonc (1980) and Broadbent (1977), van Raaij proposed a model of how the process works. This model is presented in figure 7–3. The model suggests that prior to any cognitive elaboration or thinking about an advertised product, a primary affective reaction can occur on a subconscious level. An advertisement can get people to form an overall favorable feeling about a product—which can then lead to preference for the product—even when the advertisement itself cannot be recalled. Van Raaij argued that understanding this reaction will require using new and sophisticated measurement tools in place of traditional recall measures. He proposed using new evaluation scales, physiological measures of somatic reactions, and electroencephalograms (EEGs).

MSI also published a comment on van Raaij's paper written by Brian Sternthal (1984) of Northwestern University. Sternthal did not view the evidence supporting van Raaij's model as especially persuasive. He felt that previous research had shown equivalent support for the notion that affective reactions occur after extremely limited levels of cognitive activity. However, he supported Van Raaij's call for more research on this subject, and particularly liked the notion of using physiological instrumentation to study issues such as the how the left and right sides of the brain react differentially to advertising. MSI's efforts to support studies of brain-wave activity are discussed later in this chapter.

Television Clutter

As mentioned earlier, Michael Ray became interested in the clutter issue while working with Scott Ward on a study of drug-abuse messages during his year as a Visiting Research Professor at MSI. He also found that practitioners in the advertising industry were extremely concerned about clutter at that time. They believed that television clutter was on the increase—since ten-second commercials were gaining popularity—and they feared that it was making individual advertisements less effective. Thus, when he returned to Stanford in 1973, Ray began to work with a doctoral student, Peter Webb, on three experiments on the effects of clutter.

All three studies used a naturalistic laboratory procedure in which subjects were shown television programs in a living-room-like setting with comfortable chairs, sofa, coffee table with current magazines, and refreshements. Various types of commercials were run during and between program segments. Observers behind one-way mirrors measured subjects' attention levels at ten-second intervals during the commercial and sixty-second intervals during the programs.

In their first experiment, Ray and Webb (1976) examined the effects of (1) the number of commercials presented between two programs (four

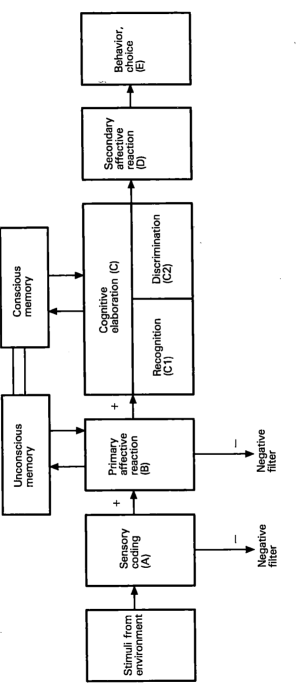

Source: Reprinted with permission from W. Fred van Raaij, "Affective and Cognitive Reactions to Advertising," Report No. 84–111, Marketing Science Institute, Cambridge, Massachusetts, p. 3.

Figure 7–3. Model of the Receiver of Information

or eight) and (2) the order in which those commercials appeared. Commercials for two "high-involvement" and two "low-involvement" products were used. The results indicated that attention, recall, and purchase intention were all reduced under more cluttered (eight messages) conditions when low-involvement products were advertised. But increased clutter did not reduce these measures for high-involvement products. In addition, attention, recall, and purchase intention were reduced for commercials that appeared at the end of "strings" of messages—especially for the low-involvement products.

The second Ray and Webb (1978) experiment looked at the effects of three different scheduling schemes for commercials (i.e., six breaks with two commercials each, three with four, and two with six) embedded within either a situation comedy or soap opera program. They found that the subjects had well-formulated expectations about when commercials would occur in these shows, and familiar schedules (i.e., six breaks with two commercials each for soap operas) produced lower levels of attention and recall. Ray and Webb interpreted the results as suggesting that the way to overcome clutter may be to vary schedules within a given program from showing to showing.

Ray and Webb (1978) completed a third study that examined the impact of "standard," "heavy," and "very heavy" (i.e., four commercials per break) clutter on attention, recall, cognitive responses (i.e., thought listing), attitude, and purchase intention. The results provided reinforcement for their earlier studies, since they found:

- First position in a string of commercials was associated with higher levels of attention and recall.
- As the amount of clutter increased, there was a consistent decrease in effectiveness scores.
- There were considerable differences among individual commercials in their ability to withstand the effects of more crowded environments. The possibility that product involvement might explain these differences was not explicitly explored in this study.

The researchers conclude by stating that "clutter can 'creep up' on the television industry" (Ray and Webb, 1978, p. 36) and seriously damage the effectiveness of individual commercials.

Advertising Repetition

Ray's interest in how involvement mediates the effects of advertising manifested itself more recently in a series of MSI-supported studies on advertising repetition he conducted in the early 1980s with Rajeev Batra, a Stanford doctoral student who later joined the faculty at Columbia University. They were interested in identifying opportunities for minimizing the number of times advertisements must be repeated to achieve effective results (Batra and Ray, 1984). Utilizing laboratory methods similar to those of Ray's previous studies, they found that under conditions of low "message response involvement"—defined to be distinct from low "product involvement" and to mean when viewers do little processing of an ad in terms of the brand attribute assertions in the ad (because of limited motivation, ability, or opportunity to do so)— repetition was helpful in building more positive attitudes and purchase intentions. However, under high message response involvement, they found that the "build" in attitudes and purchase intentions levels off after two exposures (and may decrease between two and four exposures). Batra and Ray (1984, p. 52) concluded: "The results suggest that if the product category, brand, and audience are such that viewers may be expected to think deeply about the advertised brand the first or second time they see the ad, it may be financially unsound to continue to advertise heavily."

Message Strategies and Execution

MSI has supported a variety of studies examining how certain message strategies and other executional factors enhance or detract from the effectiveness of an advertisement. Work has been done on the effects of using comparative claims, background music, humor, hard-sell statements, puffery, demonstrations, fantasy, and a host of other executional variables. An early example of work in this area was a paper on comparison advertising by William Wilkie and Paul Farris (1974) that was written while the former was a Visiting Research Professor at MSI and the latter was a doctoral student at Harvard. The paper first reviewed some of the public policy and broadcasting-industry issues that were emerging during a time of increasing use of comparative claims. The authors then explored some of the issues facing advertising strategists, and formulated several hypotheses about how comparison advertising should work, based on a review of existing literature. Among their hypotheses were the following predictions:

- The novelty of a comparison ad will cause it to receive more attention than a standard ad.
- Aggregate recall levels of comparison ads will be higher than those for standard appeals.
- Consumers will rate comparison ads as more "informative" and "interesting" than most standard ads.

- Naming a competing brand will tend to increase support arguments by users of the sponsoring brand and counterarguments by users of the competing brand.
- On the average, comparison ads are more effective in improving consumer preference for the sponsored brand than are standard advertisements. (Wilkie and Farris, 1974, p. 38)

A study which tested several of Wilkie and Farris' hypotheses was conducted by George Belch and Richard Lutz while the former was a doctoral student and the latter was a professor at UCLA in the late 1970s. Belch claims to have gotten the idea for the study while attending doctoral seminars at UCLA. He recalls developing a design with the help of UCLA faculty, and then applying to MSI for funding. A laboratory experiment presented either comparative or noncomparative messages for a fictitious brand of toothpaste within the context of a one-hour television program. The number of times this toothpaste message was repeated also varied. Belch and Lutz (1982) did not find very much support for Wilkie and Farris' thinking. Their key findings were:

- No significant differences were found between the comparative and noncomparative messages with respect to traditional measures of communication effectiveness—recall, attitudes, and purchase intention.
- There were differences in cognitive response activity for the two types of messages; recipients of comparative messages generated significantly more negative responses than recipients of noncomparative messages. But the extent of negative responses was not related to how much preference the subjects had for the named competing brand (Crest).
- Level of repetition had no significant effect on cognitive response or message acceptance measures for either the comparative or noncomparative messages. (Belch and Lutz, 1982)

Another MSI-supported study that did not generate support for Wilkie and Farris' thinking was conducted by David Aaker (Professor at the University of California—Berkeley), Donald Bruzzone (consultant), and Donald Norris (Berkeley doctoral student). Among other things, they found that comparative advertising was not perceived as substantially more informative than other advertising. But these authors also looked at eighteen other characteristics of commercials to see which ones were liked and perceived as informative. They based their conclusions on surveys that had been done on consumer reactions to 524 television commercials by Bruzzone Research Corporation. Approximately 500 randomly selected respondents had returned mail survey forms on each commercial, where photographs and scripts of commercials had been included in the forms. This huge data base was analyzed to reach the following conclusions:

- Viewers' reactions toward most commercials were generally positive. The characteristics that tended to make commercials more liked were entertainment (i.e., clever, imaginative, amusing), warmth (i.e., appealing, gentle), and personal relevance (i.e., convincing, informative, interesting).
- The characteristic that made people dislike an ad more than anything else was to have it try to sell certain products such as feminine hygiene products, female undergarments, and stomach or hemorrhoid medicines.
- The perceived informativeness of an ad seemed to increase as the ad was perceived to contain more "hard-sell" copy, a discussion of a more serious problem, and a less frequently purchased product. (Aaker, Bruzzone, and Norris, 1981)

The effect of background music in television advertisements was examined in an MSI-supported study by C. Whan Park (Professor) and S. Mark Young (doctoral student) of the University of Pittsburgh. The study was especially concerned with how involvement mediated the effects of music on attitude formation. In fact, Park claims to have become interested in doing the study out of a desire to help clarify the meaning and impact of "involvement." In a laboratory experiment, the authors manipulated (1) the presence and absence of background music in a shampoo commercial and (2) the type of involvement the subjects approached the task with— either (a) "cognitive" involvement (where differences in brand characteristics were actively processed), (b) "affective" involvement (where differences in brand characteristics were not expected, but differences in brand images or personalities were considered), or (c) low involvement. Park and Young (1974) found that music produced more favorable attitudes and purchase intentions for low involvement subjects, while it produced less favorable attitudes, weaker purchase intentions, and fewer cognitive responses for cognitively involved subjects. The effects for subjects in the affective involvement condition were unclear.

The most extensive MSI-supported study on advertising message strategies and executional factors was done by David Stewart (then at Vanderbilt) and David Furse (Nashville Consulting Group). Using data and television commercials supplied by Research Systems Corporation, Stewart and Furse (1986) content coded 1,059 commercials for 356 brands, 115 product categories, and 63 firms. Each commercial was coded on each of 153 executional factors, reflecting the information content, visual and auditory devices, appeals, characters, timing, and other characteristics it possessed. A series of regression analyses and other statistical procedures were employed to determine how the executional factors were related to measures of recall, comprehension, and persuasion (i.e., a shift in brand preference) obtained during copy tests of the commercials that Research Systems had conducted with samples of 300 to 450 people for each commercial.

Stewart and Furse (1986, p. 21) observed that the "the results obtained would appear to be consistent with much of the conventional wisdom of the advertising industry and theories of information processing." Among their overall conclusions were the following:

- The single most important executional determinant of both recall and persuasion was the presence of a brand-differentiating message—defined as a claim that was unique to the product advertised and that could not be made by other brands. However, the relationship of brand-differentiating message and persuasion was a function of the level of recall attained by the commercial and characteristics of the product being advertised. At higher levels of recall, brand-differentiating messages accounted for twice the variance accounted for at lower levels of recall. In addition, brand-differentiating messages appeared to account for more variance in persuasion among established products with a higher market share of users.
- Recall, comprehesion, and persuasion appeared to operate more independently for established product commercials, but these processes were less separable for new products. The new product response process appeared to be much more recall driven.
- Among the executional devices that seemed to enhance recall and comprehension were humor, auditory memory devices, brand sign-off, front-end impact, more time devoted to the product, use of a brand-differentiating message, and information concerning convenience in use. Devices that seemed to interfere with recall and comprehension were company identification, information about product attributes and components, and information on nutrition and health.

Brain-Wave Measurement

Herbert Krugman's ideas about low-involvement reactions to advertising have stimulated a number of people in industry and in academe to explore ways of examining how low-involvement learning occurs (Krugman, 1965,

1971, 1972, 1977). Since asking people questions can itself create involvement, the notion of using electroencephalographic (EEG) measures to study cognitive reactions to advertising has been attractive to some researchers. For instance, Krugman himself—who was an MSI trustee during his tenure at General Electric—has done research using brain-wave measures that found television advertising produced more slow, delta and theta frequency activity, and less beta activity, than print advertising (Krugman, 1970). He interpreted these results to mean that print was a more active, higher-involvement medium, whereas television was passive and lower involvement.

The work of Krugman and others influenced several MSI staff members to think about supporting more research on brain-wave measurement, and eventually one of them approached Jerry Olson of Penn State with the idea of conducting a major study in this area. Olson, who had recently worked on a consulting project analyzing brain-wave data for a major advertising agency, considered how further work on brain-wave measures might allow him to supplement the kinds of measures he was getting in his research on memory and cognitive processes. He decided to accept the invitation to write a proposal. Olson also saw it as an extremely challenging and difficult problem to pursue while serving as MSI Visiting Research Professor in 1981–82.

Working with a steering committee of representatives from MSI companies to produce "a study designed by committee," Olson conducted an extensive literature review and some testing of brain-wave measurement. In a paper that he co-authored with Penn State Psychology Professor William Ray, Olson reached somewhat pessimistic conclusions about brain-wave measurement, including:

- The latest research results from psychophysiology revealed no clear and simple relationships between recorded brain-wave activity and psychological and behavioral responses; indeed, the results were often conflicting and confusing.
- Only a few studies had been done using EEG measures of response to advertisements. Most have been limited by (1) overly simplified measures of brain-wave activity and (2) a limited range of criterion variables, usually unaided brand recall.
- To make further progress in using brain waves to understand how consumers respond to advertising, psychophysiological researchers will have to develop a comprehensive theory that will help interrelate different sets of psychological and physiological measures (Olson and Ray, 1983).

A more recent attempt to use brain-wave measurement to understand consumer reactions to advertising was carried out by Roland Rust

(University of Texas at Austin), Linda Price (Pittsburgh), and V. Kumar (Iowa). Nineteen subjects had EEG measures taken while they were exposed to advertisements from newspapers, radio, television, and magazines. In addition, a variety of recall measures were obtained after exposure to the ads. The researchers were able to conclude that:

> Consistent with previous findings, this research found that magazines produced the most beta, and that radio and TV produced higher levels of alpha than either newspapers or magazines. In addition, the research found that newspapers and magazines produced higher levels of theta, while radio and TV produced lower levels of theta. These results are consistent with the belief that beta and theta covary. (Rust, Price, and Kumar, 1985, p. 22)

They also concluded that the recall measures did not bear a consistent relationship to any brain-wave activity, since, unexpectedly, lower beta activity tended to be associated with higher recall and higher alpha activity (often thought to indicate a lack of activation) tended to be associated with higher recall.

MSI Research on Advertising: Impact and Utilization

The work reviewed in this chapter has received ample attention from both academics and practitioners. Moreover, as much as any body of research discussed in this volume, the research MSI has supported on advertising has stimulated a constructive dialogue between academics and practitioners about research findings and research needs. Academics like Ray, Aaker, and Olson have regularly communicated with practitioners and have found their interactions to be a source of inspiration and support. Practitioners, in turn, feel they have benefited from the research findings and advice. However, the practitioner community feels that much more research needs to be done in certain areas. Indeed, they expressed their views on research needs in a conference on "gaps" in advertising research sponsored by MSI in 1980 and in subsequent MSI Steering Group meetings. table 7-2 presents a summary of what practitioners have identified as priority research areas. It was prepared by Diane Schmalensee (1983), then Director and now Vice President, Research Operations at MSI.

A more detailed discussion of both the contributions and gaps in MSI's advertising research program follows.

Impact in the Academic World

The influence of Michael Ray's work on other academics has already been mentioned. He has clearly been a leader in bringing thinking from

Table 7–2

Top Priority Advertising Research Questions and Suggested Approaches

I. *Theory of Individual Consumer Response to Advertising*
   A. Questions to Be Answered:
      1. How do consumers respond to advertising? Is there a link, and if so, what kind, between advertising and resultant consumer behavior?
      2. How does advertising affect consumers? And is there any evidence to support this?
      3. What factors affect consumers' response to advertising?
   B. Suggested Approaches:
      1. Define terms and build taxonomy
      2. Critically review existing theory
      3. Identify implicit theories
      4. Develop new theory

II. *Measures of Individual Consumer Response to Advertising*
   A. Questions to Be Answered:
      1. How should individual consumer response to advertising be measured?
      2. How do alternative measures compare with each one and actual consumer behavior?
   B. Suggested Approaches:
      1. Analyze empirical interrelationships of measures and behavior
      2. Build shared advertising data bank

III. *Advertising Operating Concerns*
   A. Questions to Be Answered:
      1. What is the minimum number of repetitions required for impact? At what point does advertising wear out?
      2. What are the effects of nonverbal elements of advertising and how can the effects be measured?
      3. Under what conditions should which media (medium) be used, considering audience involvement and issues of media measurement?
      4. How can advertising concepts and whole advertising campaigns (as opposed to single commercials or executions) be measured?
      5. What consumer characteristics affect consumers' response to advertising?
      6. What is the ideal relationship between market share and share of voice?
      7. How should communications budgets be allocated over advertising sales promotion, personal selling, and corporate communications?
      8. What are the uses for and impact of corporate communications?
   B. Suggested Approaches:
      1. Empirical work and experiments
      2. Review of how firms now make these decisions
      3. Critical review of existing research on corporate communications (including definition and taxonomy)

Source: Reprinted with permission from Diane Schmalensee, "Today's Top Priority Advertising Research Questions," in *Journal of Advertising Research*, April/May 1983, pp. 49–62. Copyright ©1983 by the Advertising Research Foundation.

communications and psychology into the marketing discipline. His research on involvement, repetition, and clutter has been frequently cited, and it has led to considerable follow-up work by his students (and their students) and other researchers. Editors tended to share this favorable assesment, since three of them labeled a Ray project as a "significant" contribution" (without any prompting) and all of them chose the term "steady progress" to describe his overall contribution (with prompting).

Ray's numerous (more than a dozen) MSI working papers have often appeared in other forms in journals, conference proceedings, and books. The MSI-supported work, or closely related research, has been published in the *Journal of Marketing, Advances in Consumer Research, Communication Research, Public Opinion Quarterly, Journal of Consumer Research,* and *Journal of Advertising Research* (where an article on clutter was recently identified as a "classic" worthy of inclusion in a fiftieth anniversary issue). Ray also feels that the content of his textbook, *Advertising and Communication Management* (Prentice-Hall, 1982), was heavily influenced by the stream of research supported by MSI.

While the other researchers have not had as widespread an impact on academics as Ray, their work has definitely been recognized in the academic community. For instance, Sawyer and Belch report that they have been cited frequently for their contributions. In addition, publications such as the following have emerged from the non-Ray-MSI-supported research in advertising:

1. The van Raaij paper appeared in revised form in the *Journal of Consumer Marketing.*
2. Articles from Belch and Lutz's research appeared in the *Journal of Marketing Research* and the *Journal of Consumer Research.*
3. Articles from Aaker, Bruzzone, and Norris' research appeared in the *Journal of Advertising Research* on two occasions.
4. Park's paper appeared in the *Journal of Marketing Research.*
5. An article from Stewart and Furse's research appeared in the the *Journal of Advertising Research,* and a book on the project was published by Lexington Books.

Impact in the Practitioner World

Researcher Interviews. The authors who were interviewed generally felt that their work had influenced practitioners. Ray, Sawyer, and Olson noted that the popular business press had written stories about their research, and that this had led to a number of speaking, seminar-leading, and consulting opportunities. Ray and Sawyer also noted that their respective work had an impact in the political and public policy arena. Ray and Webb's work on clutter was used by advertisers to support their arguments against increased clutter. Sawyer and Ward's work on carryover effects became, in Sawyer's words, "reading material at the

Federal Trade Commission," as they used it to help them come to grips with how to formulate the corrective advertising remedy. In addition, Sawyer reports that the paper led to an opportunity to do some consulting on the *Burger King* v. *Wendy's* advertising case.

Practitioner Interviews. Practitioners expressed considerable appreciation when discussing the MSI-supported work in advertising. But, as suggested earlier, they expressed some disappointment over what this research had accomplished. Among the works that were praised were the Ray and Webb studies on clutter. Herbert Krugman (formerly with General Electric) sees this research as representing "the best of what MSI has done." He further states:

> I think the major decision that it affected at G.E. was that it reinforced the feelings that they should present corporate advertising within the context of their own show—and not buy spot time. It kept alive the G.E. Theater for a little longer.

Kent Mitchel (formerly at General Foods, now President of MSI) also praises the Ray and Webb research, stating that "it was a tiny little job, but it's the best thing around." According to Mitchel, "that work has been echoing around the advertising industry for ten years." And still another admirer, David Allen (Whirlpool), says "not only was it good; it was real-world and near-term applicable." Allen recalls that many companies began to seek the first commercial position after this study.

Park and Young's work on background music and Olson and Ray's work on brain-wave measurement were cited by William Cook (formerly with General Foods) as valuable. As Cook puts it:

> In both cases, they were trying to develop theory and also to push ahead the applications orientation—so they kept their heads up in the clouds and their feet on the ground at the same time.

Cook relates this experience in using Park and Young's work:

> I developed an approach to advertising copy testing and I really had to back up and develop a framework for how advertising works. A continuing dialogue with C.W. Park was very helpful to me in developing that framework and in translating it into concepts that were readily understandable by the marketing community of General Foods, and that could also be implemented by the researchers.

The Olson and Ray work also received unprompted favorable comments from Joseph Plummer (Young and Rubicam), C.J. O'Sullivan

(Shell) and Linda Alwitt (Leo Burnett). Alwitt offers an interesting perspective on the cautions that came out of this research:

> I was very involved with the Olson and Ray project, and it was unfortunate that a report did not come out on the empirical work. The reason why is that it turned out to be a very complicated subject. Just learning that and making the marketing community aware that it was a very complicated subject, and perhaps not ready to be used in business, was useful in and of itself.

Alwitt also gives high praise to the Stewart and Furse project. She states:

> I thought they did a superb job. It was quite comprehensive. MSI not only funded it, but also allowed a lot of interaction with Stewart and Furse themselves. The researchers didn't necessarily listen to everything we had to say, but I think it was a very good example of the kind of interaction that practitioners and academicians can have. I think we led them in directions that they would not have gone had we not been there to talk with them about their research.

She further states that the project helped provide support for some of the agency's copy-testing decisions. Additionally, it was used "as background for talking about copy with clients and other people in the agency.

Another MSI project that received unprompted compliments was the 1980 conference on "gaps" in advertising research. Joseph Plummer, Young and Rubicam), Philip Harding (CBS), and Philip Levine (formerly with Ogilvy and Mather) all felt that this had been a stimulating and useful experience.

But in discussing the "gaps" conference, and in discussing MSI's advertising research in general, several of the interviewed practitioners seemed frustrated with the gaps that remain in this area. One person, Larry Gibson (retired from General Mills), feels the overall quality of the research in advertising has been weak. On the other hand, David Allen (Whirlpool) displays a more typical form of frustration in saying:

> Advertising research has been one of the areas where there has been so much done, yet they always go back and ask the same questions over again. It's how do you process information? It's what makes a commercial successful? They'll pull out 800 or 900 advertising studies and do some mathematical analyses of what are the important factors. They always conclude that "it depends." And the final statement always seems to be "more expensive, more extensive research is required."

In a similar vein, Joseph Plummer (Young and Rubicam) observes:

> The problem comes in that the practitioners tend to have an interest in really tough questions that are not going to be solved with a little project. But the academic people are interested in little projects. There is a paradigm problem here. It's really hard to bring those two sides together. It seems to me that they ought to have a reduced list of issues and more longitudinal, basic stuff. It seems to me that it is not all MSI's fault. The whole publishing game for academicians has turned into a bigger debacle than has the quarterly dividend for senior management in corporations.

In general, however, practitioner comments were favorable about publication activities of academics.

8
Sales Promotion and Distribution Channels: No Longer Overlooked

This chapter covers research in two different, but somewhat related, areas—sales promotion and distribution channels. The areas are related in that many sales promotion techniques (e.g., allowances, cooperative advertising, contests) are employed by manufacturers to encourage supportive behavior by channel members. Moreover, channel members are often asked to help implement promotion efforts (e.g., in-store displays, coupons, contests). Prior to the 1970s, little empirical research was done on sales promotion, and what was done on distribution channels tended to involve descriptions of wholesale and retail institutions (Barger, 1955; Revzan, 1961). But there has been considerable growth in the amount of conceptual and empirical research in these areas over the last fifteen years.

The work done on sales promotion has tended to be rather quantitative. Beginning with some econometric modeling efforts done on store-audit data in the 1960s (Massy and Frank, 1965, 1966; Frank and Massy, 1965, 1967), a steady stream of research has been done using a variety of modeling and estimation techniques. Store-audit, panel, and, more recently, supermarket scanner data have all been analyzed to obtain a better understanding of how sales promotion influences when people buy, how much they buy, how brand loyal they are, and so forth. The bulk of the research has dealt with price promotions or discounts rather than non-price promotions.

Research on distribution channels has been less dominated by model-building and prediction concerns—and less prone to require analyses of large data bases—and has tended to involve more use of survey and experimental research. This research has been more theory-driven, because thinkers such as Bucklin (1973), Stern (1969), and Williamson (1975) have offered hypotheses and propositions about channel management and channel relations that have been grounded in theories from economics, political science, sociology, social psychology, and organizational behavior. Researchers have investigated dependency, power, conflict, cooperation, and other aspects of the dynamics of channel relationships.

MSI Research on Sales Promotion and Distribution Channels: Origins and Evolution

MSI has had a long-standing involvement with research on sales promotion, dating back to the early years in Philadelphia. MSI has supported a considerable amount of research describing promotion practices of major companies, and it has also funded work on (1) modeling the effects of promotion using archival data, (2) studying the effects of short-term promotions using experiments, and (3) developing and testing behavioral theories of the effects of promotions. In the channels area, MSI has historically devoted considerable attention to the problems of retailers, including several studies that have sought to predict what the retailing environment will be like in the future. Only recently has MSI devoted much attention to research on channel management and channel relations. The research in all these areas is reviewed later (see table 8-1).

Describing Sales Promotion Practices

One of the first projects ever supported by MSI was a study by MSI staffers Patrick Robinson and David Luck on "how funds for the promotional mix of advertising, personal selling, and sales promotion were allocated" (Robinson and Luck, 1964, p. 3). They studied the promotion planning process for twelve new products—six that were introduced by consumer

Table 8-1
Questions About Sales Promotion and Distribution Channels Addressed by MSI Researchers

Description	Explanation	Prediction	Control
1. How is sales promotion used?	1. How do promotions affect consumers and dealers?	1. How can the response to promotions be predicted?	1. How can more effective *sales promotion* strategies be formulated?
	2. How do shelf space allocations affect sales?	2. What will retailing be like in the future?	2. How can more effective *channels of distribution* strategies be formulated?
			3. How can more effective retailing strategies be formulated?

goods companies and six that were introduced by industrial goods companies. Through interviews with company executives and an examination of reports and memorandums, they found enough commonality in how the firms approached the task that they were able to propose a conceptual model of the "Adaptive Planning and Control Sequence." This sequence is presented in figure 8-1.

About a decade later, Roger Strang (then a doctoral candidate at the Harvard Business School and an MSI research assistant) began a more extensive examination of how the promotion planning process actually worked. In part, he sought to test the validity of Robinson and Luck's conceptual model. With contributions from Robert Prentice (consultant) and Alden Clayton (then MSI's Director of Research Planning, and later its President), a two-phase project was conducted that involved (1) sixty-seven personal interviews of executives from eighteen major companies and (2) a mail survey that received responses from executives from fifty-seven different major companies. A first report based on the interviews stressed the lack of promotion planning in major companies (Strang, Prentice, and Clayton, 1975). A second report (Strang, 1980) proposed the model of the planning process (for established brands) portrayed in figure 8-2. Strang further reached the following major conclusions:

- Expenditures on sales promotion had increased relative to advertising expenditures in recent years. He went so far as to say "it appears that the change in the promotional mix is not temporary and that sales promotion is likely to be the major element in the foreseeable future" (Strang, 1980, p. 7).

- Senior management were having an increased involvement with sales promotion, restricting the freedom of product managers to control this area.

- The promotion planning procedures of the respondents were not as effective as those proposed by Robinson and Luck. Budgeting for advertising and promotion tended to be treated as a residual; available information that could be used to evaluate the effectiveness of promotions was not used very extensively; and too much reliance tended to be placed on what had been done in the past.

- For brands with high growth potential and strong market positions, relatively more is spent on advertising; for brands with lower growth potential and weak market positions, relatively more is spent on sales promotion.

Trade Promotion Practices and Problems. Strang was not the only Harvard person looking at sales promotion during the mid-1970s. Michel Chevalier (a Harvard doctoral student who became a professor at INSEAD,

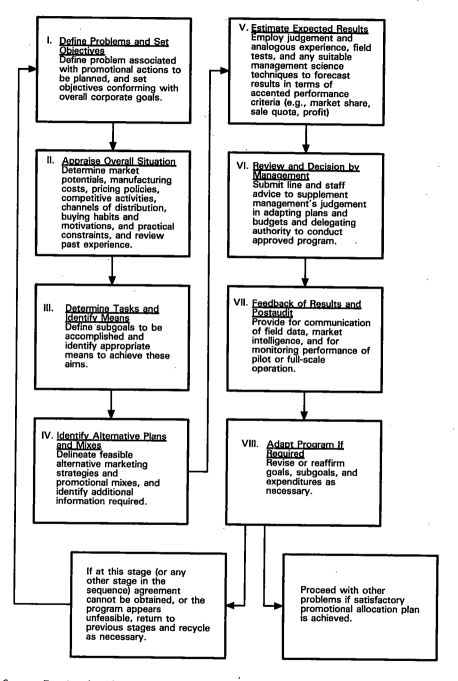

I. **Define Problems and Set Objectives**
Define problem associated with promotional actions to be planned, and set objectives conforming with overall corporate goals.

II. **Appraise Overall Situation**
Determine market potentials, manufacturing costs, pricing policies, competitive activities, channels of distribution, buying habits and motivations, and practical constraints, and review past experience.

III. **Determine Tasks and Identify Means**
Define subgoals to be accomplished and identify appropriate means to achieve these aims.

IV. **Identify Alternative Plans and Mixes**
Delineate feasible alternative marketing strategies and promotional mixes, and identify additional information required.

V. **Estimate Expected Results**
Employ judgement and analogous experience, field tests, and any suitable management science techniques to forecast results in terms of accented performance criteria (e.g., market share, sale quota, profit)

VI. **Review and Decision by Management**
Submit line and staff advice to supplement management's judgement in adapting plans and budgets and delegating authority to conduct approved program.

VII. **Feedback of Results and Postaudit**
Provide for communication of field data, market intelligence, and for monitoring performance of pilot or full-scale operation.

VIII. **Adapt Program If Required**
Revise or reaffirm goals, subgoals, and expenditures as necessary.

If at this stage (or any other stage in the sequence) agreement cannot be obtained, or the program appears unfeasible, return to previous stages and recycle as necessary.

Proceed with other problems if satisfactory promotional allocation plan is achieved.

Source: Reprinted with permission from Patrick Robinson and David Luck, *Promotional Decision Marking: Practice and Theory,* (New York: McGraw Hill, 1964), p. 21.

Figure 8–1. Adaptive Planning and Control Segments (APACS)

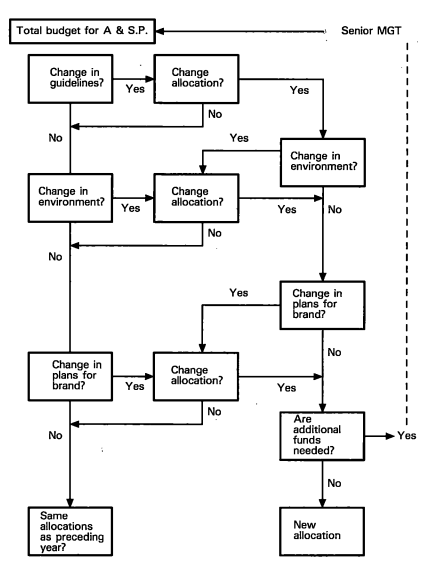

Source: Reprinted with permission from Roger A. Strang, *The Promotional Planning Process,* (New York, Praeger Publishers, Inc., 1980), p. 48, copyright ©1980 by Roger A. Strang.

Figure 8–2. Allocation Decision Process for Established Brands

France) and Ronald Curhan (a Harvard doctoral graduate who had become a professor at Boston University) collaborated on a study of how trade promotions were handled by a single major supermarket chain. They examined 1,043 different trade deals and found that this chain ignored a very high proportion of them. If deals were responded to at all, they usually led to a combination of temporary promotions for the item. However, rarely were retail price cuts equivalent to the amounts received from the deals (Chevalier and Curhan, 1975).

John Quelch was another Harvard person who noted the lack of attention being paid to sales promotion. As a new assistant professor at the Harvard Business School, he began to write cases dealing with sales promotion and found it to be an area ripe for more scholarly research. He was particularly attracted to trade promotions (i.e., allowances, short-term discounts, sales incentives), as he discovered that more was being "spent" on them than consumer promotions. As Quelch puts it:

> We had a situation where a disproportionate amount of marketing
> expenditures were going into trade promotion vis-a-vis advertising, and
> it seemed reasonable that a fair amount of academic effort should be
> devoted to that subject matter.

In the process of writing the cases, he interviewed more than thirty practitioners and became familiar with the literature on trade promotion. He used this background to write an MSI review paper describing current trade promotion practices and problems. He also followed up with more quantitative work with Dartmouth professor Scott Neslin and several Harvard doctoral students (to be discussed later).

In his review, Quelch (1982) found that managers were concerned about the rising use of trade promotion and the accompanying problems of diminished brand loyalty, inadequate merchandising support (because retailers accept deals without providing additional support or passing price reductions through to consumers), enforcement of performance requirements, and trade buying during deal periods for normal inventory or resale to other trade accounts. Shelf-space limitations and the emergence of powerful grocery chains and buying groups were seen as further aggravating these problems. Quelch concluded by stating that "many leading manufacturers are trying to reduce their commitments to trade promotion or to increase the productivity of these expenditures through improvements in promotion management, design, and evaluation" (Quelch, 1982, p. 36).

Cooperative Advertising. Another form of promotion that has received increasing usage is cooperative advertising, that is, jointly sponsored manufacturer-retailer advertising to the consumer. In an MSI-supported study by Robert Young and Stephen A. Greyser—completed at Harvard as part of Young's dissertation research—it was determined that manufacturers tend to use cooperative advertising as a means of (1) achieving immediate sales goals, (2) stimulating short-term dealer stocking, (3) ensuring general merchandising support at the store level, and (4) creating a sense of immediacy among consumers through the use of retail advertising. Young and Greyser (1982) did five case studies of appliance and fashion/soft goods manufacturers, as well as a literature review and a pilot consumer experiment. Their major findings included:

- Co-op tended to be a more important marketing tool for products characterized by infrequent consumer purchase, high perceived risk, high ego-enhancement, and low brand loyalty.
- Manufacturers' and retailers' objectives for co-op often differed, leading to conflict over execution of the programs.
- Manufacturers were concerned about the difficulties of measuring the effectiveness of spending on co-op.

They also found in their pilot study that conjoint measurement held potential as a methodology for assessing whether the manufacturer's signature or the retailer's signature in a co-op ad is a more salient and favorable cue to consumers.

Cooperative Sales Promotion. MSI also published a paper by P. Varadarajan (1984) of Texas A&M University examining "symbiosis" in sales promotion. Varadarajan developed the framework in table 8–2 to classify the various forms of cooperative sales promotion increasingly used by marketers of packaged consumer products. He focused his attention on "intercompany cooperative sales promotion"—which takes place, for example, when products like Gillette's Daisy shaver and L'eggs pantyhose are promoted together. He highlighted the potential problems that can arise when two separate companies formulate promotions designed to help two different (and sometimes unrelated) products simultaneously. He discussed the problems of developing compatibility between participants, assessing effectiveness, and other issues.

Modeling Sales Promotion Effects

Considerable effort has gone into trying to understand the effects of sales promotion on brand loyalty and purchase patterns by examining panel, scanner, and other forms of archival data. Quantitative approaches have been used to test the validity of certain models of the effects of promotions. MSI has been involved with this type of research throughout its history, and one its first publications was a monograph titled *Promotional Decisions Using Mathematical Models* (Robinson, ed., 1967). This book contained the results of four separate studies by an assortment of MSI-affiliated researchers. A probabilistic model, a distributed-lag econometric model, a discriminant function model, and an analysis-of-covariance model were

Table 8–2
Cooperative Sales Promotion: A Framework for Classification

Type of Cooperative Sales Promotion	Distinguishing Characteristics	Illustration (All illustrations presented are adaptations of real-life programs)
A. Umbrella sales promotion, Type I	Intracompany; single product category; manufacturer initiates	Cents-off store coupon good towards purchase of any of the listed brands of cigarettes manufactured by the same company
B. Umbrella sales promotion, Type II	Intracompany; multiple product categories; manufacturer initiates	Refund offer on purchase of specified brands of toothpaste, toothbrush, and mouthwash manufactured by the same company
C. Industry-level product sales promotion	Intercompany; single product category; manufacturers/industry association initiate	Cents-off store coupon good towards purchase of any brand of frozen orange juice concentrate (generally funded by the manufacturers, but planned and executed by the industry/trade association such as the Florida Orange Growers Association)
D. Horizontal cooperative sales promotion, Type I	Intercompany; multiple product categories; manufacturers initiate	Refund offer on purchase of specified brands of ground coffee and nondairy coffee creamer manufactured by different companies
E. Horizontal cooperative sales promotion, Type II	Intercompany; multiple product categories; manufacturers initiate in cooperation with the industry/trade association of a related product category	Refund offer of the purchase price of a half-gallon milk (any brand; participating trade association: American Dairy Association) on purchase of specified brands of chocolate-flavored drink mix and cookies manufactured by different companies
F. Vertical cooperative sales promotion	A, B, or D above; but channel intermediary initiates	Free-standing newspaper insert with cents-off store coupon for specific brands of bath soap, cereals, and toothpaste manufactured by the same or different firms, but distributed by the same intermediary
G. Charity-linked cooperative sales promotion	A, B, C, or D above linked with a charitable cause or charitable organization	For each coupon redeemed during a specified time period on products manufactured by a particular company, the company promises to contribute five cents to a charitable institution such as the Muscular Dystrophy Association

Source: Reprinted with permission from P. Varadarajan, "Symbiosis in Sales Promotion," in Katherine E. Jocz (ed.), *Research on Sales Promotion: Collected Papers*, Report No. 84–104, Marketing Science Institute, Cambridge, Massachusetts, pp. 108–109.

tested using various data bases. Some of the findings of these studies raise provocative implications for designing sales promotions. They include:

- A great deal of "size loyalty" was observed, with promotions frequently attracting more volume from the same sizes of competitive brands than those brand-sizes maintained on a repeat basis (Kuehn and Rohloff, 1967).
- Customers who were classified as "loyal" to a product exhibited virtually the same response to price changes and deals as did those who were classified as "nonloyal" (Frank and Massy, 1967).

Other conclusions from these studies provided insights for advertising planning and future modeling work.

In more recent times, MSI has supported an extensive series of projects and conferences on how to model the effects of sales promotions. For instance, John Quelch of Harvard has worked on two modeling projects as a follow-up to his descriptive work on sales promotion. In one project, completed with Harvard doctoral students Cheri Marshall and Dae Chang, a structural equation modeling technique called LISREL was used on data from the PIMS program to examine the relationship between promotion-to-sales ratios and other measures. Although the study was to examine the *determinants* of promotion spending in various industries—and not the *effects* of this spending—the authors observed, "It seems likely that our theories underplayed the role of promotion in inducing trial and switching in populous, high-purchase-frequency markets" (Quelch, Marshall, and Chang, 1984).

Modeling Consumer Promotions. Quelch also worked on a project with Scott Neslin and Caroline Henderson of Dartmouth. The project got started when Henderson was a doctoral student of Quelch's. Neslin became involved because the work required someone with specific quantitative skills to analyze a complex data base. Quelch simply telephoned Neslin for help, recognizing that Neslin had previously done some work on consumer promotions. Neslin offers the following comment on his experience with this project:

> MSI only funded my transportation to and from Harvard. It was actually a relatively minor outlay, but it was an important psychological lift for all of us. The idea of MSI's sponsoring something or devoting some resources to a project motivated us. It was an honor. I put it in my resume!

Neslin also has some interesting comments to offer about how he became interested in promotion in the first place. He states:

> I was talking with a colleague with whom I had done other work (Robert Shoemaker of NYU) and he mentioned that he'd been working in the

area, saw some research issues, and wondered if I was interested in thinking about them. It was serendipitous. I think Ph.D. students are taught to carefully derive the areas they should be working in by reviewing the literature, defining what it means, and so on. But I think often the area that one ends up working in results from serendipitous contacts and experiences. That's what happened to me in the area of promotion.

Neslin, Henderson, and Quelch (1984) studied whether coupon promotions lead consumers to accelerate their purchases by encouraging them to buy larger quantities or have shorter time intervals between purchases. Using data from a scanner panel that contained the toilet tissue purchases of 2,293 consumers over a twenty-eight-week period, they estimated regression equations that tested the relationship between coupon usage and both purchase quantity and purchase time interval. They then used the parameter estimates from these regressions in a simulation model that allowed them to compare what purchase quantities and time intervals would be with and without the coupons. They found that for this product category, purchase acceleration due to coupons primarily took the form of increased purchase quantity. Consumers tended to make up for larger-than-usual purchases by waiting longer rather than buying less on the next purchase. In addition, purchase acceleration induced only a very small long-term increase in total category volume. Interestingly, purchase acceleration did differ significantly from brand to brand. And, not surprisingly, purchase acceleration (larger quantities) was stronger among heavy users than light users.

Neslin (forthcoming) has done additional work by himself to study the effects of coupon promotions. Some of this work was reported at an MSI Sales Promotion Conference, October 1985. His primary concern has been with how coupons affect "incremental" sales—defined as purchases by a coupon redeemer who would have bought another brand. In this research, he has again used scanner panel data, but this time for instant coffee rather than toilet tissue. Simultaneous econometric modeling techniques have been used to examine the relationship between incremental sales per redemption and several other variables. Among Neslin's major findings were the following:

- About two-thirds of sales involving redemptions were incremental, with a fairly wide range over brands.
- Early redemptions are more likely to represent incremental sales.
- There are winners and losers in terms of longer-term impact on market share. Winners have high redemption rates and are relatively insensitive to competitive advertising.
- Incremental sales are lower for a brand with higher baseline sales.

Another MSI-supported study that examined consumer promotions was conducted by Kenneth Hardy of the University of Western Ontario. He surveyed of twenty-seven Canadian packaged goods companies to obtain information on the characteristics and performance of 216 sales promotion efforts. Attempting to identify the determinants of successful sales promotions, Hardy (1984) utilized multiple discriminant analysis to look at several potential determinants, as perceived by promotion managers. His results indicated that strong salesforce support was by far the most important determinant of successful consumer promotions.

Modeling Trade Promotions. Hardy (1984) also examined the determinants of successful trade promotions. He found the most common factor associated with success appeared to be strong trade support. The absence of competitive promotions also seemed related to success. Furthermore, in discussions with Hardy, the respondents generally thought that reasons for achieving trade support are within the control of the product manager.

Hardy's findings were noted by Harvard doctoral student Robert Kopp (now at Babson College) who found them to be consistent with his own experiences for five years as a product manager with Richardson-Vicks. With the encouragement of John Quelch and Stephen A. Greyser of Harvard, and Alden Clayton of MSI, Kopp submitted a proposal to nine MSI member companies for funding and cooperation to examine the factors that influence retailer support of trade promotions. As Kopp recalls, "obtaining the company support validated the topic in the eyes of my professors," and he was able to pursue a dissertation in this area.

Kopp's research in trade promotions took a number of different avenues, including one project done in collaboration with Boston University professor Ronald Curhan (whose own research on sales promotion is discussed later). Kopp and Curhan examined 147 trade deals of national brands in a six-week period for each of five chains in one market area. Retail audit data, SAMI data, deal sheets, price observations, and ratings provided by buyers on twenty-five trade support criteria were analyzed to determine the factors that influenced retailer support. The factors found by Curhan and Kopp (1986) to influence retailers' *acceptance* of a deal were (in order of importance):

1. judged importance of the item and likelihood that the competition will also promote it;
2. profitability of the item;
3. size of the incentive;
4. manufacturer's reputation;
5. promotion wear-out rate;

6. promotion elasticity;
7. manufacturer's support of the brand; and
8. sales turnover.

Determining what influences *compliance* with a deal was more difficult. It seemed to be most related to importance of the item, profitability, and manufacturer reputation.

Retailer Promotions. Leigh McAlister (University of Texas at Austin) has received MSI support to test how well probabilistic choice models (namely, logit) predict how households will respond to retail deals. Using scanner panel data on regular coffee, cookies, and light-duty dishwashing detergent, she determined that there was great variability in household sensitivity to deals. The panel was highly sensitive to coffee deals, moderately sensitive to cookie deals, and only mildly sensitive to detergent deals. She further determined that deal sensitivity was related to store choice patterns. Additionally, relatively small brands had an advantage over relatively big brands in terms of promotion effectiveness. Finally, she found that demographics do not separate deal-sensitive and deal-insensitive households very well.

Experimental Research on Promotions

The notion that great variability exists in consumer responses to promotions was supported in several experimental studies supported by MSI. For instance, Ronald Curhan of Boston University conducted a field experiment in four test supermarkets of a single chain. A very complex fractional factorial design was employed to examine the effects of "normal" and "featured" levels of display space, retail price, newspaper advertising, and display location quality on the sales of a variety of fresh fruits and vegetables. Curhan (1974) found that:

- Bonus display space increased unit sales of all items, especially low volume ones.
- Price reductions had a very minor effect, except that they helped sales of soft fruit significantly.
- Advertising had considerable impact in the hard fruit and cooking vegetables groups, but had a negligible impact for soft fruit and salad vegetables.
- Location quality also had mixed effects, helping hard fruit and cooking vegetables but not the other groups.

A less-complex field experiment by Michel Chevalier (1975) found a similar result with respect to the effects of display space, including the discovery of wide differences across product groups in the impact of the extra space.

Behavioral Theories and Promotion

While economic theory has provided some grounding for research on sales promotion, little has been drawn from behavioral theories to guide this research. However, MSI recently supported Alan Sawyer (Florida) and Peter Dickson (Ohio State) to write a review of relevant psychological perspectives for studying sales promotions. According to Dickson, this review was an outgrowth of experimental work both researchers had been doing on pricing. They decided that sales promotion as a topic needed its own study because it involves a different form of information transmission. Dickson was already working with MSI on some information processing research, and was able to obtain support for their sales promotion research quite readily.

Sawyer and Dickson (1984) reviewed how sales promotion research could draw on self-perception and attribution theories, price perception theory, learning and attitude theory, and noncognitive theories of induced behavior. For example, they suggested that self-perception theory implies sales promotions are likely to have negative effects on long-term attitudes and behaviors to the extent that consumers attribute their purchase of a brand to the incentive rather than to personal liking for the brand. In the same vein, they warned that noncognitive theories suggest that promotion rather than the brand may become the reinforcing stimulus for buying a product. They also discussed how price perception theories indicate how sales promotions may affect consumers' acceptable price ranges, adaption to higher prices, or the just-noticeable difference between two prices or brands.

Dickson and Sawyer (1986) followed up this review with a study of the retail environment in which consumers experience promotions. This descriptive research involved interviews with 800 consumers of margarine, coffee, cold cereal, and toothpaste in one supermarket chain. Some of the more provocative findings were:

- The point-of-purchase environment is extremely cluttered.
- One quarter of the respondents said that an item was not on special when it was, and another quarter did not know about the special. Only 13 percent knew the size of the price reduction, while half had no idea of its size.
- About 10 percent of the respondents thought an item was on special when it was not.
- Couponing may reduce point-of-purchase price checking, while in-store specials may increase point-of purchase price checking.

Perhaps their most striking finding was that half of the respondents could not correctly recall the price of an item purchased within the previous sixty seconds.

Retail Merchandising Strategies

MSI has supported a few studies that have been concerned with how retailers can merchandise their products more effectively. One such study was conducted by Ronald Curhan (Boston University) while he was a doctoral student at Harvard working with Professor Robert Buzzell (MSI's Executive Director at the time). Curhan was searching for a topic for his dissertation and was eager to do something relevant to the supermarket industry, where he had worked for ten years. He recalls:

> The National Association of Food Chains coincidentally happened to be having their national meeting in Boston that year, so I arranged an appointment with its Executive Director. We discussed what I could do as a dissertation that would be of interest to the industry. My argument was: "I'm about to embark on an arcane rite, and it seems silly to just go through the motions and have it sit on a shelf somewhere. You give me a topic that's of interest to the industry—and some financial support—and I'll produce an interesting and useful study."

The discussion produced an agreement between the two about the need for research on the impact of shelf space. Funding was then provided by the association (through MSI) to support a field experimental study in this area.

Curhan (1971) experimentally reallocated shelf space in four large supermarkets for nearly 500 representative grocery products. Sales figures for an eight-week period following a space change were compared to figures for the pre-change eight-week period. Items which had changes in retail price, shelf level, display activity, or promotions during the research period were generally excluded from the analysis. Based on this study and on a review of other recent research on shelf space, Curhan concluded that: "the impact of changes in shelf space on unit sales is very small relative to the effects of other variables" (Curhan, 1972, p. 56).

A more recent project by Curhan sought to identify more efficient ways to distribute health and beauty aids and small-ticket general merchandise (e.g., housewares, hardware, stationery). Curhan and Harvard professors Walter Salmon and Robert Buzzell collaborated in obtaining data from fifteen supermarket chains, five convenience store companies, and fifteen service merchandisers (via personal interviews and the examination of company records). They looked at dollar sales and contribution per linear foot for the chains and convenience stores, and percentage contribution and contribution per dollar of average inventory for the service merchandisers. Salmon, Buzzell, and Curhan's (1980) major findings included the following:

- For both retailers and service merchandisers, health and beauty aids were a more productive and profitable category than general merchandise. This occurred in spite of larger gross margins for the general merchandise. The general merchandise had fewer sales per unit of space and higher handling expenses.

- Retailers using service merchandisers to supply health and beauty aids and general merchandise achieved higher sales and contribution per linear foot than did firms buying these items direct. This was probably because they allocated less space to the merchandising category. The difference in performance was more marked for general merchandise.

They concluded by offering several suggestions for retailers and service merchandisers about their product lines and target markets.

Future Trends in Retailing

MSI has been involved with a long series of projects devoted to projecting how retailing institutions might be changing. Papers have been published on the "super-store" (Salmon, Buzzell, and Cort, 1974), catalog showrooms (McCammon, 1973), department stores (May, 1971), and more general trends (McNair and May, 1976). Eleanor May of the University of Virginia has played a major role in many of these projects. Her interest in retailing developed as a research assistant and research associate of Professor Malcolm McNair of the Harvard Business School (1948–1962). She followed this up with eight years as a research director for Woodward and Lothrop, a Washington, D.C. area department store. Since joining the faculty at Virginia in 1970, she has published more than a half-dozen MSI working papers, including a relatively recent effort titled "Future Trends in Retailing: Merchandise Line Trends and Store Trends 1980–1990." This project came about, according to May, because she, William Ress (consultant), and Walter Salmon (Harvard) had approached MSI about a study designed to obtain realistic projections of retail sales in 1990 by merchandise line and by type of retailer in order to guide the strategic planning of retailers and manufacturers.

May, Ress, and Salmon (1985) began their forecasts with straight-line projections from historical sales. They then refined these figures, based on a consensus of projections from leading economic forecasters. They further adjusted the merchandise line and retailer type figures for inflation and qualitative factors. Their major conclusions were:

- Sales growth expectations of most merchandise categories will be modest. Only the electronics category will enjoy exceptional growth, with an average annual increase of 14 percent. Toys, optical goods, and sporting goods will also have a higher than average growth rate. On the other hand, convenience goods (e.g., food, alcohol, drugs, tobacco, health and beauty aids) will have nearly flat or declining sales.

- Only minor shifts in sales by retailer type will occur, with the exception of the growth in computer stores. Also, mail-order will continue to grow faster than store selling. Variety stores and household maintenance outlets will decline in revenues in the 1980s.

They offered a number of explanations for their projections, including population shifts and new technology. They also pointed out that retailers had made some debatable changes in facilities and merchandise carried in recent years, and that it would take some time to recover from these moves.

Managing Channel Relationships

MSI has recently become more active in supporting theoretical and empirical research on the behavior of channel relationships. For instance, MSI published a paper by Erin Anderson (Wharton) and Barton Weitz (then at Wharton and now at Florida) that presented some new theoretical perspectives on the classic issue of whether a manufacturer should (1) contract for marketing services outside the firm (i.e., "make") or (2) vertically integrate those services within the firm (i.e., "buy"). Drawing on the thinking of economist Oliver Williamson (1975, 1979, 1981) about "transaction cost analysis," Anderson and Weitz (1983) were able to propose some conditions under which vertical integration might be preferable to contracting for outside services. These limited conditions are indicated in figure 8–3. They were identified as:

- When noncompetitive supplier markets exist either because of (1) company-specific capabilities or experiences or (2) economies of scale in supply.
- When environmental uncertainty *and* company-specific capabilities are high; but not when only environmental uncertainty exists.
- When it is difficult to assess the performance of an outside agent.
- When "free-riding" potential is high (i.e., when an outside agent can benefit from the efforts of other outside agents without having to produce much of its own effort).

However, Anderson and Weitz stress that contracting for outside services is generally a superior strategy to vertical integration. It allows the market mechanism to encourage channel coordination and control rather than reliance on the judgment of a "channel captain."

Another MSI endeavor in the channels area was a 1984 conference at Duke University. The format was innovative, with representatives from General Electric, Goodyear, IBM, and Sears opening the conference by presenting case studies of their channel management practices, and the

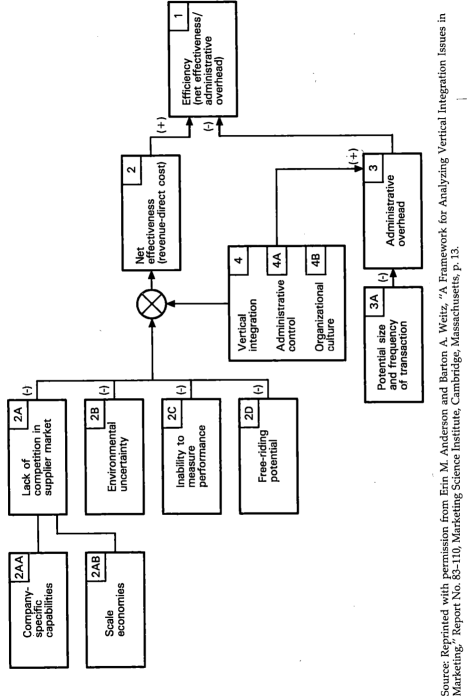

Figure 8–3. The Conditions Under Which Vertical Integration Improves Efficiency

Source: Reprinted with permission from Erin M. Anderson and Barton A. Weitz, "A Framework for Analyzing Vertical Integration Issues in Marketing," Report No. 83–110, Marketing Science Institute, Cambridge, Massachusetts, p. 13.

sessions stimulated a number of new ideas for future channel research. These ideas are summarized in a paper written by Duke doctoral student William Ross (1985). In trying to capture the essence of what was said about research needs, Ross paraphrases the comments made at the end of the conference by Louis Stern (then MSI's Executive Director and a Northwestern professor):

> There is probably no better real-world laboratory in which to study the principles of social psychology, sociology, organizational behavior, game theory, and political science in day-to-day action. For in channels management, independent organizations are forced to deal closely with each other, in both cooperation *and* competition, on a daily basis. Moreover, if perchance a company has vertically integrated, then the same act with the same conflicting individual or organizational objectives is played out, only internally (Stern, as quoted in Ross, 1985, p. 3S).

MSI Research on Sales Promotion and Channels: Impact and Utilization

MSI's long-term investment in research on sales promotion has clearly had an impact in both the academic and practitioner world, even though a large proportion of this research is still reasonably new. Moreover, the MSI-sponsored research in retailing has received considerable attention among practitioners. However, it is still too early to tell what MSI might accomplish in the channels area.

Impact in the Academic World

For a long time, most of the work done on sales promotion was done by people with long-term MSI or Harvard ties. According to Quelch, this situation is changing as a more diverse group of academics examines this area. A 1985 MSI conference on sales promotion had more than twenty-five invited academics from a variety of schools, all of whom are actively pursuing research in sales promotion. The level of sophistication in their research is improving rapidly. In fact, during the conference John Farley—MSI Executive Director and a Columbia professor—was prompted to state that "some of the best modeling work going on in marketing is being done in the promotion area."

Much of the MSI work on sales promotion has ended up in journals and other publications. Some examples include:

- The very early work by Frank and Massy led to several articles in the *Journal of Marketing Research* and a book published by M.I.T. Press.

- Curhan's experimental work on promotion was published in the *Journal of Marketing Research* and in the *Sloan Management Review.*
- Strang's work produced a *Harvard Business Review* article and a book that was published by Praeger Publishers.
- Quelch also got a *Harvard Business Review* article out of his efforts, and his work with Neslin and Henderson has been published in *Marketing Science.*

On the other hand, MSI-sponsored research related to retailing has not received much attention from academics. Curhan's work on shelf space was published in the *Journal of Marketing Research* and the *Journal of Marketing,* but little else has made it into scholarly journals or stimulated research by other academics.

The editors had little to say about the research discussed in this chapter. One labeled the Anderson and Weitz work as "significant" without any prompting, and another had favorable comments to make about the Duke distribution channel conference. But nothing else was said except for responses to the question about Curhan's research, which was described as "steady progress" by two people, "an initial step" by three people, and "a minor contribution" by one person.

Impact in the Practitioner World

Researcher Interviews. The interviews with academics revealed a feeling that practitioners had responded positively to their research. Quelch, Kopp, and Sawyer indicated that they had received several inquiries as a result of their research on sales promotion. Moreover, Curhan's work in both promotion and shelf space led to his making presentations and doing consulting for several major packaged goods manufacturers. It also led to invitations to assist a supermarket chain in Venezuela and to a lecture series before the Japanese Distribution Economics Institute.

The study by May, Ress, and Salmon received coverage in *Fortune* magazine and many other periodicals, and this helped stimulate considerable interest. May claims that several major companies are using the figures in the report for their long-range planning. Moreover, nearly 700 copies of the report were sold in 1985.

Practitioner Interviews. The practitioners who were interviewed were generally very positive about the work on sales promotion, and they reported several instances of direct utilization. For example, Kent Mitchel (then at General Foods, now MSI's President) states that there has been "a lot of helpful work in this area, which has been useful in policy decisions by goading companies into paying attention to better ways to spend their money." Similarly, Richard Elder (James River Dixie Northern) reports that "just recently we were trying to go through and think of the theory of consumer promotion, and some of the work MSI had done was very useful in terms of helping us structure our thinking and develop models to explain how things work." Others who praised MSI's involvement in promotion were Paul Fruitt (Gillette), Dudley Ruch (retired from Quaker Oats), and William Moran (formerly of Lever Brothers).

Specific projects that were cited during the interviews were the works of Roger Strang, Robert Kopp, John Quelch, and Leigh McAlister. Martin Thomas (Ore-Ida Foods) recalls using Strang's work "in setting policy and looking at the percent of dollars going to a specific type of promotion." He elaborates by saying: "With that information as background, you could reclassify your spending and see if your brands tended to be increasing or decreasing in consumer franchise-building activities."

Thomas also finds the McAlister work useful. He states:

> It helps to give you a philosophy to look at your own information. As we do our own studies, it gives us a way to approach setting them up.

A similar reaction is supplied by Charles Jacobson (formerly with Nabisco Brands), who has found the McAlister work and the Quelch, Henderson, and Neslin work to be stepping stones from which companies can take off and do their own research on promotions.

Finally, the only comment about research in distribution channels comes from Stephan Haeckel (IBM), who says:

> One of the most useful things to us is the work on distribution, particularly the conference at Duke. Out of that came a great deal of learning by us of the similarities that we face with companies in completely different industries. As a result, we held follow-up meetings with the other companies and some of the academics.

Haeckel goes on to praise this experience as "an example of how an MSI connection gave us access to ideas and insights that we otherwise wouldn't have access to."

9
Research Methodology and Model Building: From Borrowers to Innovators

This chapter focuses on research that has been oriented toward developing better tools and models for understanding a wide range of marketing phenomena. Of course, much of this methodological work has also made substantive contributions to our understanding of areas like advertising, consumer behavior, and sales management. And, likewise, some of the work discussed in other chapters has made methodological contributions. Thus, there is some overlap between what is covered here and material in other chapters. Frankly, several studies are reviewed here simply because they seemed to fit more logically here than elsewhere (e.g., the work on modeling the carryover effects of advertising).

Research in four areas is covered:

1. the measurement and scaling of attitudes and preferences;
2. research design and data collection methods;
3. quantitative modeling and analysis; and
4. utilization of models and research.

A vast amount of research has been completed in each of these areas, making it difficult to provide a concise overview of how the marketing discipline has addressed them. A source that reviews much of this research is the textbook on model-building in marketing by Lilien and Kotler (1983).

One summary comment that can be made about the research in these areas is that it has involved considerable *borrowing* of tools and methods from other academic disciplines. Social psychology, psychometrics, sociology, econometrics, management science, statistics, and diffusion of innovations are among the fields that have provided tools that marketing academics have tested on marketing problems. Some of these tools (e.g., linear programming) were found to have limited value in addressing marketing problems and have received little sustained interest following an initial flurry of attention. However, other tools—such as nonmetric multidimensional scaling, stochastic modeling, causal modeling, and decision calculus modeling—have received growing attention, and it seems fair to say that marketing academics have done as much to improve and refine these tools for use by other researchers as the people in the disciplines from which they emerged.

MSI Research on Methods and Models: Origins and Evolution

MSI has supported major research efforts in each of the four areas identified above. MSI supported work that introduced nonmetric multidimensional scaling techniques to the discipline, and it has continuously been involved with projects that have examined other measurement approaches and research design techniques. In the quantitative modeling area, MSI supported several early stochastic modeling and simulation efforts, and it has regularly assisted efforts to test out other quantitative modeling and analysis techniques on marketing problems. Furthermore, MSI has had a long history of supporting projects concerned with ways of increasing practitioners' use of marketing models and research results.

Measurement and Scaling

While MSI was still located in Philadelphia during the mid-1960s, it supported a project containing laboratory experiments designed to examine whether individuals acquired information and made choices in a manner consistent with the normative prescriptions of Bayesian decision theory (Green, Robinson, and FitzRoy, 1967). The failure of the subjects in these experiments to act like Bayesians suggested to Wharton professor Paul Green that "there seemed to be a need in marketing research for coming up with better tools for assessing people's perceptions and preference judgements." Green therefore worked with MSI to set up a lecture series at Wharton during the 1967–68 academic year at which several well-known psychological measurement researchers (including Clyde Coombs, J. Douglas Carroll, Forrest Young, and Warren Torgerson) spoke. Stimulated by these lectures and by "the intellectual aspects of what was going on," Green co-authored (with a variety of colleagues) a long series of papers and monographs on multidimensional scaling and related techniques for obtaining spatial relationships of buyer perceptions and preferences.

One of the people who collaborated with Green extensively on this research effort was a Wharton doctoral student, Vithala Rao (now at Cornell). Rao's interest in scaling had preceded his arrival at Wharton, since in the early 1960s he had done a master's degree in sociology at the University of Michigan and had been exposed to Clyde Coombs, who was working on "unfolding theory." When, after a stint in industry, he entered the Wharton doctoral program in the late 1960s, Rao was naturally drawn to Green's scaling interests. As he puts it:

> I got very excited about the prospect of doing some good mathematical work on organizing consumer theories. The connection went back to my pre-doctoral studies. Things seemed to come together, given my background in mathematics and this exposure to psychometrics.

The series of publications on multidimensional scaling by Green, Rao, and others is difficult to summarize. Their work reviewed a large assortment of measurement tools and computer programs, carefully analyzing their respective strengths and weaknesses. For instance, in a hard-cover monograph by Green and Frank Carmone (1970) of Drexel University, the authors:

- Described fully metric, fully nonmetric, and nonmetric scaling techniques. The nonmetric techniques—whereby ordinal (i.e., rank order) data about people's perceptions or preferences can be converted into metric output in the form of perceptual maps showing where objects are perceived to be located along multiple interval scales—were the focus of this book and most of Green's MSI-related work.
- Compared various ways of gathering "similarities" data to input to the programs. With these approaches, subjects are asked to rank-order pairs of objects from the most similar pair to the least similar pair in terms of an overall evaluation or in terms of possession of specific attributes.
- Compared various ways of gathering "preference" data to input to the programs. With these approaches, subjects are asked to rank-order objects based on overall liking, proximity to an "ideal" object, or possession of specific attributes.
- Reviewed methods of labeling and reducing the number of dimensions that emerge from the output of the various programs.
- Provided capsule descriptions of several computer programs that can be used to perform nonmetric multidimensional scaling and complementary cluster analysis and other analytic procedures.

Other publications from this body of work addressed issues such as the number of scales and response categories to use (Green and Rao, 1970), the effects of individual differences (Green and Rao, 1971), and the impact of stimulus context (Green and Carmone, 1970).

MSI has continued to support research using nonmetric multidimensional scaling, especially in looking at how these techniques can be used in introducing new products and in developing competitive marketing strategies. This more recent work is treated in the chapter on strategic marketing management (chapter 3).

Other than work on multidimensional scaling, MSI has only occasionally issued papers with a primary focus on measurement issues. Two papers that fit this description were written by (1) Fred Reynolds and John Neter of the University of Georgia and (2) Donald Morrison of Columbia University and his doctoral student Bruce Buchanan (now at New York University). Reynolds and Neter (1979) addressed the issue of how many response classes to use in measuring a variable such as age. A number of standardized classification systems have been used by organizations such as the Census Bureau, but little attention has been paid to whether five, six, seven, or more classes should be used in questions. Based on an analysis of data obtained from the Market Facts Consumer Mail Panel (as part of life style surveys conducted by the advertising agency Needham, Harper, and Steers), Reynolds and Neter concluded that with the variable "age," using eight classes produces better predictions of people's responses to consumer behavior questions than using fewer classes—and does not produce significantly inferior results to using more classes. However, Reynolds and Neter cautioned that with other variables and other behavior questions a different number of response classes might be more effective. They concluded by calling for more research on these issues.

Buchanan and Morrison (1985) examined the problem of obtaining data on people's preferences using blind, forced-choice product testing (e.g., blind taste tests). A host of issues were addressed in their research including the relative efficiency of different test formats and the needed sample sizes for these tests. Their major contribution was to offer an analytic approach that a researcher could use to evaluate the efficiency of different test formats. Among their more interesting conclusions was the strong suggestion that forced-choice test data reported in many comparative advertisements may be unreliable because of woefully inadequate sample sizes.

Research Design and Data Collection

MSI has supported a number of projects where the major focus has been on identifying improved types of experimental, quasi-experimental, or survey research designs. For example, Michael Ray of Stanford worked on a project that sought to stimulate interest in unobtrusive research techniques. Ray (1973) stressed that taking obtrusive measurements can produce invalidity by stimulating interviewee reactance, interviewer bias, or a host of other problems. He recommended serious consideration of the use of unobtrusive techniques such as (1) entrapment approaches (e.g., using coupon returns to evaluate advertising), (2) observation, (3) archival records (e.g., content analysis of editorial material), and (4) physical traces (e.g., measuring carpet wear). He also urged the use of multiple measures in marketing research.

Another MSI-supported project that suggested new research design ideas was conducted by Lynn Phillips of Stanford University while he was a Northwestern doctoral student. Phillips (1978) assessed the research designs used in several evaluations of consumer protection reforms—a project that is also discussed in chapter 10. In writing up his assessment, Phillips provided an introduction to several useful research designs for conducting evaluations of public policy actions and of marketing actions as well. In particular, he discussed the strengths and weaknesses of the "pretest-posttest design with a no-reform, non-equivalent control group" and of various forms of "interrupted time series" designs.

MSI also supported research on the nonresponse problem in survey studies. Frederick Wiseman and Philip McDonald of Northeastern University headed up this effort. Wiseman claims to have become interested in this issue through reading media reports, hearing comments at an American Statistical Association conference, and reading a journal article that lamented the increased number of survey refusals. After contacting MSI, Wiseman and McDonald used the cooperation of MSI member companies and the Council of American Survey Research Organizations to help them examine the response rates of 182 telephone survey studies, encompassing approximately one million attempted telephone interviews. Their most striking conclusion was that "a large percentage of designated respondents/households [is] not contacted." Furthermore, "when contact is made, there is more than a one in four chance that a refusal will result" (Wiseman and McDonald, 1978, p. 63). They further argued—in a follow-up paper (Wiseman and McDonald, 1980)—for more standardized definitions, methods of calculation, and reporting procedures for response rates, contact rates, completion rates, refusal rates, and so forth.

Quantitative Modeling and Analysis

MSI has supported a wide range of quantitative research, much of which is discussed in other chapters of this book (e.g., the work on market structure analysis in chapter 3, on sales management in chapter 4, on sales promotion in chapter 8). What is covered here is research that sought to introduce new modeling and statistical analysis approaches to the discipline.

MSI was involved with quantitative research from its early days in Philadelphia. This earlier activity tended to focus on sales promotion (see chapter 8). After MSI moved to Cambridge, research on a broader range of quantitative topics began to be supported. For example, Jerome Herniter of Boston University conducted a series of projects that looked at stochastic models (Cook and Herniter, 1970), an entropy model (Herniter, 1972), and the commercially-marketed "Hendry model" (Herniter, 1973) as ways of predicting consumer brand choice behavior. Similarly, Frank Bass (then at Purdue University) wrote papers on decomposable regression models (Bass, 1971) and on multivariate regression analysis (Bass and Beckwith, 1971). In the same vein, Vithala Rao (Cornell) and James Cox (Virginia Tech) presented a review of various sales forecasting techniques, including an examination of Box-Jenkins time series methods, brand-switching methods, and conjoint analysis methods (Rao and Cox, 1978).

Perhaps the biggest step MSI took to broaden its involvement with quantitative research was to bring in Professor David Montgomery as a visiting researcher for the 1969–70 academic year, while he was between appointments at M.I.T. and Stanford. With a Ph.D. in management science from Stanford and several years of experience on the faculty at M.I.T., Montgomery had already distinguished himself by introducing innovative modeling approaches to the discipline. Working with people like William Massy at Stanford, and John Little, Glenn Urban, and Alvin Silk at M.I.T., Montgomery found it natural to immerse himself in modeling efforts. As he recalls: "I looked around me and everybody I knew was a model builder." Among his early (pre-MSI) exploits, was a book he wrote with Urban, titled *Management Science in Marketing* (Montgomery and Urban, 1969). Montgomery claims this project got started as follows:

> I'd been at M.I.T. about six months—and Urban had been there about six weeks—and we decided that we were going to build a whole new course for M.I.T.; and that we were going to write a book to use in the course. We would pay for it all by running a summer program called "Management Science in Marketing." We pulled it off. In six months we had six of nine chapters written and the summer program was a financial success.

Montgomery came away from this book-writing experience with a wealth of new research ideas. He therefore sought out help from MSI to allow him to pursue these ideas. He recalls:

> When I heard that MSI was moving to Harvard, I called Buzzell (its Executive Director) and said: "Buzz, I need a year off to work on some things. How would you like to make me a research associate?" Fortunately for me, he didn't think that this was the most outrageous idea he'd ever heard. And so, MSI essentially worked out a deal where they bought my time away from teaching at M.I.T. and I basically moved into MSI.

Montgomery worked on a host of projects during that year. He began his work on a "hierarchical thresholding" model of choice that enabled him to predict the actions of supermarket buyers (Montgomery, 1973). He also worked on a paper estimating the dynamic effects of marketing communications expenditures (Montgomery and Silk, 1972). This effort developed largely as the result of an encounter with a pharmaceutical company executive at an American Marketing Association meeting. This person offered Montgomery some interesting data in response to hearing his plea for industry-academic cooperation. The same contact person also stimulated work on a multiple-product sales force allocation model (Montgomery, Silk, and Zaragoza, 1971).

Through the years, MSI has published a large number of Montgomery's papers, including some that did not result from direct MSI financial support. Montgomery has welcomed MSI publication because he feels it has forced him to think more broadly about the implications of his research. Topics that have been covered in his MSI papers include stochastic models of consumer choice (Montgomery and Ryans, 1971), the predictive validity of conjoint analysis (Montgomery and Wittink, 1980), the use of distributed lag models for understanding communication effects (Montgomery and Silk, 1970), and experience curves (Montgomery and Day, 1985).

Analyzing the Cumulative Effects of Advertising. The use of distributed lag models to study the effects of advertising also drew the interest of Professor Darral Clarke (now at Brigham Young University) when he was a doctoral student at Purdue in the early 1970s. Clarke had been a research analyst in industry, where he had been assigned the task of coming up with sales forecasts, given various levels of advertising. His recollection of how he handled the assignment is:

> I sort of made up the model myself. Then it was a surprise later to find that people had been writing about it in the past.

Clarke went on to write several papers in graduate school on the subject. After he joined the faculty at the Harvard Business School, he commenced an extensive review of all the previous research that had used distributed lag models as well as other techniques to study the cumulative effects of advertising. MSI published this review, although it did not provide direct support for the project. The major conclusion of this review was as follows:

> The published econometric literature indicates that 90 percent of the cumulative effects of advertising on sales of mature, frequently purchased, low priced products occurs within three to nine months of the advertising. The conclusion that advertising's effect on sales lasts for months rather than years is strongly supported. (Clarke, 1977, p. 60)

MSI did support Clarke in putting together a volume to follow up his review and examine cumulative advertising from a variety of perspectives (Clarke, 1977). One of the papers in this volume looked at the issue from a behavioral perspective and is discussed in chapter 7 (Sawyer and Ward, 1976). Other papers addressed the managerial (Palda and Turner, 1977) and public policy (Beckwith, 1977) implications of advertising's having certain cumulative effects.

One other MSI-supported study that examined cumulative advertising effects was conducted by Paul Farris (Virginia) and David Reibstein (Wharton) while both were colleagues at the Harvard Business School. Farris and Reibstein (1978) critically evaluated distributed lag models and, in particular, took exception to the popular Koyck model that many previous studies had employed (Koyck, 1954). They argued that the Koyck model has an important assumption that is inappropriate, namely linearity in the advertising-sales response function. They recommended an alternative procedure that employed a nonlinear response function, and showed that this approach will provide more reliable estimates of the extent to which advertising effects carry over from one measurement to another. The authors warn, however, that "there are good reasons to believe that wide variations in the carry-over effects of advertising exist across product categories." (Farris and Reibstein, 1978, p. 12)

Utilization of Models and Marketing Research Results

MSI has regularly provided support for projects that have been concerned with increasing practitioner utilization of marketing models and marketing research information. Some of these projects have been normative or prescriptive in orientation, presenting thoughts on setting up better information systems or decision support systems. Other projects have been more descriptive, identifying actual usage of models or research techniques.

David Montgomery of Stanford has written a number of papers in the "prescriptive" category. In one paper, he argued that a "balanced" marketing information system with the features shown in figure 9-1 is desirable (Montgomery, 1970). A balanced system would not overemphasize data generation, storage, and retrieval, with the attendant risk of overloading managers with data. Effective and efficient utilization of data would be a priority.

A follow-up paper explored some of the issues in implementing such a system. It also endorsed a "decision calculus" approach to building information or decision-support systems, defined as a "model-based set of procedures for processing judgments and data to assist a manager in his decision making" (Montgomery, 1973, p. 18). Positive results with using decision-calculus systems like "DETAILER" (for sales management), "BRANDAID" (for marketing mix planning), and "SPRINTER" (for new product introductions) are reported in this paper and in a third paper (Montgomery and Weinberg, 1974).

More "descriptive" research on utilization has been carried out in several projects. For example, in the early 1970s James Taylor of the University of Michigan conducted in-depth interviews with personnel from five major companies to determine how widely nonmetric multidimensional scaling and other perceptual mapping techniques were used. The companies were all rather sophisticated enterprises (e.g., DuPont, Procter and Gamble), that liked to experiment with new methods, and so it was difficult to generalize from their experiences. Nevertheless, Taylor found the following quote from Robert Lavidge of the research firm of Lavidge and Steiner to provide a good summary of what he discovered:

> Our experience with mapping indicates that it does not bring light to an otherwise dark situation. Rather, it brings additional illumination to situations where there already was some light. Consequently, we have not experienced major surprises from the mapping results. We have found mapping a very helpful research tool that managers and researchers should make use of. (Lavidge as quoted in Taylor, 1971, p. 37)

In a much broader look at utilization of sophisticated marketing research techniques—done for the Commission on the Effectiveness of Research and Development for Marketing Management (co-sponsored by the American Marketing Association and MSI)—John Myers (Berkeley), William Massy (Stanford), and Stephen A. Greyser (Harvard) reported the following results from a survey on utilization of thirteen techniques done with 1,271 members of the American Marketing Association:

> Overall, market segmentation, time-series analysis, and focus groups seem to be most widely used. In contrast, the level of usage of more complex techniques such as cluster analysis, conjoint analysis,

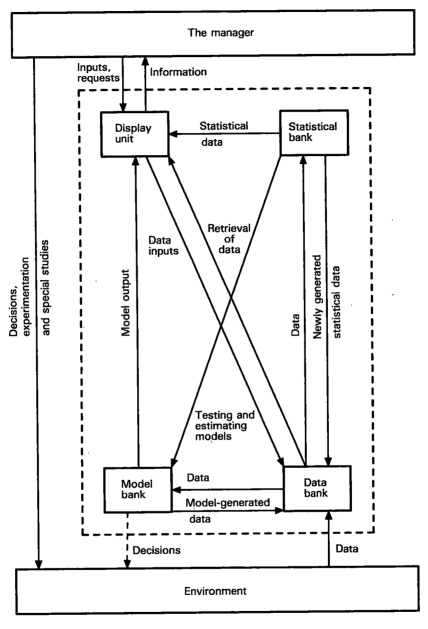

Source: Reprinted with permission from David B. Montgomery, "Developing a Balanced Marketing Information System," Report No. 70–111, Marketing Science Institute, Cambridge, Massachusetts, p. 3.

Figure 9–1. Decision-Information System Structure

multidimensional scaling, Bayesian analysis, and factor analysis is very low (Myers, Massy, and Greyser, 1980, p. 215).

The Commission also looked at utilization of other "products" (e.g., theories, empirical results) of the knowledge development system in marketing and came away, in total, with a reasonably pessimistic view about utilization. Their conclusion, which has already been reported and critiqued in chapter 2 of this volume, is repeated here:

> The major and disturbing finding from these [Commmision] efforts is the discrepancy between the amount of new knowledge developed and available, and the amount being applied in day-to-day marketing management operations. A significant amount of marketing research effort, new-knowledge development, model building, and theorizing has had relatively little impact on improving marketing management practice (Myers, Massy, and Greyser, 1980, pp. 279–280).

Of course, this author is addressing many of the same issues the Commission addressed, but has come to somewhat different conclusions (see chapter 11 for a summary.).

An MSI-supported project that reached a more positive conclusion about the use of marketing research—at least for the type of research done by commercial suppliers—was completed by Gerald Zaltman of the University of Pittsburgh and his doctoral student Rohit Deshpande (now at Dartmouth). This project was an outgrowth of a long-standing interest of Zaltman's in the diffusion of new ideas and innovations. His work on diffusion had drawn the attention of someone who recommended him as a consultant to the National Institute of Mental Health. The Institute was looking for help in organizing a research program on improving the use of new ideas and information by government officials and private-sector managers. Zaltman began working with the Institute and eventually received a major grant to explore knowledge use issues more extensively. He feels that winning this grant caused him to focus his energies more precisely on this topic. But he also claims:

> It's a topic that I saw as being relevant to a lot of different settings. That rather intrigued me because I could pursue it in different contexts. I find that kind of fun. It also represented a convergence for me of a lot of other interests—both diffusion interests and marketing interests, since the issue of using anything, whether information or a physical manifestation of information, is in many ways a marketing problem.

Zaltman further states that "the MSI funding made a very big difference in enabling us to pursue interests with respect to marketing management." Deshpande expands on this thought by recollecting:

The MSI support had a very significant impact for two major reasons. One was that the funding indicated that there were other people interested in what we were doing, and this was a strong encourager. The second reason was that it enabled us to do things that we would not have been able to do. It widened the scope of our study. We could go to a wider sample of firms across the nation with a mail survey.

Zaltman and Deshpande (1980) obtained responses from eighty-six marketing managers from large consumer-oriented companies and ninety market researchers from commercial research firms. The respondents' answers dealt with their perceptions about what factors influence use of research results. Besides finding overall high usage of marketing research results, the authors determined the following:

- The managers indicated that the most important variables explaining low research use were: (1) having a high degree of formalization and centralization in the organization and (2) having an exploratory purpose for the research.
- The managers revealed these variables as explaining high research use: (1) quality of the report content, (2) interaction between researchers and managers, and (3) political acceptability of the results.
- The researchers thought research use was enhanced by interaction, political acceptability, exploratory research purpose, and quality of report content and form.

Among their final conclusions, Zaltman and Deshpande warned that:

> Researchers who favor a more exploratory style of research should be especially sensitive to managers' tendencies to want confirmatory research containing little surprise. Special efforts will be necessary to widen "comfort zones" among managers if the results of the exploratory research are to be accepted. (Zaltman and Deshpande, 1980, p. 45)

Another MSI study that obtained data from both marketing managers and marketing researchers—although in this case both groups came from large corporations—was completed by David Luck and James Krum of the University of Delaware. They interviewed seventy-three persons from ten large companies while exploring the conditions that facilitate or impede the effective use of marketing research. They concluded that research tended to be used more effectively if it was designed to help strategic rather than tactical thinking. They also concluded that delivery of marketing research services was uneven, that planning for research was often unsystematic, and that funds for research in the studied firms were inadequate (Luck and Krum, 1981).

MSI Research on Methods and Models: Impact and Utilization

The work MSI has supported on research methodology and model building has had considerable impact in both the academic and practitioner worlds. Several of the techniques first introduced through these research projects have become extremely popular with academic and commercial researchers.

Impact in the Academic World

Most of the research discussed in this chapter seemed to spark academics to do follow-up or similar research. But the work by Green, Rao, and their colleagues on nonmetric multidimensional scaling probably sparked more academic activity than any of the other projects. Among other things, it laid the groundwork for research on conjoint measurement and market structure analysis (see chapter 3). As Rao states:

> I believe that it has had a great impact. It has given a way of looking at consumer's perceptions of themselves and products in a descriptive and sometimes normative way. Practitioners and academics alike have integrated these ideas into their normal day-to-day work. Multidimensional scaling brought consumer behavior from a qualitative to a more quantitative approach.

Numerous journal articles—several of which appeared in the *Journal of Marketing Research* and the *Journal of Marketing*—and at least two books came out of this activity. Moreover, this body of work has been cited and reprinted extensively. In fact, in a study done by Robinson and Adler (1979), Green was found to be the most-cited author in the marketing discipline—with a high proportion of those citations coming from his MSI-supported work.

Montgomery's work on model building has left nearly as impressive a legacy. Articles that came out of MSI-supported projects have appeared in the *Journal of Marketing Research* (five times), *Management Science* (twice), the *Journal of Marketing*, the *Journal of Advertising Research*, the *Journal of Finance*, and several other publications. He feels these articles have been reprinted and cited very frequently.

Although it came from a much smaller stream of research, Clarke's paper on cumulative advertising effects—which was also published in the *Journal of Marketing Research*—probably had as much impact on marketing academics as any individual paper written by Green or Montgomery. Besides winning the William F. O'Dell award for the best article in the *Journal of Marketing Research*, his paper, according to Clarke, stimulated "thirty or forty papers based on it or discussing it in one way or another."

Other publications have also come out of the work discussed in this chapter:

- Wiseman and McDonald had articles based on their response rate research published in the *Journal of Marketing Research, Journal of Data Collection, Survey Methodology,* and several conference proceedings. This work also has been summarized in several marketing research texts.
- Zaltman and Deshpande had articles based on their knowledge use research published in the *Journal of Marketing Research* (twice), the *Journal of Marketing, Knowledge* (twice), and several conference proceedings. This work has been cited frequently in other disciplines, and occasionally in marketing.

The interviews with the editors only provided comments on the work of Green and his colleagues. Two labeled this work a "significant contribution" without any prompting and, after prompting, five labeled it as a "major contribution" and four labeled it as "steady progress."

Impact in the Practitioner World

Researcher Interviews. All of the interviewed researchers feel that their MSI-supported work has been extensively used by practitioners. Some highlights of their comments follow:

- Green and Rao offer an impressive list of companies using multidimensional scaling techniques (with and without their consulting assitance). These companies range from major consumer products firms, to pharmaceutical companies, to an auto company and an office equipment supplier. Rao claims that these techniques are "like a drug that was patented in the beginning and then became generic."
- Wiseman feels his work with McDonald had an impact through helping the Council of American Survey Research Organizations formulate uniform definitions.
- Montgomery knows the pharmaceutical company that supplied him with data used his work extensively. He has also seen many other applications, particularly as spin-offs of the more than 120 executive programs he has conducted in the last fifteen years.

- Clarke has done many seminars for major corporations on measuring advertising effects. He has also provided consulting services in this area to a few of these companies.
- Zaltman and Deshpande report that several major consumer products companies have had them present special seminars on their work. A few of these companies have apparently adopted many of their ideas about improving the marketing intelligence function.

Practitioner Interviews. The interviews with the practitioners revealed very little recall of the work covered in this chapter, even when the respondents were prompted to comment on MSI work in "model building and quantitative areas." This prompt tended to stimulate comments about the sales promotion research discussed in chapter 8. The failure to cite the work covered in this chapter should not be surprising, since much of it was conducted before most of the interviewees had become involved with MSI.

About the only specific comment on something from this chapter was provided by Paul Fruitt (Gillette), who praised Darral Clarke's work on measuring advertising effectiveness. At the same time, Robert Bergen (formerly with the Royal Bank of Canada) expressed frustration with the marketing field's inability to provide more guidance on how to measure the effectiveness of advertising.

10

Marketing and Public Policy: Broadening the Perspectives of Economists and Lawyers

The activities of government regulators and policy makers have been of considerable interest to marketing scholars for many decades. A steady stream of writing has appeared in which anti trust, consumer protection, and other policies have been described, interpreted, analyzed, and critiqued. Until the early 1970s, the bulk of this writing did not draw on empirical research. Most of the work contained either descriptions of policies, analyses of legal precedents and developments (e.g., court decisions, enforcement actions), or discussions of relevant economic theories. Books and articles by Grether (1966), Howard (1964), and Stern and Grabner (1970) were among the most significant contributions of this type.

The 1970s brought a major increase in both the quantity of writing on public policy issues and the amount of that writing that was based on empirical research. An activist Federal Trade Commission, a powerful consumer movement, and other political developments all created interesting research opportunities, and numerous authors began examining topics such as measuring the effects of corrective advertising, assessing the effects of advertising on children, and providing more usable comparative product information to consumers. Having rapidly discovered the relevance to public policy of empirical research traditions in several other disciplines, they drew heavily on the theories and methods of fields like industrial organization economics, human information processing, child development, and evaluation research.

Some of the responsibility for this increase in public policy research can be attributed to the FTC itself. The agency started a program of bringing in "visiting" marketing professors to assist its staff economists and lawyers in understanding marketing and marketing research methods. Professors like William Wilkie, David Gardner, H. Keith Hunt, Harold Kassarjian, and others spent periods of time at the FTC and then went off and urged the rest of the academic marketing community to pursue research that could have relevance to FTC decision-making (see, for example, the MSI paper by Wilkie and Gardner, 1974). The FTC also became involved with funding several research projects and in conducting hearings and conferences that included many marketing academics.

Research by marketing academics on public policy issues has diminished during the 1980s. The deregulation emphasis of the Reagan Administration has dampened the activism of agencies like the FTC. Controversial actions or proposed actions—such as the proposal to eliminate all television advertising to children that the FTC staff issued in the mid-70s—have all but disappeared. Thus, research formulated specifically to address public policy questions does not appear to be needed or wanted as much as it once was. Nevertheless, researchers are still pursuing more basic research in areas such as consumer socialization and consumer information processing. In the process, they have made discoveries that have public policy implications.

MSI Public Policy Research: Origins and Evolution

MSI has supported research on public policy questions throughout its history. As the consumer movement and the FTC increased their activism at the beginning of the 1970s, MSI supported research to help its member companies and others interpret what was happening and how they might respond. MSI also got heavily involved with empirical research on controversial issues such as the impact of television advertising on children and the improvement of information disclosures to consumers. The major questions that have been addressed in MSI-supported research are summarized in table 10-1.

As the table shows, the MSI work has basically sought (1) to provide input to the formulation of more effective public policies and (2) to suggest ideas to help businesses respond most effectively to public policy developments. Under the first heading, MSI has supported considerable amounts of work on the effects of advertising to children and on consumer information processing. Both of these areas have been reviewed in chapter 6. In addition, MSI has devoted much support to research designed to interpret and test thinking from the field of industrial organization economics. This subfield of economics is concerned with the relationships among the structure, conduct, and performance of markets. A major issue in this subfield has been how advertising affects competition and prices in certain markets, and MSI has devoted particular attention to this issue. Finally, MSI has supported research to develop methods for evaluating consumer protection laws and has funded several studies which evaluated specific laws.

Table 10–1
Questions About Public Policy Addressed by MSI Researchers

Description	Explanation	Prediction	Control
1. Who are the dissatisfied and activist consumers?	1. How does television advertising affect children? (See chapter 6)	1. What new laws and regulations are likely to emerge?	1. How can more effective *public policy* toward marketing be formulated?
	2. How are industry structure, conduct, and performance related?	2. What will happen to consumerism?	2. How should information be presented to consumers in labels, advertising, and elsewhere to facilitate usage? (See chapter 6)
	3. What are the social and economic effects of advertising?		3. How can companies respond most effectively to public policy developments?
	4. What has been the impact of various laws and regulations?		

To help businesses respond more effectively to public policy developments, MSI has supported research seeking to describe the characteristics of dissatisfied and activist consumers. The topic of how to measure consumer satisfaction/dissatisfaction has also received support. Moreover, several projects have been funded which seek to predict where consumerism and public policy will head in future years. Lastly, a major MSI project investigated how businesses and governments might work together, rather than as adversaries, in formulating policies.

Structure, Conduct, and Performance

The field of industrial organization economics has had considerable influence over antitrust and consumer protection policy in the United States. Industrial organization economists have occupied prominent positions within the FTC and the Antitrust Division of the Department of Justice, and their thinking has led to many controversial initiatives (e.g., the antitrust cases against IBM and the cereal industry, both of which were eventually dropped). These economists have studied issues such as whether structural features such as having few sellers, extreme product differentiation, or high barriers to entry tend to lead to less competition and higher prices. They have also examined a myriad of other issues, including evaluating the role that advertising plays in competition and in determining consumer welfare.

When Robert Buzzell took over as Executive Director of MSI in the late 1960s, he recognized the influence of industrial organization over public policy. He steered MSI toward several projects designed to interpret this discipline for marketing academics and practitioners. For example, MSI and the U.S. Department of Agriculture supported work by Louis W. Stern (1970) which basically summarized the major concepts and research findings from industrial organization up to that point. Stern— who later served as MSI's Executive Director—reviewed definitions of market structure and market performance, discussed the strengths and weaknesses of these definitions, evaluated the theories that proposed a linkage between elements of market structure and market performance, and briefly reviewed empirical tests that had been conducted of those theories. Stern (1970) concluded:

> The notion that market structure, often defined in terms of seller concentration, barriers to entry, and product differentiation, influences various aspects of performance is not a recent concept. However, despite the obvious expectation that this influence would be susceptible to empirical verification, past efforts have been frequently inconclusive, conflicting, or extremely tenuous. (pp. 52–53)

Market performance was seen by Stern (1970) as a multi-dimensional concept reflecting the degree to which the firms in an industry achieve allocative efficiency (i.e., reasonable industry profits), technical efficiency (i.e., reasonable industry production costs), low selling costs, product performance, technological progress, and equitable income distribution.

A more extensive examination of the same body of literature was conducted by Duke University economist John Vernon, who spent the 1969–70 year as a visiting professor at MSI. Vernon (1972) wrote a textbook-like volume for MSI which defined certain industrial organization concepts more completely and reviewed more of the empirical research in the field. Like Stern, he also failed to detect much evidence in support of a link between market structure and market performance. He stressed: "The overwhelming conclusion would appear to be that solid, factual support for public policy in this area does not exist." (Vernon, 1972, p. 117) He based this conclusion on weaknesses he perceived in both the statistical models that had been employed in this research (i.e., mostly cross-sectional, single-equation regression studies) and in the data that were analyzed (i.e., mostly government census data).

Vernon (1970), while affiliated with MSI, also conducted an empirical study of his own which examined the relationship of structure, conduct, and performance in a single industry, pharmaceuticals. By looking at relationships in eighteen different "therapeutic classes" of drugs, he hoped to be able to obtain a clearer picture of the relationships among concentration, promotion spending, market share, and other variables than was obtainable by looking across a group of less homogeneous markets. His results led him to the following primary conclusions:

> There is no evidence that high promotion leads to high concentration within therapeutic markets . . . higher promotion/sales ratios are likely to be found in therapeutic markets with higher market share instability, lower brand loyalty, and (more active competition). (Vernon, 1970, p. 21–22)

This study was the first of a long line of MSI-supported work that found little support for the often-heard argument that advertising and promotion are harmful to competition. The following section reviews the highlights of this research.

The Effects of Advertising on Competition

Many industrial organization economists have argued that advertising can inhibit competition by helping firms establish entry barriers, accumulate market power, and avoid pressures to keep prices low. They have argued that advertising hurts the welfare of consumers in these ways and that public policy should seek to rectify the situation. This argument fell on many sympathetic ears during the early 1970s, and it served as a basis for the ill-fated FTC antitrust case against the major manufacturers of ready-to-eat breakfast cereals. Research supported by MSI did not tend to support this argument—neither did research on this issue conducted under other auspices—and today the prevailing view among industrial organization economists and policy makers is much less anti-advertising.

Robert Buzzell himself was active in writing about this issue. For instance, a paper he wrote in 1971—which was based on testimony he delivered to the FTC—stressed that advertising should not be picked on as being anti-competitive, especially since it only serves as one element of the marketing mix of most products (Buzzell, 1971). Buzzell and Professor Stephen A. Greyser, his Harvard colleague and successor as Executive Director of MSI, also supervised a study prepared for the FTC hearings titled *Appraising the Economic and Social Effects of Advertising* (Pearce, Cunningham, and Miller, 1971). Buzzell later urged two of his Harvard doctoral students, first Paul Farris and later Mark Albion, to become involved with investigating this and related issues. They produced a large volume of work, both with Buzzell and by themselves. Professor Greyser also had much to do with encouraging Farris and Albion, both in his role as MSI Executive Director and as a Harvard colleague.

Farris was a research assistant at MSI for several years while pursuing his doctorate. It was natural for him to become involved with research with Buzzell, who eventually became his dissertation chairman. The notion of looking at advertising expenditures and their impact interested him for several reasons, including the fact that he had worked as 'a product manager and was experienced in making advertising budgeting decisions. At first, he and Buzzell collaborated on several projects that looked at marketing costs in a variety of industries (Buzzell and Farris, 1976a, 1976b, 1976c). They were interested in describing exactly how much was being spent on advertising and promotion and in determining what variables seemed to explain variations in those expenditures across industries (Farris, 1977). From there, Farris made what he views as a logical progression to studying the relationship between advertising and profitability, using the PIMS data base (Farris and Buzzell, 1976; Farris and Reibstein, 1978), to studying advertising's impact on consumer prices and welfare (Farris and Albion, 1979; Albion and Farris, 1979, 1982). Farris describes his research program in this way: "I tried to approach the field from an avenue that allowed me to capitalize on some of my accumulated intellectual capital."

Farris credits his closeness to MSI with helping to encourage and facilitate this research activity. A similar, but stronger acknowledgement is offered by Mark Albion, who began working with Farris after Farris had received his doctorate and become a faculty member at Harvard. Albion reports that he first became interested in studying the economic effects of advertising when Buzzell approached him with an opportunity to earn money with MSI on a summer research project (with Farris) that amounted to an update of the Pearce, Cunningham, and Miller (1971) report. Albion saw it as a way of making some money while doing research that would help him prepare for his doctoral orals. After delving into the subject, Albion found it to be inherently interesting, and this, combined with enjoying the collaboration with Farris and the support and facilities of MSI, led him to make a strong commitment to doing research in the area. Albion also credits MSI trustee Paul Fruitt (Gillette) as someone who had a major influence on the direction of his research activity.

The first publications from Farris and Albion's collaboration were essentially literature reviews of previous research on the effects of advertising on competition. They identified two prevailing schools of thought in the literature—the "advertising equals market power" and the "advertising equals information" schools—and summarized and critiqued the theoretical and empirical research that could help evaluate these points of view. The arguments of both schools, as interpreted by Farris and Albion (1979, p. 7), are presented in table 10-2. Both schools were seen as having limited empirical support, leading Albion and Farris to conclude that:

> . . . little conclusive evidence exists on any of the varied economic effects of advertising. Some relationships have been identified on a case-by-case basis for particular sets of data, but no general model has been able to explain the range- of these effects. Advertising is but one of the interdependent communications devices used by diverse managements, in a variety of strategic corporate environments, to influence, in some manner, the purchasing behavior of consumers with different preferences and processes of obtaining information. Advertising's behavioral and economic implications for the consumer, brand, firm, industry, and economy as a whole have remained an enigma to social scientists. (Albion and Farris, 1979, p. 168)

With respect to advertising's specific effects on consumer prices, Albion and Farris concluded:

> We strongly believe that advertised products charge higher prices, on average, than comparable unadvertised products. However, we also believe retailers earn lower profit margins on advertised brands than on unadvertised brands. Further, advertising seems to contribute to the viability of self-service retail outlets. *Because of these nonprice effects,* we do not know whether advertising contributes to higher average prices paid by consumers for products; the stage of the product life cycle and the distribution network employed seem critical. Yet, even if advertising does raise average prices, the value of advertising in reducing consumer search costs and building markets must be weighed against the higher prices to measure the true *social* cost and benefits. (Albion and Farris, 1979, pp. 172–173)

In later empirical research using a data base obtained from a major supermarket chain and additional funding from the Association of National Advertisers, Albion and Farris (1982) found support for the contention that manufacturers' advertising has the "hidden" effect (Albion, 1983) of lowering retailer margins, suggesting that at least advertising stimulates competition among retailers. This positive feature of advertising had been overlooked in most previous research—the exception to this being Robert Steiner's MSI-supported work that discussed how mass advertising had helped stimulate lower prices for consumers in the children's toy and other industries by, in part, assisting the development of much more efficient and competitive large-scale retailers (Steiner, 1974). To quote Albion and Farris again:

Table 10-2
Two Schools of Thought on Advertising's Role in the Economy

Advertising = Market Power		*Advertising = Information*
Advertising affects consumer perferences and tastes, changes product attributes, and differentiates the product from competitive offerings.	*Advertising*	Advertising informs consumers about product attributes and does not change the way they value those attributes.
Consumers become brand loyal and less price sensitive, and perceive fewer substitutes for advertised brands.	*Consumer Buying Behavior*	Consumers become more price sensitive and buy best "value." Only the relationship between price and quality affects elasticity for a given product.
Potential entrants must overcome established brand loyalty and spend relatively more on advertising.	*Barriers to Entry*	Advertising makes entry possible for new brands because it can communicate product attributes to consumers.
Firms are insulated from market competition and potential rivals; concentration increases, leaving firms with more discretionary power.	*Industry Structure and Market Power*	Consumers can compare competitive offerings easily and competitive rivalry is increased. Efficient firms remain, and as the inefficient leave, new entrants appear; the effect on concentration is ambiguous.
Firms can charge higher prices and are not as likely to compete on quality or price dimensions. Innovation may be reduced.	*Market Conduct*	More informed consumers put pressure on firms to lower prices and improve quality. Innovation is facilitated via new entrants.
High prices and excessive profits accrue to advertisers and give them even more incentive to advertise their products. Output is restricted compared to conditions of perfect competition.	*Market Performance*	Industry prices are decreased. The effect on profits due to increased competition and increased efficiency is ambiguous.

Source: Reprinted with permission from Paul W. Farris and Mark S. Albion, "An Investigation into the Impact of Advertising on the Price of Consumer Products," Report No. 79–109, Marketing Science Institute, Cambridge, Massachusetts, p. 7.

. . . by increasing competition among retailers and by easing their selling task, manufacturer advertising of consumer goods may stimulate the development of more efficient retail operations and contribute to the productivity of our distribution systems. . . . both manufacturer and retail gross margins need to be considered in advertising policymaking, for it is the total profit margin of these two business entities combined that is the relevant criterion of consumer welfare. Too many past policies have seriously overestimated the impact of advertising on the total gross profit margin and the absolute retail price level of a market by neglecting the effect of manufacturer advertising on retail pricing behavior. (Albion and Farris, 1982, pp. 12–13)

Evaluating Public Policy Initiatives

MSI has been involved with several research efforts in which the impact of specific laws and regulations has been evaluated. For example, Wilkie looked at the corrective advertising remedy and other forms of consumer information disclosures in a series of projects that were reviewed in chapter 6. In addition, an evaluation of the repeal of the fair trade law in Rhode Island was conducted by Hourihan and Markham (1974). This study found repeal to have important benefits for consumers—benefits which were apparently recognized by national policy makers, who in the late 1970s repealed fair trade in all states. Perhaps the most ambitious MSI evaluation project was conducted by Louis W. Stern and his colleagues at Northwestern University during the mid-1970s. Stern et al (1977) examined the Fair Credit Reporting Act as a way of demonstrating a rigorous methodology for evaluating public policy actions.

Stern originally became interested in this project as a result of some hard self-reflection about his own career and developments within society and the marketing discipline. As he states:

> I really did sit down and contemplate my navel. I really did say, "What do I want to do in the next step of my career?" I felt that I could help society by doing this kind of research. I had gotten to a particular stage in my career where I wasn't so much trying to manage my publication stream as trying to make a general contribution to society. I know that this sounds terribly highfalutin, but it was the motivating force behind taking on this project. I said to myself, "There are just thousands upon thousands of pieces of legislation year after year dealing with marketing in one form or another. Wouldn't it be great if we could develop a multidisciplinary methodology to evaluate these laws?"

One of Stern's Northwestern students at the time, Lynn Phillips, was instrumental in encouraging pursuit of the project. Phillips had just completed a course with social psychologist Donald Campbell on quasi-experimental research designs, and he was very enthused about applying what he had learned to the study of the impact of consumer protection laws. In fact, he wrote a research proposal in a doctoral seminar that had a major influence on the eventual project. Stern and Phillips also enlisted the collaboration of Professors Brian Sternthal (marketing), Robert Dewar (organizational behavior), and Allan Drebin (accounting).

Early in the project, the researchers recognized that large amounts of funding would be necessary to conduct a comprehensive evaluation of the typical consumer protection law. Thus, they limited the funding they were seeking from MSI to what would allow them to complete a pilot study. They hoped to take the methods and instruments developed in the pilot study to the National Science Foundation or other large agency and obtain funding for an extensive project. Although they never received substantial funding from NSF or anyone else, Stern has great praise for how people from MSI and its member companies treated them during their execution of the project and their quest for greater funding. He states:

> The whole process that we went through and our failure is a story for an Uncle Remus tale. But MSI's willingness to fund us without enormous red tape—going basically on faith after we'd written the proposal—gave us a great shot in the arm or push off. And the supportiveness of Alden Clayton, Steve Greyser, and the MSI trustees gave us more motivation. Alden even accompanied us on several trips to Washington to seek funding.

The project produced two MSI working papers. The first was a literature review by Phillips (1978) that evaluated previous evaluations of consumer protection laws. Phillips identified threats to the internal validity of many of the previous studies that made it hard to isolate the true effects of a law. He provided a comprehensive examination of a variety of evaluation research designs, pointing out their strengths and weaknesses (see chapter 9 also). The second paper by Stern et al. (1977) describes the evaluation methodology developed in the pilot study. This methodology was appropriate for doing *retrospective* evaluations, where ample data about prelaw and postlaw situations cannot be analyzed and where it is too late to set up some type of controlled experiment or quasi-experiment to detect a law's effects. The proposed methodology consisted of four parts:

1. *analysis of the legislative and litigative history*—to understand a law's objectives, potential effects, judicial interpretations, and so forth;
2. *analysis of consumer response*—to see if consumers utilized and benefitted from the law in the intended manner;
3. *analysis of organizational response*—to determine the level of compliance of affected organizations; and
4. *analysis of costs*—to calculate the costs of compliance and enforcement of the law.

Demonstrations of how each of these analyses could be performed with the Fair Credit Reporting Act were offered. As part of this effort, survey instruments were developed for obtaining information from consumers and organizations. No definitive conclusions were reached about the Fair Credit Reporting Act, since extensive surveys were needed before any judgments about the law's effects could be made.

One other evaluation project was funded by MSI during the mid-1970s. This study by Alan Andreasen and his Illinois doctoral student, Gregory Upah, looked at the effects of the FTC's Creditors' Remedies Rule. Andreasen's involvement in this project was an outgrowth of a long-standing commitment to studying the problems of disadvantaged consumers. He had been a faculty member during the late 1960s at a campus that had experienced considerable student unrest, and he had become interested at that time in doing research that might contribute toward making the university "more relevant to the broader society."

The FTC had proposed a Trade Regulation Rule designed to protect disadvantaged consumers from entering into credit arrangements where they could be charged unreasonable late fees, have threats communicated to their employers, have their wages assigned, or have other confusing, degrading, or unfair actions taken against them. Andreasen and Upah (1978) reviewed the history of this rule and the content of several studies that had been completed for the FTC while developing the rule. They did not reach any firm conclusions about the impact of the rule, since it was not yet being enforced. But they had several strong statements to make about how the rule was developed. They saw a need to be much more attentive to the feelings and comments of the disadvantaged *themselves*, rather than looking primarily toward so-called "experts" about the problems of the disadvantaged. Therefore, they recommended that more systematic research be conducted on the decision-making processes, problems, and satisfaction levels of the disadvantaged.

Consumer Satisfaction and Dissatisfaction

MSI was involved with several projects during the 1970s which sought to understand (1) the characteristics of dissatisfied consumers and (2) how consumer dissatisfaction could be measured. One project in this area was an outgrowth of more basic research conducted at Purdue University on the use of attitude and activity (i.e., life style) measures for understanding consumer behavior. Hustad and Pessemier (1971, 1972), along with several other Purdue faculty and doctoral students, were interested in using multivariate statistical techniques for developing improved ways of segmenting and describing markets. In one of their studies, they accumulated a very large data base that contained several measures of people's attitudes toward business, marketing, and a variety of political issues. Hustad saw a chance to use the data in a new way. As he describes it: "We were not being visionary, but opportunistic." He saw a fit between their data and the "issues of the times," and he decided to see what the data would reveal about the characteristics of anti-business and activist consumers. Financial support and encouragement from MSI also played a significant role in motivating them to use the data in this way.

The major conclusion, stated in their paper titled "Will the Real Consumer-Activist Please Stand Up?" was:

> The principal findings of this analysis offer little comfort to the business community. Anti-business consumers cannot be written off as a dissident element among life's losers. They are more accurately described as an activist, avant-garde segment of society, with both the motivation and the capacity to institute change—largely through correcting what they view as the defects in current institutions and practices. The size of the anti-business cluster (18 percent of the sample population) clearly demonstrates that attitudes unfriendly to business have achieved wide acceptance among the educated/activist element of society. (Hustad and Pessemier, 1972, pp. 34–35)

Findings like those in the Hustad and Pessemier (1972) study contributed to having academics, practitioners, and public policy makers recognize the importance of being able to accurately monitor the extent and nature of consumer discontent. H. Keith Hunt was someone who saw the need for better techniques to monitor consumer feelings, especially after he completed a year as a visiting professor at the FTC and witnessed numerous situations where people had difficulty defining and assessing consumer satisfaction and dissatisfaction. He decided to approach MSI about funding a workshop on consumer satisfaction, found a warm reception, and then worked through MSI to apply to the National Science Foundation for substantial funding. Hunt credits MSI with being extremely supportive in his efforts to obtain NSF money. He states: "I wrote a proposal that was very much with Steve Greyser and Alden Clayton's blessings and help along the way—they sure did a lot of hand holding." The NSF funding was eventually secured, and in April 1976 a workshop titled "Conceptualization and Measurement of Consumer Satisfaction/Dissatisfaction" was held in Chicago.

The workshop covered much ground and served to highlight several issues that have continued to concern researchers in this area (Hunt, 1977). The difficulty of defining satisfaction and dissatisfaction was a prominent topic, as was the need for widely accepted techniques for measuring these concepts. Other topics included the social and personal factors that affect satisfaction, the base of comparison used by consumers in making satisfaction judgments (i.e., norms or expectations), and the implications of research in this area for public policy.

Consumerism and Consumer Affairs

MSI has funded a great deal of work that has sought to describe, interpret, and predict the activities of the consumer movement. Moreover, the manner in which business firms can organize consumer affairs functions to help them respond most effectively to consumerism has received considerable attention from MSI. Professor Stephen A. Greyser of Harvard—a former Executive Director of MSI—has been the focal point of this research activity. Greyser first became interested in the consumer movement prior to his relationship with MSI. He and his senior colleague at Harvard, Raymond Bauer, had collaborated on several studies in the 1960s that alerted him to a number of external forces that were impinging on marketing. In work that they did on the opinions of Americans toward advertising (Bauer and Greyser, 1968) and in exploring the poor state of relations between business leaders and public policy makers, which they characterized as "The Dialogue That Never Happens" (Bauer and Greyser, 1969), Greyser was persuaded that it was "clear that consumerism was going to have a major set of impacts."

Once he became Executive Director of MSI, Greyser launched three streams of research that touched on consumerism. Much of the work was done in collaboration with doctoral students at Harvard, but others were also involved. First, he conducted a series of attitude surveys to learn more about both the public's and the business community's feelings about consumerism (Greyser and Diamond, 1974; Greyser, 1977; Greyser, Bloom, and Diamond, 1982). Through these studies, evidence was accumulated about the fairly widespread support consumerism received during the 1970s. In addition, support for consumerism from the business community—where it apparently began to be seen as more of an opportunity than a threat—was also detected. Second, Greyser encouraged and participated in research on how businesses were responding to consumerism, particularly in terms of how they were mounting consumer affairs functions to handle consumer complaints, promote consumer education, and advise management about consumer issues. Several case studies and other pieces were written in this area (Greyser, 1970, 1974). Third, Greyser became involved with trying to forecast what consumerism might do in the future. One of his efforts in this area was in collaboration with this author (Bloom and Greyser, 1981).

The future of consumerism was a subject that had interested me before I became involved with Greyser or MSI. I had been interested in public policy toward marketing for many years and, as a natural outgrowth of that interest, had co-authored an article on the future of consumerism with one of my former professors at Northwestern, Louis W. Stern, in the mid-1970s. In late 1979, I was looking for a place to spend a sabbatical year away from the University of Maryland and inquired about the possibility of becoming a visiting professor at MSI. Alden Clayton and Steve Greyser responded to my inquiry by encouraging me to write a proposal for research I might conduct. They told me that my chances would be better if I proposed a project that fit well with the "research priorities" MSI had published. So I paged through the research priorities booklet, looking for a suitable topic. I discovered that work on consumerism was a priority area. I therefore proposed an update of the work I had done with Stern on the future of consumerism. It was a topic that I had retained much interest in, and I was eager to have the chance to write something that made a better set of predictions, since Stern and I had incorrectly forecast a rather rapid demise of consumerism (Bloom and Stern, 1977).

My proposal was received favorably by MSI, since Steve Greyser suggested that he would like to collaborate with me on the project. Our research proceeded in a number of directions, including a review of a few research studies that had been done on public attitudes toward consumerism. In addition, we conducted several interviews with consumer leaders. Our predictions for the future of consumerism were based on a "life cycle" model (Bloom and Greyser, 1981). We saw consumerism in a mature stage of its life cycle at that time, experiencing considerable fragmentation and heavy competition among the diverse organizations and institutions competing in the consumerism "industry." We predicted that local and grass-roots organizations would compete more effectively in this fragmented market in the future, and that national organizations would diminish in importance. We also predicted that "pocketbook" issues (e.g., getting lower prices) would be more likely to capture the imagination of consumers than issues having to do with consumer representation, consumer information, or regulatory reform.

As a follow-up to the work with Greyser, I organized a conference for MSI and the Center for Business and Public Policy at the University of Maryland, funded by Chesebrough-Pond's, Inc. The conference explored questions about consumerism's future in more depth. My feeling was that forecasting the future of the movement required in-depth information about the strength of individual consumer organizations and the environment in which they functioned, and that bringing together a group of experts on the movement would serve to provide this information. Considerable consensus emerged among the academics, business managers, consumer activists, and government officials who attended the conference, which was held in Maryland in April 1982. The major conclusions reached were:

1. Consumerism still retains and can be expected to maintain a considerable amount of vitality.
2. "Reaganomics" may actually be healthy for consumerism.
3. Consumer organizations of all types will face continual problems with funding.
4. Grass-roots and "participative" consumerism will predominate over "spectator" consumerism.
5. The most hotly debated consumer issues will stem from public concern about:
   a. how far regulatory reform should go.
   b. what should be done about the influence and impact of big businesses and other large institutions.
   c. how to control the various "information priests" in our society who determine the nature and content of consumer information.
   d. what can be done to help less-privileged consumers in this country and in the Third World.
6. New approaches to managing corporate consumer affairs and social responsibility programs will be required to meet tomorrow's challenges. (Bloom, 1982)

Regulatory Reform

The basic process by which public policy is formulated was the focus of research conducted by G. David Hughes. He was interested in discovering whether there are ways to make the process less adversarial and more research-based and rational. Hughes became interested in this topic when he observed all the complaining the business community was doing about the costs and paperwork involved with complying with many of the regulatory initiatives of the 1970s. He had been teaching and writing about antitrust and other public policy issues, and he was eager to show that the thinking of marketing academics and practitioners could help formulate public policy more effectively and efficiently. He saw this as a risky area for a marketing academic to research, since the work needed to be multi-disciplinary and there were limited publication outlets, but he felt that a chaired professor at the University of North Carolina could afford to take some risks.

Support and encouragement from MSI also influenced Hughes. He spent a semester in 1978 as a visiting research professor at MSI and found the interactions with MSI staff and member company personnel very stimulating. He comments: "It took someone courageous, like the people at MSI, to put risk capital into what I was doing. I think MSI frequently fills the niche where something is too applied for the academics and too theoretical for the business world."

Working with MSI, Hughes organized a workshop in which representatives from regulatory agencies, academia, business, corporate law firms, and federal agencies met to explore their differences about regulatory matters. Hughes was encouraged by this experience, which he labeled "The Dialogue That Happened" (Hughes and Williams, 1979), to explore ways to encourage more frequent and productive dialogues. He especially thought that such non-adversarial discussion would help the process of serious regulatory reform that began in the late 1970s. He argued that marketers should take part in this discussion, since marketing thinking could be extremely helpful in guiding the use of incentives, performance standards, voluntary programs, information disclosures, and other approaches that limit the need for centralized and bureaucratic control of business behavior. In concluding a report on his findings, Hughes claimed:

> [Marketers'] knowledge of communication theory and consumer behavior could be appropriately applied to the areas of information disclosure and the communication and diffusion of regulatory innovation. The marketing of rights that derive from performance standards would draw on a wide range of marketers' talents, including their knowledge of marketing institutions, communications, price and negotiation strategies, and the general economics of exchange. The development of alternative dispute resolution systems requires a knowledge of the conflict management literature, legal procedures, and methods for value clarification. Marketers may contribute to value clarification through their knowledge of the measurement of beliefs, values, and attitudes. Marketers with a knowledge of information systems, regulations, and strategic planning could participate nicely in the development of corporate regulatory strategies. (Hughes, 1980, p. 19)

MSI Public Policy Research: Impact and Utilization

Many of the researchers who were interviewed had begun their investigations with hopes of making a contribution to society. However, they found that society's interest in what they were doing diminished substantially after the deregulation-oriented Reagan Administration came into office, and their initial aspirations for the impact of their research may not have been achieved. Nevertheless, this work seemed to have a noticeable impact on both academics and practitioners.

Impact in the Academic World

The public policy research programs MSI has supported have produced numerous journal articles and books and, in a few cases, large amounts of additional academic research. Publications that have emerged from these programs include:

1. Stern and Grabner's 1970 book, *Competition in the Marketplace* (published by Scott, Foresman and Co.), which was a seminal piece for introducing thinking from industrial organization economics and antitrust law to the marketing profession;
2. articles by Farris and Albion in the *Journal of Marketing* and *Harvard Business Review*; and two books published by Auburn House, *The Advertising Controversy* (by Albion and Farris) and *Advertising's Hidden Effects* (by Albion);
3. a pair of articles by Phillips and Calder in the *Journal of Consumer Affairs*;
4. an article by Andreasen and Upah in the *Journal of Marketing*;
5. an article by Hustad and Pessemier in the *Journal of Marketing Research*; and
6. several articles by Greyser and others in the *Harvard Business Review*; and a book edited by Bloom and Smith (published by Lexington Books) that contained updated papers from the 1982 conference.

This list does not include the many publications that came out of the previously discussed MSI-sponsored work on children's television advertising and consumer information processing.

The interviews revealed a feeling among most of the authors that their work had been consistently cited by the limited number of others who had done research in similar areas. Stronger responses were provided by Hustad and Hunt, who both felt that their work had helped pave the way for much additional work on consumer satisfaction and dissatisfaction. Hunt points out that nine additional conferences—with proceedings— have been held on "Consumer Satisfaction and Complaining Behavior" and that the topic has "come to have acceptability in the area of consumer research."

It can also be argued that the work on structure, conduct, and performance had a major impact on marketing academics. Thinking from industrial organization economics has not only become influential in work on public policy issues, but also has influenced research and writing on marketing strategy (see chapter 3), advertising, pricing, and distribution. Without the introduction to this field provided by the early MSI work, the diffusion of its ideas may have taken a longer time.

The editors limited their comments on the work covered in this chapter to two unprompted compliments about Albion and Farris' research and some prompted responses about the work of Greyser and his colleagues. The latter work was not rated as highly as some others, with two editors calling it a "minor contribution," five calling it an "initial step," and two calling it "steady progress."

Impact in the Practitioner World

Researcher Interviews. Only a few of the interviewed researchers felt their work had influenced either public policy makers or marketing managers. Farris and Albion report that their research received some coverage in the business press and that they have been asked to give several seminars and speeches on their findings. Most frequently, they have been asked to discuss the implications of their findings in order to help managers set advertising strategies and budgets. However, Albion feels their work may have been influential in the cereal antitrust case.

Greyser and Bloom also feel that their work has influenced practitioners. Their ideas about consumerism and consumer affairs have received ample coverage in the business press, and both have given numerous speeches to audiences of managers, consumer affairs professionals, consumer activists, and policy makers. They believe their work has helped encourage companies to mount more serious consumer affairs programs. Moreover, they feel they hold at least a small responsibility for the shift that some consumer organizations have taken toward emphasizing local and pocketbook issues.

Practitioner Interviews. The research covered in this chapter probably did not have as much influence on marketing managers and public policy makers as the work in chapter 6 on consumer socialization and information processing. Nevertheless, the interviews revealed appreciation for several projects covered in this chapter. In general, the practitioners saw MSI as Kent Mitchel (formerly with General Foods, now MSI's President) describes it—as "an excellent place to deal with public policy issues because it is generally regarded as truly neutral ground." Sam Thurm (retired from the Association of National Advertisers) also feels that MSI can make important contributions to public policy debates, especially because he's "never heard a bad commentary on MSI in terms of integrity, which is excellent and most unusual in the business." But Thurm raises the possibility that this has happened because MSI has failed to be critical enough, and he would like to see more difficult issues (e.g., political advertising or the relationship between advertising and alcohol consumption) addressed in the future.

One specific project that was cited in the interviews was the work of Albion and Farris. Paul Fruitt (Gillette) comments that he "wouldn't say that it has been a specific citation or source of action, but it was a good piece that gets into your frame of reference and way of thinking." Another comment suggesting appreciation, but not direct usage, came from Larry Gibson (retired from General Mills) in talking about the evaluation work of Stern and his colleagues:

> We didn't use it specifically. General Mills is not particularly heavily into retail credit. But the concept that public policy legislation has costs and that one should measure benefits and costs—and that this is possible to do—seemed to us a vitally important principal that needed to be established before the various government agencies.

Other positive comments came from Joseph Plummer (Young and Rubicam), who praised Greyser's stream of consumerism research, and Philip Harding (CBS), who complimented the conference on consumerism organized by this author.

11
Concluding Insights and Assessments

The preceding eight chapters have presented considerable descriptive material on how academic research in marketing has been initiated, pursued, disseminated, and utilized. This chapter contains an attempt to synthesize and interpret this material, going beyond the mere reporting of summary figures that was done in chapter 2. The first part of the chapter covers· what has been learned about the knowledge development process in marketing, while the latter part focuses on assessing MSI's contributions. The chapter closes with a final, personal, subjective statement about MSI's role in knowledge development in marketing.

Insights About Knowledge Development

Seven questions about the knowledge development process in marketing were posed at the beginning of chapter 2. Each question is repeated below, followed by some insights about answering the question that came from the exploratory research that produced this volume.

1. *Where and how do the ideas for research efforts originate?*

The integrated model of the knowledge-creation process presented in chapter 2 (figure 2-3) seems to incorporate most of the factors that sparked the research projects discussed in this book. The ideas for MSI-supported studies often came from:

a. *Previous research experiences*—such as Green's turning to new scaling techniques after being disappointed by his decision theory experiments; or Ray's building on the stream of research he had completed on repetition and involvement.

b. *Previous work or consulting experiences*—such as Curhan's drawing on his earlier employment with a supermarket chain; or Day's building on strategy consulting work with companies like General Electric.

c. *Previous teaching experiences*—such as Quelch's extending the case teaching and writing he had done on trade promotions; or Corey's being stimulated by his assignment to teach a course on purchasing.

d. *Discussions with colleagues*—such as Churchill, Ford, and Walker's agreeing that doing research on sales management would be a way of keeping their collaboration going after Walker's graduation; or Bonoma and Shapiro's recognizing their mutual interest in industrial market segmentation.

e. *Careful observation of societal events*—such as Ward's noticing the broad interest in children's television advertising; or Greyser's recognizing the widespread interest in consumerism.

f. *Careful assessments of an area's research needs*—such as Stern's deciding that new evaluation research methods were needed; or Wiseman's seeing the lack of uniformity in the way survey response rates were reported.

In a large number of cases, a serendipitous event or encounter had something to do with sparking the original ideas. Thus, research programs have gotten started after unexpected encounters during:

a. *Conferences*—such as Lovelock's having his interest in services heightened by meeting Eiglier and Langeard at a European Conference; or Montgomery's learning of the avaliability of valuable data from an executive attending an American Marketing Association conference.

b. *Casual conversations*—such as Buzzell's learning of GE's forerunner to PIMS through a comment by a colleague; or Dickson's learning of valuable Census data on durable goods purchases by chatting with someone sitting next to him at a meeting.

c. *Job interviews*—such as Spekman's meeting Moriarty and discovering a mutual interest in testing hypotheses about industrial buying.

Often projects were sparked by MSI itself, as researchers became interested in topics after reading MSI's research priorities or talking to MSI personnel. MSI seemed to have much to do with the initiation of projects such as Pessemier's new product development work, Shapiro and Moriarty's national account management work, Olson's brain-wave study, Webster's top management study, and Bloom and Greyser's consumerism work.

2. *Why are certain topics and projects pursued?*

The factors that seemed to lead people to make an investment in a particular research idea are also captured in the integrated model in figure 2-3. Intrinsic motivation seemed to have a big influence, since many researchers stated innate curiosity and/or a desire to make a contribution to the literature were strong motivating factors. However, they also recognized that making a contribution, and getting highly regarded pub-   ⌐ lications, could enhance their careers.

Obtaining support from MSI, and sometimes other sources, was a motivating factor for going ahead with several projects. Besides providing a means for paying for necessary research expenses—which certainly made a difference to the completion of research like the service quality studies by Parasuraman, Zeithaml, and Berry or the sales management work by Churchill, Ford, and Walker—the support from MSI frequently facilitated collaboration among researchers. For example, it helped teams of researchers such as Lovelock, Bateson, Eiglier, and Langeard (on services) or Quelch, Henderson, and Neslin (on sales promotion) get together more frequently. To some researchers, such as Ward, Montgomery, and others, MSI represented a supportive atmosphere and facilities, and a nice office with friendly, interesting people and good secretarial support where they enjoyed working. MSI also provided practitioner access and encouragement, such as for the strategy research done by Day, the top management work by Webster, or the clutter research by Ray.

Finally, an important reason why several of the projects moved ahead was that a talented doctoral student was often pressed into service. This use of "extrinsic motivation"—at least early on in some of the projects— seemed to help amplify the studies worked on by Bateson, Albion, Phillips, and Deshpande. Of course, these four "student" researchers became extremely interested in their MSI projects, and they all went on to do other, more intrinsically motivated, work in the same areas.

3. *Who and what influences researchers in their decisions about what topics, theories, and methods to employ in conducting their investigations?*

As mentioned, many researchers were influenced by their academic colleagues during the knowledge creation process, and several others were greatly influenced by MSI and its affiliated marketing practitioners. In the latter category, several of the study designs were shaped to a considerable extent by a dialogue between the researchers and MSI staff and steering group members. For example, this "shaping" occurred with the brain-wave study by Olson, the services quality work by Parasuraman, Zeithaml, and Berry, the promotion work of McAlister, and several other projects.

Depending on the topic, the previous research in marketing may have been of much or little value to the researchers. Many of them claimed to have found more useful material in psychology, organizational behavior, and management science, particularly for the many projects that essentially broke new ground in marketing. Much of the consumer behavior, sales management, and model building research could be described in this way. However, several projects in industrial buying, sales management, and advertising drew heavily from previous marketing research.

4. How do the results of research projects tend to be disseminated?

All of the projects discussed in this volume had working papers issued by MSI, and some of these received rather widespread distribution. Particularly noteworthy was the distribution given Webster's top management paper, Shapiro and Moriarity's national account management papers, and May et al.'s future trends in retailing report.

Most of this work was also presented at MSI-organized conferences—before audiences of (primarily) practitioners—and a high proportion of the work was presented at academic conferences. Additionally, numerous published papers, articles, and books emerged directly or indirectly from this research. Many of the articles were accepted in the most highly regarded journals in the discipline, and several of the articles were even award winners.

5. What research has stimulated further research by other individuals?

Many of the studies reviewed here seemed to serve as stepping stones for major streams of research. Among the projects that stimulated the most follow-up work were the ones by Buzzell and his colleagues on PIMS, Day and Shocker on product-market boundaries, Churchill, Ford, and Walker on sales management, Eiglier et al. on services, Ward and his colleagues on consumer socialization, Wilkie and his colleagues on consumer information processing, Ray and his colleagues on low-involvement response to advertising, and Green and his colleagues on multidimensional scaling.

6. How do practitioners utilize the findings of scholarly research efforts?

The preceding chapters contain numerous quotes from practitioners describing how they have used the findings of specific projects. There are also a large number of comments from researchers about usage of their research. Many of the comments were about usage for making decisions (i.e., instrumental usage). For example, Stephan Haeckel (IBM) and Robert Pratt (Avon) talked about how they have often brought MSI-supported researchers into their companies to consult or speak on specific problems. Some of the projects where this kind of follow-up took place were Day's work in strategic planning, Shapiro and Moriarty's work on national account management, Parasuraman, Zeithaml, and Berry's work on services quality, McAlister's work on sales promotion, and Green's work on multidimensional scaling.

A large number of comments from the practitioners were less specific about how a given project had helped them, but they seemed to suggest that the research had been useful for general enlightenment (i.e., conceptual usage). In fact, several practitioners seemed to feel that general knowledge building is all they could really expect from the kind of research supported by MSI. Paul Fruitt (Gillette) expresses this view when he says:

> I don't think any of the work that gets done by MSI is tailor-made to fit any company-specific problems. That's not the kind of work it is intended to be. It's not a problem-solving exercise. But it does heighten the level of sophistication that some of the marketing people have in thinking about larger problems. How they apply it to their own situations will vary. To the extent that a number of your people have absorbed this sort of thing and agree with it or have thought about it, it makes the communication and decision-making process a little easier because you are operating from a common base of knowledge. It is building up this base of knowledge that is one of the more important contributions you get out of the stream of MSI research.

Several recurrent themes suggested this type of appreciation for the enlightenment provided by MSI-supported research. One theme was that exposure to the research allows, in the words of Philip Levine (formerly with Ogilvy and Mather), "practitioners to step back now and then from the day-to-day projects and think more about the theory of what they are doing." This "breaking away" benefit was seen as helping practitioners develop themselves intellectually and indirectly, benefitting their companies. For instance, Linda Alwitt (Leo Burnett) relates the following experience:

> One of the roles of the advertising steering committee is to review research proposals. Just in the process of reviewing them, you get to think about issues that you might not consider otherwise. I've found that very useful in my day-to-day work because it sparks other ways of thinking that I might not have used. It's an informal and unexpected plus that you get from MSI, but it's extremely useful.

A second recurrent theme was that MSI supports research that a single company could not do on its own. People appreciated the ability to do cross-company research and other broader types of studies which, in the words of Harry Sunenshine (Kentucky Fried Chicken), "are of such general interest and so fundamentally interesting to the whole marketing process that I've found them very useful whether they were directly applicable to my company or not."

A third recurrent theme was that the MSI-supported research is helpful in company training programs. People like Dudley Ruch (retired from Quaker Oats) commented on how the company distributed MSI papers and sent subordinates to MSI mini-conferences and workshops to help people obtain backgrounds in certain areas.

A final recurrent theme was that MSI publications are useful for supporting the speaking and teaching activities of executives. C.J. O'Sullivan (Shell) relates his experiences with this form of usage in the following comment:

> I know that several Shell people are on the faculty of the business colleges around town. I've often gotten materials from MSI for those people. They've used them to give to the students or to incorporate in the curriculum.

7. Who and what influence research utilization by practitioners?

Personal contact with researchers, either through MSI workshops and conferences or through follow-up speaking and consulting assignments, seemed to facilitate usage a great deal. The distribution of working papers also seemed to encourage usage in a few situations.

Almost all of the interviewed practitioners and several of the editors and researchers praised MSI for providing a means by which academics and practitioners can meet with one another and learn about mutual interests and concerns. Gerald Mayfield (formerly with AT&T) sees particular benefits for academics from this when he says:

> I believe that MSI serves a very important role of providing an avenue for people, primarily with academic backgrounds, to be exposed to some very pragmatic business problems and opportunities. Through that interaction, both the business people and the academics have a better understanding of what the opportunities are. I think it is this ability to interact in the forum that MSI provides that's a unique benefit.

Robert McNulty (formerly with AT&T) commented on the rewards practitioners gain from the interaction:

> I think that they've drawn some practical business decision makers to work with some very fine academicians. I think that this role is very

important, particularly in companies that are high tech like IBM and AT&T—the two companies I have worked for—where people really do not believe that there is such a thing as "marketing science." You are dealing with people who have Ph.D.'s or master's degrees in electrical engineering who don't understand the role of a marketing executive. They don't understand the difference between marketing and sales.

Several practitioners also commented on the usable knowledge that can be acquired by interacting on a regular basis with other forward-thinking and influential marketing executives. Kent Mitchel (formerly with General Foods, now MSI's President) expresses this feeling as follows:

MSI has clearly meant a set of contacts with interesting people in different industries with which to rub elbows and keep networking going. It attracts the best people from about forty corporations in the United States—an impressive group of companies and trustees.

Prescriptions for Knowledge Development in Marketing

In summary, the findings of this project seem to suggest several rather obvious, general prescriptions for improving knowledge development in the marketing discipline. These are:

1. Encourage academics to research what they personally find stimulating and interesting, not just what they think they can get published.
2. Encourage academics to interact frequently and in various ways with other academics and practitioners. They should not isolate themselves in "ivory towers."
3. Provide increased amounts of funding and other forms of support for academic researchers. Even small amounts of support can lead to excellent work.
4. Disseminate research results through vehicles other than scholarly journals—such as series of working papers, small conferences, and consulting presentations—to facilitate use of academic research.
5. Encourage practitioners to appreciate the possiblity that academic research can provide them with valuable forms of general enlightenment.

Since the intent of this project was to be primarily descriptive rather than prescriptive, the formulation of more specific prescriptions will not be attempted here. However, those readers who are interested in considering some more specific reform proposals should refer to the position papers created by the American Marketing Association's Development of Marketing Thought Task Force (Monroe, 1986).

Assessing MSI

It seems clear that MSI has helped the initiation, pursuit, dissemination, and utilization of the body of research reviewed in this volume. But does this mean that MSI has made an overall strong contribution to knowledge development in the marketing discipline? The possibility exists that much of the research MSI has supported over the last twenty-five years might have been done anyway. And it is also possible that the body of research has added a relatively small amount to the discipline's knowledge base relative to all the other research that has been completed.

Unfortunately, as discussed at the beginning of this volume, it is impossible to make an accurate determination of just what MSI has contributed. There is no way of knowing what would have happened without MSI. Moreover, there is no way of validly judging whether the MSI-related published works—which undeniably make up a rather small proportion of the discipline's printed words—have added a greater share of knowledge than their share of words. Citation analysis, which provides one way of assessing the knowledge contribution of a piece of research, could not really be used to evaluate MSI (without an unreasonable amount of labor), since MSI working papers are generally not listed in the *Social Science Citation Index* and many of the studies were not published in any other form. (It should be noted, however, that several of the journal articles and books that came out of MSI-supported research have been extremely widely cited.)

About all that can be used to evaluate MSI is what people say about it. On this basis, MSI comes out looking rather good. The researchers and practitioners who were interviewed tended to be quite approving, and the interviewed journal editors, in spite of a few reservations, tended to speak highly of specific projects and of how the institution has evolved in recent years. In each of the knowledge development areas discussed in this volume—initiation, problem pursuit, dissemination, and utilization—the admittedly limited sample of people who were interviewed seemed to feel that MSI had made a substantive difference.

MSI as Initiator

In terms of helping the initiation of research, several of the editors and a few of the researchers offered favorable comments about how MSI has made contributions by helping new research areas to "grow" and by providing a boost to promising young researchers in the field. For example, two of the editors compliment MSI's ability to initiate research in areas that then proceed to experience "multiplier" or "second-order" effects, with many non-MSI studies following the initial MSI-supported work. A third editor states:

> MSI plays a proactive role in stimulating research in particular areas where it is very difficult. They do it with more than just funding. They do it by stimulating dialogue and direct contact between academics and businesses. It is very difficult for a conference coordinator or journal editor to stimulate work in a specific area without displaying favoritism or creating other problems.

The "career boost" aspect of MSI support was mentioned by several of the researchers. Lynn Phillips (Stanford) offers the most elaborate thoughts on this subject in saying:

> MSI affects the discipline quite a bit by giving seed money to doctoral students to help inculcate values of research in them, and that has an impact beyond whatever articles or papers might come out of a study. The work I did as a doctoral student really was formative in terms of my career later on. It was instrumental in shaping my attitudes toward research. And it was also instrumental, I think, in helping me get a job at the type of institution I wanted. MSI had a major impact on me and my career.

Of course, by seeking to "fertilize" new ideas and emerging researchers, MSI has taken some risks, and this has possibly produced fewer journal articles than might have been the case if only old topics and established researchers had been funded. But in the sub-areas of the discipline where MSI made an early and active support attempt, such as in services and industrial marketing, the risks seemed to yield considerable payoff, since the interviewees consistently recognized that MSI support produced key, seminal studies.

MSI as Pursuit Enhancer

MSI has made the pursuit of research problems easier for many researchers by providing money, research design advice, and access to key practitioners and data. It has not made everybody happy in the way it has allocated its support, since people who have had proposals rejected or who have received only small amounts of funding or access have naturally felt that better decisions might have been made. But, in general, the interviewees felt that MSI has done a good job of balancing the diverse self-interests of its member companies and the academic community. Professor Vithala Rao (Cornell) sums up this view in saying:

> They are trying to get a portfolio of projects—some with long-term payoff, some with short-term. I think it's laudable, and they are doing a superb job of maintaining balance in the portfolio.

MSI as Disseminator

Several of the interviewees praised the conferences and workshops MSI has conducted, and they generally seemed satisfied with the working paper series. It seems that MSI does better at getting practitioners and academics together than the professional associations in the marketing discipline. MSI has tried innovative conference formats—such as having practitioners present papers to be discussed by academics—and has generally kept its events small. These might be approaches that the associations could imitate.

MSI as Utilization Facilitator

The consistent impression obtained from the interviewees was that, at the very least, MSI has found a way to affect how practitioners think about their problems. The dissemination vehicles used, and the process of having practitioners get involved with designing the research when working with the steering groups, have seemed to help research projects receive attention they might not have received otherwise. It seems possible to create research that is both academically rigorous and practically relevant.

A Personal, Subjective Assessment of MSI

Given the exploratory nature of the research methods employed in this study and the limited sample of people who were interviewed, it is not possible to offer a firm, "bottom-line" conclusion about MSI's accomplishments. Moreover, since MSI commissioned this study and has had a close association with the author, attempting to present any final comments as unbiased or objective would be dishonest. Thus, what follows is simply a statement of what one academic, who has been relatively pro-MSI for a number of years, has come to feel about MSI after spending a substantial amount of time and energy learning about its operations and hearing what other knowledgable people think about what it has done.

My feelings about MSI are very positive, and I am tempted to give it the kind of endorsement provided by Victor Cook (Tulane), one of MSI's first staff members, who states:

> I think MSI invented marketing science, beginning with the first dissertation it sponsored. I think Thomas McCabe's wildest dreams were more than satisfied. If it hadn't been for MSI, I think marketing would still be in the dark ages today.

Since I lack Cook's historical perspective and feel less capable of speculating where the discipline would have headed in MSI's absence, I must be a little more modest in my conclusions. Moreover, I have to confess that what I have discovered about the importance of intrinsic motivation in driving research activity makes me wonder whether many of the researchers MSI has supported through the years would have somehow found a way to get relatively similar research studies completed.

Nevertheless, I feel MSI should be heartily commended for initiating many important studies—including projects such as the early PIMS work, some of the sales promotion work, Webster's top management study, and Shapiro and Moriarty's national account management work—and for *being there* to help out all the other studies. MSI has been very creative in how it has "leveraged" its resources to provide small amounts of support for a substantial number of projects. Marketing academics have really had practically no place else to turn for research funds, and having MSI's support has probably allowed many studies to be completed faster and more competently. Certainly, much of the work has been of the highest technical quality and has been acceptable to the most prestigious journals in the field.

I also feel MSI deserves considerable praise for what it has done to encourage usage of academic research. The MSI staff has somehow found a way to help many academics—who often come from a culture that places little emphasis on serving practitioners—learn how to communicate persuasively to this group. At the same time, MSI has conducted conferences and published papers, research summaries, newsletters, and other materials that manage to generate some excitement about academic research with some very busy and often skeptical practitioners. Keeping both "sides" happy, interested, and cooperating is, in my opinion, a noteworthy achievement.

Finally, I feel MSI should be commended for its flexibility. It has changed dramatically throughout its twenty-five years, and it is even very different today from what it was five years ago when I spent a year in residence as its Visiting Research Professor. I am impressed by the organization's ability to adapt to changing desires on the part of both its member companies and academics. For instance, the relatively new steering-group approach seems to be getting rave reviews from all concerned. Maintaining this flexibility should allow MSI to prosper for at least another twenty-five years.

References

Aaker, David A., Bruzzone, Donald E., and Norris, Donald (1981), "Viewers' Perceptions of Prime Time Television Advertising and Characteristics of Commercials Perceived as Informative," Report No. 81-103, Marketing Science Institute, Cambridge, Massachusetts.

Abell, Derek F. (1975), "Competitive Market Strategies: Some Generalizations and Hypotheses," Report No. 75-107, Marketing Science Institute, Cambridge, Massachusetts.

Albion, Mark S. (1983), *Advertising's Hidden Effects* (Boston: Auburn House Publishing Company).

———, and Farris, Paul W. (1979), "Appraising Research on Advertising's Economic Impacts," Report No. 79-115, Marketing Science Institute, Cambridge, Massachusetts.

———, and ——— (1982), "The Effect of Manufacturer Advertising on Consumer Prices: A Managerial Overview," Report No. 82-108, Marketing Science Institute, Cambridge, Massachusetts.

Alderson, Wroe (1957), *Marketing Behavior and Executive Action* (Homewood, Illinois: Richard D. Irwin, Inc.).

———, "The Analytical Framework ·for Marketing," in Delbert Duncan (Ed.), *Proceedings: Conference of Marketing Teachers from Far Western States* (Berkeley: University of California).

———, and Green, Paul E. (1964), *Planning and Problem Solving in Marketing* (Homewood, Illinois: Richard D. Irwin, Inc.).

Amabile, Theresa (1983), "The Social Psychology of Creativity: A Componential Conceptualization," *Journal of Personality and Social Psychology*, 45 (2), pp. 375–396.

——— (1985), "Motivation and Creativity: Effects of Motivational Orientation on Creative Writers," *Journal of Personality and Social Psychology*, 48 (2), pp. 393–395.

Anderson, Carl R., and Paine, Frank T. (1978), "PIMS: A Re-Examination," *Academy of Management Review*, 3, pp. 602–611.

Anderson, Erin M., and Weitz, Barton A. (1983), "A Framework for Analyzing Vertical Integration Issues in Marketing," Report No. 83-110, Marketing Science Institute, Cambridge, Massachusetts.

212 · *Knowledge Development in Marketing*

Anderson, Paul (1986), "On Method in Consumer Research: A Critical Relativist Perspective," *Journal of Consumer Research*, 13 (September), pp. 155–173.

Andreasen, Alan R. (1965), "Attitudes and Consumer Behavior: A Decision Model," in Lee Preston (Ed.), *New Research in Marketing*, Institute of Business and Economic Research, University of California, Berkeley, CA.

————, and Upah, Gregory (1978), "Regulation and the Disadvantaged: The Case of the Creditors' Remedies Rule," Report No. 78–110, Marketing Science Institute, Cambridge, Massachusetts.

Arndt, Johan (1985), "On Making Marketing Science More Scientific: Role of Orientations, Paradigms, Metaphors and Puzzle Solving," *Journal of Marketing*, 49 (Summer), pp. 11–23.

Bagozzi, Richard P. (1979), "Sales Management: New Developments from Behavioral and Decision Model Research," Report No. 79–107, Marketing Science Institute, Cambridge, Massachusetts.

Barger, Harold (1955), *Distribution's Place in the American Economy Since 1869* (Princeton, N.J.: Princeton University Press).

Bass, Frank M. (1971), "Decomposable Regression Models in the Analysis of Market Potentials," Report No. 71–110, Marketing Science Institute, Cambridge, Massachusetts.

————, and Beckwith, Neil E. (1971), "A Multivariate Regression Analysis of the Responses of Competing Brands to Advertising," Report No. 71–126, Marketing Science Institute, Cambridge, Massachusetts.

Bateson, John E.G., Eiglier, Pierre, Langeard, Eric, and Lovelock, Christopher H. (1978), "Testing a Conceptual Framework for Consumer Service Marketing," Report No. 78–112, Marketing Science Institute, Cambridge, Massachusetts.

Batra, Rajeev, and Ray, Michael L. (1984), "Identifying Opportunities for Repetition Minimization," Report No. 84–108, Marketing Science Institute, Cambridge, Massachusetts.

Bauer, Raymond A., and Greyser, Stephen A. (1968), *Advertising in America: The Consumer View* (Boston: Division of Research, Harvard Business School).

————, and ———— (1969), "The Dialogue That Never Happens," *Harvard Business Review*, (Jan-Feb), pp. 122–128.

Beckwith, Neil E. (1977), "Public Policy Implications of the Duration of Cumulative Advertising Effects," in Darral Clarke (Ed.), *Cumulative Advertising Effects: Sources and Implications*, Report No. 77–111, Marketing Science Institute, Cambridge, Massachusetts.

Belch, George E., and Lutz, Richard J. (1982), "A Multiple Exposure Study of the Effects of Comparative and Noncomparative Television Commercials on Cognitive Response, Recall, and Message Acceptance," Report No. 82–107, Marketing Science Institute, Cambridge, Massachusetts.

Bell, Daniel (1973), *The Coming of Post-Industrial Society* (New York: Basic Books).

Berry, Leonard L. (1981), "The Employee as Customer," *Journal of Retail Banking*, (March) pp. 24–28.

Biggadike, Ralph (1977), "Entering New Markets: Strategies and Performance," Report No. 77–108, Marketing Science Institute, Cambridge, Massachusetts.

Bliss, Perry (1963), *Marketing and the Behavioral Sciences* (Boston: Allyn and Bacon).

Bloom, Paul N. (1982), "Consumerism and Beyond: Research Perspectives on the Future Social Environment," Report No. 82–102, Marketing Science Institute, Cambridge, Massachusetts.

————, and Greyser, Stephen A. (1981), "Exploring the Future of Consumerism," Report No. 81–102, Marketing Science Institute, Cambridge, Massachusetts.

————, and Stern, Louis W. (1977), "Consumerism in the Year 2000: The Emergence of Anti-Industrialism," in Norman Kangun and Lee Richardson (Eds.), *Consumerism: New Challenges for Marketing* (Chicago: American Marketing Association).

Bonoma, Thomas V., and Shapiro, Benson P. (1983), "Industrial Market Segmentation: A Nested Approach," Report No. 83–100, Marketing Science Institute, Cambridge, Massachusetts.

————, Zaltman, Gerald, and Johnston, Wesley J. (1977), "Industrial Buying Behavior," Report No. 77–117, Marketing Science Institute, Cambridge, Massachusetts.

Brinberg, David and Hirschman, Elizabeth C. (1986), "Multiple Orientations for the Conduct of Marketing Research: An Analysis of the Academic/Practitioner Distinction," *Journal of Marketing*, 50 (October), pp. 161–173.

Broadbent, D. E. (1977), "The Hidden Preattentive Processes," *American Psychologist*, 32, pp. 222–231.

Buchanan, Bruce S., and Morrison, Donald G. (1985), "Measuring Simple Preferences: An Approach to Blind, Forced-Choice Product Testing," Report No. 85–103, Marketing Science Institute, Cambridge, Massachusetts.

Bucklin, Louis P. (1973), "A Theory of Channel Control," *Journal of Marketing*, 37 (January), pp. 39–47.

Business-Higher Education Forum (1983), *America's Competitive Challenge: The Need for a National Response* (Washington, D.C.: American Council on Education).

Buzzell, Robert D. (1971), "Role of Advertising in the Marketing Mix," Report No. 71–135, Marketing Science Institute, Cambridge, Massachusetts.

———— (1985), *PIMS Research Bibliography* (Cambridge: The Strategic Planning Institute).

———— and Farris, Paul W. (1976), "Marketing Costs in Consumer Goods Industries," Report No. 76–111, Marketing Science Institute, Cambridge, Massachusetts.

———— and ———— (1976), "Industrial Marketing Costs: An Analysis of Variations in Manufacturers' Marketing Expenditures," Report No. 76–118, Marketing Science Institute, Cambridge, Massachusetts.

———— and ———— (1976), "Marketing Costs in Industrial Businesses," Report No. 76–120, Marketing Science Institute, Cambridge, Massachusetts.

————, Gale, Bradley T., and Sultan, Ralph G.M. (1974), "Market Share, Profitability, and Business Strategy," Report No. 74–116, Marketing Science Institute, Cambridge, Massachusetts.

Campbell, John P., Daft, Richard L., and Hulin, Charles H. (1982), *What to Study: Generating and Developing Research Questions* (Beverly Hills: Sage Publications).

Caplan, Nathan, Morrison, A., and Stambaugh, R.J. (1975), "The Use of Social Science Knowledge in Policy Decisions at the National Level: A Report to

Respondents," Center for Research on Utilization of Scientific Knowledge, Institute for Social Research, University of Michigan, Ann Arbor, Michigan.

Chevalier, Michel (1975), "Increase in Sales Due to In-Store Display," *Journal of Marketing Research*, 12 (November), pp. 426–431.

———, and Curhan, Ronald C. (1975), "Temporary Promotions as a Function of Trade Deals: A Descriptive Analysis," Report No. 75-109, Marketing Science Institute, Cambridge, Massachusetts.

Churchill, Gilbert A. Jr., Ford, Neil M., and Walker, Orville C. Jr. (1974), "Measuring the Job Satisfaction of Industrial Salesmen," *Journal of Marketing Research*, 11, (August) pp. 254–260.

———, ———, and ——— (1976), "Motivating the Industrial Salesforce: The Attractiveness of Alternative Rewards," Report No. 76-115, Marketing Science Institute, Cambridge, Massachusetts.

———, ———, and ——— (1983), "Organizational Climate and Job Satisfaction in the Salesforce," in N. Ford, O. Walker, and G. Churchill (Eds.), *Research Perspectives on the Performance of Salespeople: Selected Readings*, Report No. 83-107, Marketing Science Institute, Cambridge, Massachusetts.

Clarke, Darral G. (1977), "Cumulative Advertising Effects: Sources and Implications," Report No. 77-111, Marketing Science Institute, Cambridge, Massachusetts.

Cohen, D., et al. (1972), "A Garbage Can Model of Organizational Choice," *Administrative Science Quarterly*, 17, pp. 1–25.

Colley, Russell (1961), "Defining Advertising Goals for Measured Advertising Results," Association of National Advertisers, New York, New York.

Comer, James, and Dubinsky, Alan (1985), *Managing The Succussful Sales Force* (Lexington, Massachusetts: Lexington Books).

Cook, Victor J., and Herniter, Jerome D. (1970), "A Multidimensional Stochastic Model of Consumer Purchase Behavior," Report No. 70-127, Marketing Science Institute, Cambridge, Massachusetts.

———, and Schutte, Thomas (1967), *Brand Policy Determination* (Boston: Allyn and Bacon).

Corey, E. Raymond (1978), "The Organizational Context of Industrial Buying Behavior," Report No. 78-106, Marketing Science Institute, Cambridge, Massachusetts.

Coughlan, Anne, and Sen, Subrata (1986), "Salesforce Compensation: Insights from Management Science," Report No. 86-101, Marketing Science Institute, Cambridge, Massachusetts.

Curhan, Ronald C. (1971), "The Relationship Between Shelf Space and Unit Sales in Supermarkets: A Model Proposed and Tested," Report No. 71-132, Marketing Science Institute, Cambridge, Massachusetts.

——— (1972), "The Relationship of Shelf Space to Unit Sales: A Review," Report No. 72-122, Marketing Science Institute, Cambridge, Massachusetts.

——— (1974), "The Effects of Merchandising and Temporary Promotional Activities on the Sales of Fresh Fruit and Vegetables in Supermarkets," Report No. 74-110, Marketing Science Institute, Cambridge, Massachusetts.

_____, and Kopp, Robert J. (1986), "Factors Influencing Grocery Retailers' Support of Trade Promotions," Report No. 86–104, Marketing Science Institute, Cambridge, Massachusetts.

Czepiel, John A. (1980), "Managing Customer Satisfaction in Consumer Service Businesses," Report No. 80–109, Marketing Science Institute, Cambridge, Massachusetts.

Day, George S. (1980), "Strategic Market Analysis: Top-Down and Bottom-Up Approaches," Report No. 80–105, Marketing Science Institute, Cambridge, Massachusetts.

_____ (1984), *Strategic Market Planning: The Pursuit of Competitive Advantage* (Saint Paul: West Publishing Company).

_____, and Shocker, Alan D. (1976), "Identifying Competitive Product-Market Boundaries: Strategic and Analytical Issues," Report No. 76–112, Marketing Science Institute, Cambridge, Massachusetts.

_____, and Wensley, Robin (1983), "Priorities for Research in Strategic Marketing," Report No. 83–103, Marketing Science Institute, Cambridge, Massachusetts.

_____, Massy, William F., and Shocker, Allan D. (1978), "The Public Policy Context of the Relevant Market Question," in J. F. Cody (Ed.), *Marketing and the Public Interest*, Report No. 78–105, Marketing Science Institute, Cambridge, Massachusetts.

Dickson, Peter R., and Sawyer, Alan G. (1986), "Point-of-Purchase Behavior and Price Perceptions of Supermarket Shoppers," Report No. 86–102, Marketing Science Institute, Cambridge, Massachusetts.

_____, and Wilkie, William L. (1978), "The Consumption of Household Durables: A Behavioral Review," Report No. 78–117, Marketing Science Institute, Cambridge, Massachusetts.

Eiglier, Pierre, Langeard, Eric, Lovelock, Christopher H., Bateson, John E. G., and Young, Robert F. (1977), "Marketing Consumer Services: New Insights," Report No. 77–115, Marketing Science Institute, Cambridge, Massachusetts.

Engel, James F., Kollat, David T., and Blackwell, Roger D. (1968), *Consumer Behavior* (New York: Holt, Rinehart, and Winston).

Farley, John U., Hulbert, James M., and Weinstein, David (1980), "Price Setting and Volume Planning by Two European Industrial Companies: A Study and Comparison of Decision Processes," *Journal of Marketing*, 44 (Winter), pp. 46–54.

Farris, Paul W. (1977), "Determinants of Advertising Intensity: A Review of the Marketing Literature," Report No. 77–109, Marketing Science Institute, Cambridge, Massachusetts.

_____, and Albion, Mark S. (1979), "An Investigation into the Impact of Advertising on the Price of Consumer Products," Report No. 79–109, Marketing Science Institute, Cambridge, Massachusetts.

_____, and Buzzell, Robert D. (1976), "Relationships Between Changes in Industrial Advertising and Promotion Expenditures and Changes in Market Share," Report No. 76–119, Marketing Science Institute, Cambridge, Massachusetts.

———, and Reibstein, David J. (1978), "Using a Nonlinear Response Function in Estimating Advertising's Carry-Over Effects," Report No. 78-107, Marketing Science Institute, Cambridge, Massachusetts.

Fisk, Raymond P., and Silpakit, Patriya (1985), *Services Marketing: An Annotated Bibliography* (Chicago: American Marketing Association).

———, ———, and Hromas, James G. (1985), "The Services Marketing Literature: A Twenty-Year Status Report," Working Paper, Oklahoma State University, Stillwater, Oklahoma.

Ford, Neil M., Walker, Orville C. Jr., and Churchill, Gilbert A. Jr. (1981), "Differences in Attractiveness of Alternative Rewards Among Industrial Salespeople: Additional Evidence," Report No. 81-107, Marketing Science Institute, Cambridge, Massachusetts.

———, ———, and ——— (1983), "Research Perspectives on the Performance of Salespeople: Selected Readings," Report No. 83-107, Marketing Science Institute, Cambridge, Massachusetts.

Frank, Ronald G., and Massy, William F. (1965), "Market Segmentation and the Effect of a Brand's Price and Dealing Policies," *Journal of Business*, 38 (April), pp. 186-200.

———, and ——— (1967), "Estimating the Effects of Short-Term Promotional Strategy on Selected Market Segments," in Patrick Robinson (Ed.), *Promotional Decisions Using Mathematical Models* (Boston: Allyn and Bacon), pp. 146-225.

Frey, Albert W. and Howard, John (1960), "A Proposal for The Institute of Science in Marketing," unpublished paper of the Marketing Science Institute.

Galper, Morton (1979), "Communications Spending Decisions for Industrial Products: A Literature Review," Report No. 79-111, Marketing Science Institute, Cambridge, Massachusetts.

Garvey, William D. (1979), *Communication, the Essence of Science: Facilitating Information Exchange among Librarians, Scientists, Engineers, and Students* (Oxford, NY: Pergamon Press).

George, William R., and Barksdale, Hiram C. (1974), "Marketing Activities in Service Industries," *Journal of Marketing*, 38 (October), pp. 65-70.

Green, Paul E., and Carmone, Frank J. (1970), "Stimulus Context and Task Effects on Individuals' Similarities Judgements," Report No. 70-139, Marketing Science Institute, Cambridge, Massachusetts.

———, and Rao, Vithala R. (1970), "Rating Scales and Information Recovery— How Many Scales and Response Categories to Use," Report No. 70-136, Marketing Science Institute, Cambridge, Massachusetts.

———, and Rao, Vithala R. (1971), "Multidimensional Scaling and Individual Differences," Report No. 71-123, Marketing Science Institute, Cambridge, Massachusetts.

———, Robinson, Patrick, and Fitzroy, Peter (1967), *Experiments on the Value of Information in Simulated Marketing Environments* (Boston: Allyn and Bacon).

Grether, E.T. (1966), *Marketing and Public Policy* (Englewood, NJ: Prentice Hall, Inc.).

Greyser, Stephen A. (1977), "Americans' Attitudes Toward Consumerism," Report No. 77-113, Marketing Science Institute, Cambridge, Massachusetts.

——— (1970), "Consumer Affairs and Marketing Management," Report No. 70-109, Marketing Science Institute, Cambridge, Massachusetts.

_____ (1974), "Marketing and the Future: The Response to Consumerism," Report No. 74-117, Marketing Science Institute, Cambridge, Massachusetts.

_____ (1980), "Marketing Issues—Challenges for the 1980s," Report No. 80-102, Marketing Science Institute, Cambridge, Massachusetts.

_____ , Bloom, Paul N., and Diamond, Steven L. (1982), "Assessing Consumerism: The Public's and Expert's Views," in Paul Bloom (Ed.), *Consumerism and Beyond: Research Perspectives on the Future Social Environment*, Report No. 82-102, Marketing Science Institute, Cambridge, Massachusetts.

_____ , and Diamond, Steven L. (1974), "Marketing and Responsiveness to Consumerism," Report No. 74-101, Marketing Science Institute, Cambridge, Massachusetts.

Gronroos, Christian (1983), "Strategic Management and Marketing in the Service Sector," Report No. 83-104, Marketing Science Institute, Cambridge, Massachusetts.

Hardy, Kenneth G. (1984), "Factors Associated with Successful Manufacturer Sales Promotions in Canadian Food and Drug Businesses," in Katherine E. Jocz (Ed.), *Research on Sales Promotion: Collected Papers*, Report No. 84-104, Marketing Science Institute, Cambridge, Massachusetts.

Hauser, John R. (1985), "Theory and Application of Defensive Strategy," Report No. 85-107, Marketing Science Institute, Cambridge, Massachusetts.

Heeler, R.M. (1972), "The Effects of Mixed Media, Multiple Copy, Repetition, and Competition in Advertising: A Laboratory Investigation," Ph.D. Dissertation: Graduate School of Business, Stanford University.

Henderson, Caroline, Kopp, Robert J., Isler, Leslie, and Ward, Scott (1980), "Influences on Children's Product Requests and Mother's Answers: A Multivariate Analysis of Diary Data," Report No. 80-106, Marketing Science Institute, Cambridge, Massachusetts.

Hendrix, Philip E., Kinnear, Thomas C., and Taylor, James R. (1983), "Consumer's Time Expenditures: A Behavioral Model and Empirical Test," Report No. 83-109, Marketing Science Institute, Cambridge, Massachusetts.

Herniter, Jerome (1972), "An Entropy Model of Brand Purchase Behavior," Report No. 72-111, Marketing Science Institute, Cambridge, Massachusetts.

_____ (1973), "A Comparison of the Entropy and Hendry Model," Report No. 73-101, Marketing Science Institute, Cambridge, Massachusetts.

Hirschman, Elizabeth C. (1986), "Humanistic Inquiry in Marketing Research: Philosophy, Method, and Criteria," *Journal of Marketing Research*, 23 (August), pp. 237-249.

Hofer, Charles W., and Schendel, Dan (1978), *Strategy Formulation: Analytical Concepts* (St. Paul: West Publishing).

Hourihan, Anthony P., and Markham, Jesse W. (1974), "The Effects of Fair Trade Repeal: The Case of Rhode Island," Report No. 74-109, Marketing Science Institute, Cambridge, Massachusetts.

Howard, John A., and Sheth, Jagdesh N., (1969), *A Theory of Buyer Behavior* (New York: John Wiley and Sons).

Howard, M. (1964), *Legal Aspects of Marketing* (New York: McGraw-Hill).

Hughes, G. David (1980), "Marketers' Potential Contribution to Regulatory Reform," Report No. 80-113, Marketing Science Institute, Cambridge, Massachusetts.

————, and Williams, E. Cameron (1979), "The Dialogue That Happened," Report No. 79–108, Marketing Science Institute, Cambridge, Massachusetts.

Hunt, H. Keith (1977), "Consumer Satisfaction and Disatisfaction: Perspectives and Overview," Report No. 77–112, Marketing Science Institute, Cambridge, Massachusetts.

Hustad, Thomas P., and Pessemier, Edgar A. (1971), "A Review of Current Developments in the Use of 'Attitude and Activity Measures in Consumer Marketing Research'," Report No. 71–134, Marketing Science Institute, Cambridge, Massachusetts.

————, and ———— (1972), "Will the Real Consumer-Activist Please Stand Up: An Examination of Consumers' Opinions About Marketing Practices," Report No. 72–126, Marketing Science Institute, Cambridge, Massachusetts.

Hutton, R. Bruce, and Wilkie, William L. (1980), "'Life Cycle Cost': A New Form of Consumer Information," Report No. 80–116, Marketing Science Institute, Cambridge, Massachusetts.

Isler, Leslie, Popper, Edward, and Ward, Scott (1979), "Children's Purchase Requests and Parental Responses: Results from a Diary Study," Report No. 79–110, Marketing Science Institute, Cambridge, Massachusetts.

Journal Citation Reports (1984), (Philadelphia: Institute for Scientific Information).

Kassarjian, Harold, and Robertson, Thomas S. (1968), *Perspectives in Consumer Behavior* (Glenview, Illinois: Scott, Foresman, and Company).

Kotler, Philip, and Levy, Sidney (1969), "Broadening the Concept of Marketing," *Journal of Marketing*, 33 (January) pp. 10–15.

————, and Zaltman, Gerald (1971), "Social Marketing: An Approach to Planned Social Change," *Journal of Marketing*, 35, pp. 3–12.

Koyck, L.M. (1954), *Distributed Lags and Investment Analysis* (Amsterdam: North Holland Publishing Company).

Krugman, Herbert E. (1965), "The Impact of Television Advertising: Learning Without Involvement," *Public Opinion Quarterly*, 29, pp. 349–356.

———— (1970), "Electroencephalographic Aspects of Low Involvement: Implications for the McLuhan Hypothesis," Report No. 70–113, Marketing Science Institute, Cambridge, Massachusetts.

———— (1971), "Brain Wave Measures of Media Involvement," *Journal of Advertising Research*, 11, pp. 3–9.

———— (1972), "Why Three Exposures May Be Enough," *Journal of Advertising Research*, 11, pp. 11–14.

———— (1977), "Memory Without Recall, Exposure Without Perception," *Journal of Advertising Research*, 17, pp 7–12.

Kuehn, Alfred A. and Rohloff, Albert C. (1967), "Consumer Response to Promotions," in Patrick Robinson (Ed.), *Promotional Decisions Using Mathematical Models* (Boston: Allyn and Bacon), pp. 43–145.

Kulka, Richard A. (1982), "Idiosyncrasy and Circumstance: Choices and Constraints in the Research Process," in J. McGrath, J. Martin, and R. Kulka (Eds.), *Judgement Calls in Research* (Beverley Hills: Sage Publications), pp. 41–68.

Langeard, Eric, Bateson, John E. G., Lovelock, Christopher H., and Eiglier, Pierre (1981), "Services Marketing": New Insights from Consumers and Managers," Report No. 81–104, Marketing Science Institute, Cambridge, Massachusetts.

Lasswell, Harold (1948), "The Structure and Function of Communication in Society," in L. Bryson (Ed.), The *Communication of Ideas* (New York: Harper and Row).

Lilien, Gary L., and Kotler, Philip (1983), *Marketing Decision Making: A Model Building Approach* (New York: Harper and Row).

Lovelock, Christopher H. (1973), "Consumer Oriented Approaches to Marketing Urban Transit," Ph.D. Dissertation, Stanford University.

_____ (1975), "A Market Segmentation Approach to Transit Planning, Modeling, and Management," *Proceedings of the Sixteenth Annual Meeting of the Transportation Research Forum* (Oxford, Indiana: Richard B. Cross Company), pp. 247–258.

Lovelock, Christopher, and Weinberg, Charles (1975), "Contrasting Private and Public Sector Marketing," in R. C. Curhan (Ed.), *1974 Combined Proceedings,* (Chicago: AMA).

Luck, David J., and Krum, James R. (1981), "Conditions Conducive to Effective Use of Marketing Research in the Corporation," Report No. 81–100, Marketing Science Institute, Cambridge, Massachusetts.

March, J.G., and Olsen, J.P. (1976), *Ambiguity and Choice in Organizations* (Bergen, Norway: Universitels Forlaget).

Marketing Science Institute (1985), *MSI Annual Report: 1985–86,* Marketing Science Institute, Cambridge, Massachusetts.

Martin, Joanne (1982), "A Garbage Can Model of the Research Process," in J. McGrath, J. Martin, and R. Kulka (Eds.), *Judgement Calls in Research* (Beverly Hills: Sage Publications).

Massy, William F., and Frank, Ronald E. (1965), "Short-Term Price and Dealing Elasticities in Selected Market Segments," *Journal of Marketing Research,* 2 (May), pp. 171–185.

_____ , and _____ (1966), "An Analysis of Retailer Advertising Behavior," *Journal of Marketing Research,* 3 (November), pp. 378–383.

Matthews, William E. (1972), "Challenge for Industrial Marketers: Changing Channels of Distribution," Report No. 72–104, Marketing Science Institute, Cambridge, Massachusetts.

May, Eleanor G. (1971), "Image Evaluation of a Department Store," Report No. 71–117, Marketing Science Institute, Cambridge, Massachusetts.

May, Eleanor G., Ress, C. William, and Salmon, Walter J. (1985), "Future Trends in Retailing: Merchandise Line Trends and Store Trends 1980–1990," Report No. 85–102, Marketing Science Institute, Cambridge, Massachusetts.

McAlister, Leigh, and Lattin, James M. (1984), "Identifying Competitive Brand Relationships When Consumers Seek Variety," Report No. 84–105, Marketing Science Institute, Cambridge, Massachusetts.

McCabe, Thomas (1961), "The Institute for Science in Marketing: A Proposal," unpublished paper of the Marketing Science Institute.

McCammon, Bert Jr. (1973), "The Future of Catalog Showrooms: Growth and Its Challenge to Management," Report No. 73–104, Marketing Science Institute, Cambridge, Massachusetts.

McCann, John M., and Reibstein, David J. (1978), "Incorporating Marketing into Corporate Planning Models," Report No. 78–111, Marketing Science Institute, Cambridge, Massachusetts.

McNair, Malcolm P., and May, Eleanor (1976), "The Evolution of Retail Institutions in the United States," Report No. 76–100, Marketing Science Institute, Cambridge, Massachusetts.

McNeill, Dennis L. and Swinyard, William R. (1980), "Comparative Product Information and Its Interaction with Brand Name and Product Type," Report No. 80–114, Marketing Science Institute, Cambridge, Massachusetts.

Monroe, Kent B. (1986), "Report of the Marketing Thought Task Force," Working Paper, Virginia Tech University, Blacksburg, Virginia.

Montgomery, David B. (1970), "Developing a Balanced Marketing Information System," Report No. 70–111, Marketing Science Institute, Cambridge, Massachusetts.

—— (1973), "Marketing Information and Decision Systems: Coming of Age in the '70's," Report No. 73–113, Marketing Science Institute, Cambridge, Massachusetts.

——, and Day, George S. (1985), "Experience Curves: Evidence, Empirical Issues, and Applications," Report No. 85–101, Marketing Science Institute, Cambridge, Massachusetts.

——, and Ryans, Adrian B. (1971), "Stochastic Models of Consumer Choice Behavior," Report No. 71–140, Marketing Science Institute, Cambridge, Massachusetts.

——, and Silk, Alvin J. (1970), "Distributed Lag Models of Response to a Communications Mix," Report No. 70–112, Marketing Science Institute, Cambridge, Massachusetts.

——, and —— (1972), "Estimation of Dynamic Effects of Market Communications Expenditures," Report No. 72–112, Marketing Science Institute, Cambridge, Massachusetts.

——, ——, and Zaragoza, Carlos E. (1971), "A Multiple-Product Sales Force Allocation Model," Report No. 71–125, Marketing Science Institute, Cambridge, Massachusetts.

——, and Urban, Glen L. (1969), *Management Science in Marketing* (Englewood Cliffs, NJ: Prentice-Hall).

——, and Urban, Glen L. (1969), "Marketing Decision-Information Systems: An Emerging View," Report No. 70–123, Marketing Science Institute, Cambridge, Massachusetts.

——, and Weinberg, Charles B. (1974), "Modeling Market Phenomena: A Managerial Perspective," Report No. 74–118, Marketing Science Institute, Cambridge, Massachusetts.

——, and Wittink, Dick R. (1980), "Market Measurement and Analysis," Report No. 80–103, Marketing Science Institute, Cambridge, Massachusetts.

Moriarty, Rowland T., and Galper, Morton (1978), "Organizational Buying Behavior: A State-of-the-Art Review and Conceptualization," Report No. 78–101, Marketing Science Institute, Cambridge, Massachusetts.

——, and Reibstein, David J. (1982), "Benefit Segmentation: An Industrial Application," Report No. 82–110, Marketing Science Institute, Cambridge, Massachusetts.

——, and Spekman, Robert E. (1983), "Sources of Information Utilized During the Industrial Buying Process: An Empirical Overview," Report No. 83–101, Marketing Science Institute, Cambridge, Massachusetts.

Myers, John G., Massy, William F., and Greyser, Stephen A. (1980), *Marketing Research and Knowledge Development* (Englewood Cliffs, NJ: Prentice-Hall).

Naylor, Thomas H. (1978), "PIMS: Through A Different Looking Glass," *Planning Review*, 6, pp. 15–16, 32.

Neslin, Scott A., Quelch, John, and Henderson, Caroline (1984), "Consumer Promotions and the Acceleration of Product Purchases," in Katherine E. Jocz (Ed.), *Research on Sales Promotion: Collected Papers*, Report No. 84–104, Marketing Science Institute, Cambridge, Massachusetts.

Nicosia, Francesco M. (1966), *Consumer Decision Processes: Marketing and Advertising Implications* (Englewood Cliffs, NJ: Prentice-Hall).

Olson, Jerry C., and Ray, William J. (1983), "Using Brain-Wave Measures to Assess Advertising Effects," Report No. 83–108, Marketing Science Institute, Cambridge, Massachusetts.

Palda, Kristian S., and Turner, Ranald E. (1977), "Managerial Implications of Long-Lasting Advertising Effects," in Darral Clarke (Ed.), *Cumulative Advertising Effects: Sources and Implications*, Report No. 77–111, Marketing Science Institute, Cambridge, Massachusetts.

Parasuraman, A., Zeithaml, Valarie A., and Berry, Leonard L. (1984), "A Conceptual Model of Service Quality and Its Implications for Future Research," Report No. 84–106, Marketing Science Institute, Cambridge, Massachusetts.

———, ———, and ——— (1986), "SERVQUAL: A Multiple Item Scale for Measuring Customer Perceptions of Service Quality," Report No. 86–108, Marketing Science Institute, Cambridge, Massachusetts.

Park, C. Whan, and Young, S. Mark (1984), "The Effects of Involvement and Executional Factors of a Television Commercial on Brand Attribute Formation," Report No. 84–100, Marketing Science Institute, Cambridge, Massachusetts.

Pearce, Michael, Cummingham, Scott M., and Miller, Avon (1971), "Appraising the Economic and Social Effects of Advertising," Report No. 71–103, Marketing Science Institute, Cambridge, Massachusetts.

Pessemier, Edgar A. (1975), "Managing Innovation and New Product Development," Report No. 75–122, Marketing Science Institute, Cambridge, Massachusetts.

——— (1976), "Market Structure Analysis of New Product, Market, and Communication Opportunities," Report No. 76–106, Marketing Science Institute, Cambridge, Massachusetts.

——— (1979), "Managerial Aspects of Market Structure Analysis and Market Maps," Report No. 79–101, Marketing Science Institute, Cambridge, Massachusetts.

——— (1979), "Simulation Methods as an Aid to Designing Market Map Studies: A Managerial Review," Report No. 79–102, Marketing Science Institute, Cambridge, Massachusetts.

———, and McAlister, Leigh (1982), "Varied Consumer Choice Behavior: A Theory, some Empirical Results, and Their Practical Consequences," Report No. 82–111, Marketing Science Institute, Cambridge, Massachusetts.

Peter, J. Paul, and Olson, Jerry C. (1983), "Is Science Marketing?" *Journal of Marketing*, 47 (Fall), pp. 111–125.

Phillips, Lynn (1978), "Threats to Validity in Quasi-Experimental Evaluations of Consumer Protection Reforms: A Critical Review of Extant Research," Report No. 78–102, Marketing Science Institute, Cambridge, Massachusetts.

Polli, Rolando, and Cook, Victor (1969), "Validity of the Product Life-Cycle," *Journal of Business*, (October), pp. 385–400.

Porter, Michael E. (1980), *Competitive Strategy: Techniques for Analyzing Industries and Competitors* (New York: Free Press).

Quelch, John A. (1978), "Behavioral and Attitudinal Measures of the Relative Importance of Product Attributes: The Case of Cold Breakfast Cereals," Report No. 78–109, Marketing Science Institute, Cambridge, Massachusetts.

———— (1982), "Trade Promotion by Grocery Products Manufacturers: A Managerial Perspective," Report No. 82–106, Marketing Science Institute, Cambridge, Massachusetts.

————, Marshall, Cheri T., and Chang, Dae R. (1984), "Structural Determinants of Ratios of Promotion and Advertising to Sales," in Katherine E. Jocz (Ed.), *Research on Sales Promotion: Collected Papers*, Report No. 84–104, Marketing Science Institute, Cambridge, Massachusetts.

Ramanujam, V., and Venkatraman, N. (1984), "An Inventory and Critique of Strategy Research Using the PIMS Data Base," *Academy of Management Review*, 9, pp. 138–151.

Rao, Vithala, and Cox, James E. (1978), "Sales Forecasting Methods: A Survey of Recent Developments," Report No. 78–119, Marketing Science Institute, Cambridge, Massachusetts.

Rathmell, John M. (1966), "What is Meant by Services," *Journal of Marketing*, 30 (October), pp. 32–36.

Ray, Michael L. (1974), "Consumer Initial Processing: Definitions, Issues, and Applications," in G. David Hughes and Michael L. Ray (Eds.), *Buyer/Consumer Information Processing* (Chapel Hill: The University of North Carolina Press).

———— (1973), "Marketing Communication and the Hierarchy-of-Effects," Report No. 73–112, Marketing Science Institute, Cambridge, Massachusetts.

———— (1982), *Advertising and Communication Management* (Englewood Cliffs, NJ: Prentice-Hall).

————, Sawyer, A. G., and Strong, E. C. (1971), "Frequency Effects Revisited," *Journal of Advertising Research*, 11, pp 14–20.

————, Ward, Scott, and Lesser, Gerald (1973), "Experimentation to Improve Pretesting of Drug Abuse Education and Information Campaigns," Report No. 73–103, Marketing Science Institute, Cambridge, Massachusetts.

————, and Webb, Peter H. (1976), "Experimental Research on the Effects of TV Clutter: Dealing With A Difficult Media Environment," Report No. 76–102, Marketing Science Institute, Cambridge, Massachusetts.

————, and Webb, Peter H. (1978), "Advertising Effectiveness in a Crowded Television Environment," Report No. 78–113, Marketing Science Institute, Cambridge, Massachusetts.

Revzan, David A. (1961), *Wholesaling in Marketing Organizations* (New York: John Wiley).

Reynolds, Fred D., and Neter, John (1979), "Age Classification," Report No. 79–100, Marketing Science Institute, Cambridge, Massachusetts.

Rich, Robert F. (1977), "Uses of Social Science Information by Federal Bureaucrats: Knowledge for Action vs. Knowledge for Understanding," in C. H. Weiss (Ed.), *Using Social Research in Public Policy Making* (Lexington, MA: D. C. Heath).

Robinson, Larry M., and Adler, Roy D. (1979), "Citations Provide Objective Ratings of Schools, Scholars," *Marketing News*, 12 (July), p. 8.

Robinson, Patrick (Ed.), (1967), *Promotional Decisions Using Mathematical Models* (Boston: Allyn and Bacon).

———, Dalbey, Homer, Gross, Irwin, and Wind, Yoram (1968), *Advertising Measurement and Decision Making* (Boston: Allyn and Bacon).

———, Faris, Charles W., and Wind, Yoram (1967), *Industrial Buying and Creative Marketing* (Boston: Allyn and Bacon).

———, and Luck, David (1964), *Promotional Decision Making: Practice and Theory* (New York: McGraw-Hill).

———, and Stidsen, Bent (1967), *Personal Selling in A Modern Perspective* (Boston: Allyn and Bacon).

Ross, William T. (1985), "Managing Marketing Channel Relationships," Report No. 85–106, Marketing Science Institute, Cambridge, Massachusetts.

Rothschild, Michael L. (1974), "The Effects of Political Advertising upon the Voting Behavior of a Low Involvement Electorate," Ph.D. Dissertation, Graduate School of Business, Stanford University.

Ruekert, Robert W., Walker, Orville C., and Roering, Kenneth J. (1985), "The Organization of Marketing Activities: A Contingency Theory of Structure and Performance," Report No. 85–104, Marketing Science Institute, Cambridge, Massachusetts.

Russo, J. Edward, Staelin, Richard, Russel, Gary J., and Metcalf, Barbara L. (1985), "Nutrition Information in the Supermarket," Report No. 85–100, Marketing Science Institute, Cambridge, Massachusetts.

Rust, Roland T., Price, Linda L., and Kumar, V. (1985), "EEG Response to Advertisements in Print and Broadcast Media," Report No. 85–111, Marketing Science Institute, Cambridge, Massachusetts.

Ryans, Adrian B., and Weinberg, Charles B. (1979), "Determinants of Salesforce Performance," Report No. 79–113, Marketing Science Institute, Cambridge, Massachusetts.

———, and ——— (1981), "Sales Force Management: Integrating Research Advances," *California Management Review* (Fall), pp. 82–104.

Salmon, Walter J., Buzzell, Robert D., and Cort, Stanton G. (1974), "Today the Shopping Center, Tomorrow the Superstore," Report No. 74–124, Marketing Science Institute, Cambridge, Massachusetts.

———, ———, and Curhan, Ronald C. (1980), "The Economics of Health, Beauty Aids, and General Merchandise Distribution Among Retailers and Service Merchandisers," Report No. 80–110, Marketing Science Institute, Cambridge, Massachusetts.

Sasser, W. Earl (1976), "Match Supply and Demand in Service Industries," *Harvard Business Review*, 54, pp. 133–141.

Sawyer, Alan G. (1971), "A Laboratory Experimental Investigation of the Effects of Repitition in Advertising," Ph.D. Dissertation, Graduate School of Business, Stanford University.

———, and Dickson, Peter R. (1984), "Psychological Perspectives on Consumer Response and Sales Promotion," in Kathrine E. Jocz (Ed.), *Research on Sales Promotion: Collected Papers*, Report No. 84-104, Marketing Science Institute, Cambridge, Massachusetts.

———, and Ward, Scott (1976), "Carry-Over Effects in Advertising Communication: Evidence and Hypotheses from Behavioral Science," Report No. 76-122, Marketing Science Institute, Cambridge, Massachusetts.

Saxe, Robert, and Weitz, Barton A. (1982), "The SOCO Scale: A Measure of the Customer Orientation of Salespeople," Report No. 82-113, Marketing Science Institute, Cambridge, Massachusetts.

Schmalensee, Diane (1983), "Today's Top Priority Advertising Research Questions," *Journal of Advertising Research*, 23 (April/May), pp. 49-62.

——— et al. (1982), "Determinants of Food Consumption in American Households," Report No. 82-112, Marketing Science Institute, Cambridge, Massachusetts.

Schoeffler, Sidney, Buzzell, Robert D., and Heany, Donald F. (1973), "PIMS: A Breakthrough in Strategic Planning," Report No. 73-120, Marketing Science Institute, Cambridge, Massachusetts.

Shapiro, Benson P. (1977), "Industrial Product Policy: Managing the Existing Product Line," Report No. 77-110, Marketing Science Institute, Cambridge, Massachusetts.

———, and Moriarty, Rowland T. (1980), "National Account Management," Report No. 80-104, Marketing Science Institute, Cambridge, Massachusetts.

———, and ——— (1982), "National Account Management: Emerging Insights," Report No. 82-100, Marketing Science Institute, Cambridge, Massachusetts.

———, and ——— (1984), "Organizing the National Account Force," Report No. 84-101, Marketing Science Institute, Cambridge, Massachusetts.

———, and ——— (1984), "Support Systems for National Account Management Programs: Promises Made, Promises Kept," Report No. 84-102, Marketing Science Institute, Cambridge, Massachusetts.

Sheth, Jagdish (1973), "A Model of Industrial Buying Behavior," *Journal of Marketing*, 37, pp. 50-56.

——— (1979), "The Surpluses and Shortages in Consumer Behavior Theory and Research," *Journal of the Academy of Marketing Science*, 7 (Fall), pp. 414-426.

Shocker, Allan D. (1979), "Analytic Approaches to Product and Marketing Planning," Report No. 79-104, Marketing Science Institute, Cambridge, Massachusetts.

Shostack, G. Lynn (1977), "Breaking Free from Product Marketing," *Journal of Marketing*, 41 (April), pp. 73-80.

Silk, Alvin J., and Vavra, Terry (1974), "Advertising's Affective Qualities and Consumer Response," Report No. 74-100, Marketing Science Institute, Cambridge, Massachusetts.

Snyder, Watson Jr., and Gray, Frank B. (1971), "The Corporate Marketing Staff: Its Role and Effectiveness in Multi-Division Companies," Report No. 71-108, Marketing Science Institute, Cambridge, Massachusetts.

Srivastava, Rajendra K., and Shocker, Allan D. (1982), "Analytic Approaches to Product and Marketing Planning: The Second Conference," Report No. 82-109, Marketing Science Institute, Cambridge, Massachusetts.

Stanton, William J. (1967), *Fundamentals of Marketing* (New York: McGraw-Hill).

Stein, Morris S. (1974), *Stimulating Creativity: Volume 1* (New York: Academic Press).

Steiner, Robert L. (1974), "Economic Theory and the Idea of Marketing Productivity," Report No. 74-108, Marketing Science Institute, Cambridge, Massachusetts.

Stern, Louis W. (1969), *Distribution Channels: Behavioral Dimensions* (Boston: Houghton Mifflin).

———— (1970), "Market Structure as a Measure of Market Performance," Report No. 70-121, Marketing Science Institute, Cambridge, Massachusetts.

————, Dewar, Robert, Drebin, Allan R., Phillips, Lynn W., and Sternthal, Brian (1977), "The Evaluation of Consumer Protection Laws: The Case of the Fair Credit Reporting Act," Report No. 77-114, Marketing Science Institute, Cambridge, Massachusetts.

————, and Grabner, John R. (1970), *Competition in the Marketplace* (Glenview, Illinois: Scott, Foresman, and Company).

Sternthal, Brian (1984), "Comment on the Role of Affect and Cognition," in W. F. van Raaij, "Affective and Cognitive Reactions to Advertising," Report No. 84-111, Marketing Science Institute, Cambridge, Massachusetts.

Stewart, David and Furse, David (1986), *Effective Television Advertising* (Lexington, MA: Lexington Books).

Strang, Roger A. (1980), *The Promotional Planning Process* (New York: Praeger Publishers, Inc.).

————, Prentice, Robert M., and Clayton, Alden G. (1975), "The Relationship Between Advertising and Promotion in Brand Strategy," Report No. 75-119, Marketing Science Institute, Cambridge, Massachusetts.

Sujan, Harish, and Weitz, Barton (1985), "The Amount and Direction of Effort: An Attributional Study," Report No. 85-105, Marketing Science Institute, Cambridge, Massachusetts.

Taylor, James R. (1971), "Management Experience with Applications of Multidimensional Scaling Methods," Report No. 71-120, Marketing Science Institute, Cambridge, Massachusetts.

Tyebjee, Tyzoon T., Bruno, Albert V., and McIntyre, Shelby H. (1983), "Growing Ventures Can Anticipate Marketing Stages," Report No. 83-102, Marketing Science Institute, Cambridge, Massachusetts.

Van de Ven, Andrew (1985), "Central Problems in the Management of Innovation," Report No. 85-109, Marketing Science Institute, Cambridge, Massachusetts.

van Raaij, W. Fred (1984), "Affective and Cognitive Reactions to Advertising," Report No. 84-111, Marketing Science Institute, Cambridge, Massachusetts.

Varadarajan, P. (1984), "Symbiosis in Sales Promotion," in Katherine E. Jocz (Ed.), *Research on Sales Promotion: Collected Papers*, Report No. 84-104, Marketing Science Institute, Cambridge, Massachusetts.

Vernon, John (1970), "Concentration, Promotion, and Market Share Stability in the Pharmaceutical Industry," Report No. 70-108, Marketing Science Institute, Cambridge, Massachusetts.

———— (1972), *Market Structure and Industrial Performance: A Review of Statistical Findings* (Boston: Allyn and Bacon).

von Hippel, Eric (1984), "Novel Product Concepts from Lead Users: Segmenting Users by Experience," Report No. 84-109, Marketing Science Institute, Cambridge, Massachusetts.

Ward, Scott (1971), "Effects of Television Advertising on Children," Report No. 71–114, Marketing Science Institute, Cambridge, Massachusetts.
———— (1974), "Consumer Socialization," Report No. 74–106, Marketing Science Institute, Cambridge, Massachusetts.
————, and Wackman, Daniel B. (1972), "Children's Purchase Influence Attempts and Parental Yielding," *Journal of Marketing Research*, 9 (3), pp. 316–319.
————, ————, and Wartella, Ellen (1977), *How Children Learn to Buy* (Beverly Hills: Sage Publications).
Webster, Frederick E., Jr. (1980), "Top Management Views of the Marketing Function," Report No. 80–108, Marketing Science Institute, Cambridge, Massachusetts.
————, and Wind, Yoram (1972), *Organizational Buying Behavior* (Englewood Cliffs, NJ: Prentice-Hall).
Weiss, Carol H. (1980), "Knowledge Creep and Decision Accretion," *Knowledge: Creation, Diffusion, Utilization*, 1 (March), pp. 381–404.
Weitz, Barton A., and Wright, Peter (1978), "The Salesperson as a Marketing Strategist: The Relationship Between Field Sales Performance and Insight About One's Customers," Report No. 78–120, Marketing Science Institute, Cambridge, Massachusetts.
Wiersema, Frederik D. (1982), "Strategic Marketing and the Product Life Cycle," Report No. 82–103, Marketing Science Institute, Cambridge, Massachusetts.
Wilkie, William L. (1975), "Applying Attitude Research in Public Policy," Report No. 75–117, Marketing Science Institute, Cambridge, Massachusetts.
———— (1975), "Consumer Information Processing Research: Product Labeling," Report No. 75–104, Marketing Science Institute, Cambridge, Massachusetts.
———— (1986), "Structural Impediments to the Development of Marketing Knowledge," working paper, University of Florida.
————, and Dickson, Peter R. (1985), "Shopping for Appliances: Consumers' Strategies and Patterns of Information Search," Report No. 85–108, Marketing Science Institute, Cambridge, Massachusetts.
————, and Farris, Paul L. (1974), "Comparison Advertising: Issues and Prospects," Report No. 74–103, Marketing Science Institute, Cambridge, Massachusetts.
————, and ———— (1976), "Consumer Information Processing: Perspectives and Implications for Advertising," Report No. 76–113, Marketing Science Institute, Cambridge, Massachusetts.
————, and Gardner, David M. (1974), "The Role of Marketing Research in Public Policy Decision Making," *Journal of Marketing*, 38 (January), pp. 38–47.
————, and Pessemier, Edgar A. (1973), "Issues in Marketing's Use of Multi-Attribute Attitude Models," Report No. 73106, Marketing Science Institute, Cambridge, Massachusetts; also in *Journal of Marketing Research*, 10 (November), pp. 428–441.
Williamson, Oliver E. (1975), *Markets and Hierarchies: Analysis and Anti-Trust Implications* (New York: Free Press).
———— (1979), "Transaction-Cost Economics: The Governance of Contractual Relations," *Journal of Law and Economics*, 22 (October), pp. 233–262.
———— (1981), "The Economics of Organization: The Transaction-Cost Approach," *American Journal of Sociology*, 87, pp. 548–577.

Wiseman, Frederick, and McDonald, Philip (1980), "Toward the Development of Industry Standards for Response and Nonresponse Rates," Report No. 80-101, Marketing Science Institute, Cambridge, Massachusetts.

———, and ——— (1978), "The Nonresponse Problem in Consumer Telephone Surveys," Report No. 78-116, Marketing Science Institute, Cambridge, Massachusetts.

Yip, George S. (1984), "The Role of Strategic Planning in Consumer-Marketing Businesses," Report No. 84-103, Marketing Science Institute, Cambridge, Massachusetts.

Young, Robert F., and Greyser, Stephen A. (1982), "Cooperative Advertising, Its Uses and Effectiveness: Some Preliminary Hypotheses," Report No. 79-112, Marketing Science Institute, Cambridge, Massachusetts.

Zajonc, R. B. (1980), "Feeling and Thinking. Preferences Need No Inferences," *American Psychologist*, 35, pp. 151-175.

Zaltman, Gerald (1965), *Marketing: Contributions from the Behavioral Sciences* (New York: Harcourt, Brace, and World).

———, and Deshpande, Rohit (1980), "The Use of Market Research: An Exploratory Study of Manager and Researcher Perspectives," Report No. 80-115, Marketing Science Institute, Cambridge, Massachusetts.

——— and Vertinsky, Ilan (1971), "Health Services Marketing: A Suggested Model," *Journal of Marketing*, 35 (July), pp. 19-27.

Index

About the Author

Paul N. Bloom is professor of marketing at the University of North Carolina at Chapel Hill. He holds a Ph.D. in marketing from Northwestern University and also has degrees from Lehigh University and The Wharton School of the University of Pennsylvania. His research on public policy toward marketing, services marketing, marketing strategy, and several other topics has produced numerous articles and books, including the recently released *The Future of Consumerism* (Lexington Books, 1986). Dr. Bloom was the Visiting Research Professor at the Marketing Science Institute during the 1980–81 academic year and has worked on several MSI projects. He is currently serving as a member of the American Marketing Association's "Development of Marketing Thought" Task Force.